Passenger Airliners of the United States
1926-1986
A Pictorial History

Passenger Airliners of the United States
1926-1986 A Pictorial History

TWA's giant wooden-winged Fokker F-32 was the first four-engine passenger aircraft. Courtesy Trans World Airlines.

Noel Wien shows off his Hamilton Metalplane in a February 1929 photograph autographed to fellow Alaskan airline pioneer Bob Reeve, founder of Reeve Aleutian Airways. Courtesy Reeve Aleutian Airways.

This unidentifiable PKA S-40 was photographed in the water shortly after a launching. The gentlemen on the ramp indicate the aircraft's size. Note the open windows on the starboard side of the fuselage. Courtesy Pan American World Airways

An American Airways Lockheed Orion in flight. This aircraft was probably the first passenger transport with fully retractable landing gear, although the tail wheel remained stationary. Courtesy American Airlines

by Myron J. Smith, Jr.

Library of Congress
Catalog Card No. 86-90432

ISBN 0-933126-72-7

First Printing July 1987

Typography: Arrow Graphics, Missoula, Montana
Layout: Stan Cohen

FRONT COVER:
A DC-3 silhouetted at Miami, Florida in March 1984. Courtesy Robert E. Garrard.

Dedicated to Jay.

PICTORIAL HISTORIES PUBLISHING COMPANY
713 South Third West
Missoula, Montana 59801

CONTENTS

INTRODUCTION

BACKGROUND

IN THE BEGINNING, aviation as a means of passenger transport in America was considered wildly impractical. Critics and cynics derided the few who speculated positively on the concept and even Orville Wright was once heard to describe the chances of transatlantic flight as "a bare possibility." By 1986, however, all doubt concerning the value of domestic and international air commerce has long since been removed. Today, the miracle of airborne mobility continues to receive its greatest tribute in the fact that millions of people daily simply take it for granted. Much of that confidence rests with the sophistication of the airliners involved and the skill with which they are managed in the air and on the ground. Such was not the case sixty years ago.

During the "barnstorming" years immediately following World War I, flying—as pilot or passenger—was a dream for most Americans and an adventure for the few who were lucky or brave enough to become involved. American passenger air transport as an industry did not really begin until the mid-to-late 1920s, somewhat behind European development. Among the reasons for this tardiness were geography, excellent ground transportation, lack of appropriate aircraft, and somewhat spotty public relations. The United States in the second decade of the twentieth century, as previously, was a single, continent-wide nation possessed of advanced intrastate and interstate rail and road networks. Little immediate need was seen by travelers—and virtually none by ground transportation magnates—for the introduction of that period's relatively small and slow aircraft into either internal or international commerce. Additionally, America, late into World War I, had not produced larger combat planes on anything approaching the scale of the Europeans and therefore was not left with a large reservoir of surplus machines convertible into airliners. Thus it was that efforts to provide sustained scheduled air service in this country began in the only area where the air offered any real advantage over surface transport—faster mail delivery.

The U.S. Post Office Air Mail Service dominated air commerce in the United States between 1918 and 1927. Its experiments in routes and schedules led the way for later developments and, together with barnstormers, racers, distance flyers, and military air arms, helped to sell the

Backbone of the Post Office—An exceedingly rare flying picture of a U.S. Air Mail Service DeHavilland DH-4B. Introduced in late 1918, 100 of the modified former World War I bombers were built in America under license and operated until the Post Office retired from active flight in 1927. Courtesy American Airlines

possibilities of aviation to the public. Following passage of the 1925 Kelly Act, which authorized the eventual transfer of airmail service to private operators, the Post Office began to exit from the flying business. Certain segments of its established network were designated Contract Air Mail (C.A.M.) Routes and were put up for bids from prospective private carriers capable of meeting the government's requirements. In return for their involvement, successful applicants would be paid on the basis of mail weight carried. Airlines as an American industry were thus born in the spring of 1926 and within two years of the Kelly Act, 15 carriers were fulfilling Post Office mail contracts. Mail would remain the major source of revenue for most of these new airlines throughout the remainder of the 1920s and into the 1930s, but, if not at the forefront, passengers were not entirely left out.

The changeover from government to private operation of the airmail routes greatly aided the advancement of America's civil-aircraft-building industry. These now stepped forward to offer new designs to the

On April 6, 1926, pilot Leon Cuddeback, flying a Curtiss Swallow similar in all respects except engines to this one photographed in June, inaugurated Varney Airlines' mail service. Varney would eventually evolve into that giant carrier of today, United Airlines. Courtesy United Airlines

Square-tailed Mail Bird – Fifteen Curtiss Carrier Pigeons were built for air mail operations. Equipped with Liberty or Conqueror engines, they began to enter National Air Transport Service on May 12, 1926. Like the Curtiss Swallow, the Carrier Pigeon was not designed to accommodate passengers. Courtesy United Airlines

Pitcairn PA-5 Mailwing of Colonial Western Airways – A total of 120 Pitcairn PA-5 mailwings were built; their initial service began with Texas Air Transport on February 6, 1928. The PA-5 and improved PA-6 equipped a number of early carriers including the American Airlines ancestors T.A.T., Southern Air Transport, Colonial Western Airways, and Universal Aviation Corporation; the United Airlines predecessor National Air Transport; and the Eastern Airlines ancestor, Pitcairn Aviation. Courtesy American Airlines

Army Aircraft in Civil Service – Some 450 Curtiss Falcons were constructed for the U.S. Army as O-1Bs or A-3s. At the close of 1928, National Air Transport acquired eight Falcons for use on its main New York-Chicago-Dallas mail route. Powerful and roomy, the Falcon, equipped with a Liberty or Conqueror engine, could accommodate 1-2 passengers on folding chairs in its forward mail compartment; however, the practice was not common. Courtesy United Airlines

Western Air Express Douglas M-2 – When WAE launched passenger service in May 1926, two people could be carried in the forward mail compartment. This refurbished example was recently donated to the National Air and Space Museum. Courtesy McDonnell Douglas

operators and, as the decade progressed, created new machines to meet carrier and public expectations – the latter boosted considerably by such record individual feats as Charles A. Lindbergh's New York to Paris flight in 1927. Yet, owing to the overriding importance to the airlines of their mail contracts, initial commercial aircraft were not built to handle large numbers of passengers.

Even after Western Air Express and Ryan Airlines introduced distinct passenger services in 1926, customers were normally carried by airlines with great reluctance. Mail-conscious operators at first saw passengers primarily as bonus income, which could be cleared above that received from the Post Office contracts. Thus those passengers able to book passage were initially seated on folding chairs among the letter sacks in the forward mail compartments of such planes as the Douglas M-1 or M-2 or Ryan M-1. As might be imagined, such rides were very uncomfortable, lacked all amenities, and offered only one advantage – rapid intercity transport. Still, efforts toward pure passenger service were made and among the most exciting experiments of the 1920s were the Guggenheim Fund-sponsored, first-class service between Los Angeles and San Fran-

cisco operated by Western Air Express. Equally inspiring achievements were scored in the air-rail operations of Standard Airlines and Transcontinental Air Transport (T.A.T.). In that challenging developmental decade, (and in the opening of the Caribbean by Pan American Airways) ended by the Stock Market Crash, at least a few far-sighted individuals and concerns had come to value the concept of passenger air commerce. Additionally, as the decade advanced, newer and larger transport aircraft began to replace the relatively small, single-seat biplanes, which had droned on for grueling hours getting the mail through.

By today's standards, the civil aircraft manufactured prior to the early 1930s were, for the most part, rather primitive. Despite the addition of more sophisticated engines and the builders' development of new structural and aero-dynamic concepts, some traditional features died slowly. For example, even after cabins were accepted, cockpit enclosures were adopted with great reluctance. Biplanes remained common and wooden and fabric construction was normal. Still, design progress was steady and a host of models with passenger-carrying capability (some minimum) were introduced during the years 1925 through 1931. These included the famous and rugged Ford Tri-Motors; the infamous wooden-winged Fokkers from Model 4 up through Model 32, one of the largest early aircraft assembled in America; the go-anywhere utility Fairchilds FC-2, FC-2W, Model 71, and Model 100; little-remembered types like the Bach 3-CT, Buhl CA, and Hamilton H series; sleek beauties such as the Lockheed Vega and Orion and the Northrop Alpha; early examples of Boeing airliners, the Models 40 and 80 biplanes; transports from Stinson, including the SB-1 SM-1, and SM-6000; diverse entries from Curtiss and Consolidated such as the B-20, the Commodore flying boat, and the Fleetster; progressively more advanced over-water Sikorskys like the S-26, S-38, S-40, and S-41; and commercial passenger aircraft built upon the success of pioneer distance planes like the Ryan B-5 and Bellanca CH series. There were others, many of which are individually treated below.

PASSENGER AIRLINERS, 1926-1931

Name	Year of Initial Service	Seating
Stout 2-AT	1925	8
Douglas M-1/M-2	1926	3
Fokker Model 4 Universal	1926	4
Fokker F-VIIA/3M	1926	8
Ford 4-AT	1926	14
Ryan M-1	1926	3

Stinson SB-1	1926	4
Boeing 40A	1927	3
Fairchild FC-2	1927	4
Stinson SM-1	1927	4-5
Bach 3-CT-6	1928	10
Boeing 80	1928	20
Fokker F-10/F-10A	1928	12-14
Ford 5-AT	1928	16
Hamilton H	1928	8
Lockheed Vega	1928	6
Ryan B-5	1928	5
Sikorsky S-38	1928	8
Bellanca CH-300	1929	6
Boeing 40B	1929	3
Fairchild FC-2W	1929	6
Fairchild 71	1929	7
Fokker Model 8 Super Universal	1929	6
Fokker F-14	1929	8
Travel Air 6000	1929	6
Consolidated Commodore	1930	22
Consolidated 17	1930	6
Curtiss 13-20	1930	18
Fokker F-32	1930	32
Stinson SM-6000	1930	10
Lockheed Orion	1931	6
Northrop Alpha	1931	5
Sikorsky S-40/41	1931	40-11
Buhl CA	1931	8
Fairchild 100	1931	8

Mr. Pan Am – Juan Terry Trippe, founder and President of Pan American World Airways, one of the world's outstanding personalities in the field of commercial aviation. He was decorated by 18 countries, including the U.S. Medal of Merit, for his contributions to the enhancement of world aviation. Courtesy Pan American World Airways

By Air and Rail – Employing Ford Tri-Motors, Standard Airlines, in cooperation with several railroads, was able to introduce transcontinental air-rail service in February 1929. Courtesy American Airlines

Meanwhile, under the forceful prodding of President Hoover's postmaster general, Walter Folger Brown, the airlines were encouraged to pay even greater attention to passenger transport. Using – and some critics claimed overusing – powers derived from his control of airmail-contract awards, Brown presided over the establishment of an integrated-route system across the country. The McNary-Watres Act of 1930 encouraged carriers to invest in better equipment and to expand passenger services by changing the manner in which airmail payments were made.

Fokker and Stinson Tri-motors in Ohio – A Fokker F-10A of Trans-America Airlines Corp. at Columbus Airport, ca. early 1931, with a Stinson SM-6000B of Pennsylvania Airlines in the background. The crash of a wooden-winged TWA F-10 in 1931, which caused the death of coach Knute Rockne, resulted in the first airliner grounding ordered by the U.S. government and the demise of Fokker manufacturing in America until the 1960s. Only 55 of the little-remembered Stinson SM-6000s were built, with the first entering service with the Ludington Line on September 1, 1930. Courtesy American Airlines

Auto Maker's Airliner – A Ford Tri-Motor of United Airlines. Courtesy United Airlines

The streamlined Lockheed Vega – admired by West Virginia aviation enthusiasts at Charleston's Wertz Field, the Lockheed Model 5B *Winnie Mae* of Wiley Post/Harold Gathy clearly shows off its portside door. Courtesy West Virginia Dept. of Culture and History

Henceforth, government subsidies would be given on the basis of aircraft space available, not weight carried. Behind this legislation was the idea that operators having purchased greater-capacity aircraft would fill them with people simply to earn revenues for what might otherwise be carried as empty space or space occupied by a few express packages. Given the requirements of equipment financing under this arrangement, many smaller carriers in the deepening depression began to fail or were taken over by larger consortiums whose interests also included airframe-power-plant production. Believing these larger operations more efficient in their handling of the airmail, Postmaster General Brown gave them somewhat preferential treatment in contract awards.

Although Brown's approach had the effect of helping to establish airline giants, it was roundly condemned by the succeeding Roosevelt Administration. In 1934, all airmail contracts were canceled and the U.S. Army Air Corps was called upon to fly the mail. After a month of disasters, the government decided to invite civil carriers to rebid for the routes. But prior to their participation, it forced the "Big Four" airlines—American, Eastern, TWA, and United—to sever their connections with the conglomerates that had previously supported and equipped them. Now, with the airlines and manufacturers separated and compelled to stand on their own feet, competition by the latter to produce and sell aircraft that would give a competitive edge would become fierce—and would remain so to the present day. Interestingly enough, however, one of the longest-lasting cases of manufacturer rivalry had its beginning in 1933, a full year before the airmail emergency, and came about precisely because of a perceived lack of competition.

In response to an order from the United Air Lines division of United Aircraft and Transport Corporation, the Boeing Airplane Company (also owned by UATC) flew the first "modern airliner," its Model 247, on February 8, 1933. A twin-engined, low-wing monoplane with stressed metal skin and seating for 10 passengers, the 247 was a marvel of its time. Boeing/United's insistence that all of the $50,000 aircraft be delivered on the original order before any could be produced for rival carriers caused an almost-predictable reaction by the other airlines. Responding to a request from TWA, the manufacturing firm of Donald Douglas entered the lists and produced a larger, twin-engined transport with all the features of the 247 and many others besides, including roomier fuselage, seating for 12, and better aerodynamic shape and mechanics. The Douglas Commercial (DC) 1, as the plane was designated, first flew on July 1, 1933, and

United Boeing 247D—The use of two engines and the modern structure of the Boeing 247D rendered exceptional aerodynamic qualities. Boeing's total first run production commitment to United led TWA to seek the Douglas DC-1. Courtesy United Airlines

from it stemmed all of the pre-jet Douglas airliners to follow. So successful were these Douglas products that, within a few months of their appearance, many carriers were forced to begin acquiring them and the great design competition that exists today between Boeing and Douglas (presently McDonnell-Douglas) was launched.

Only one DC-1 was built, and it was followed by the slightly "stretched" and more powerful DC-2 with seating for 14. The second DC was followed by the remarkable DC-3, which featured more powerful engines still, a better shaped fuselage allowing seating for 21 passengers, and extended wings of multi-spar construction, which gave unprecedented efficiency. By 1936, the year after its introduction and fifty years ago, the DC-3 was becoming the air-transport industry's standard airliner and by the time of Pearl Harbor, much of the world's passenger air commerce was handled by this airplane. Efforts were made by the competitors of Boeing and Douglas to offer airlines something of a choice during the middle 1930s. Between 1934 and 1937 the last great biplane airliner, a good bush aircraft, and several transports faster than the 247 or DC-2 were introduced. American Airlines inaugurated operations with the 14-passenger biplane Curtiss T-32 Condor II in 1934. That same year, Jack Northrop's speedy Gamma and Delta were delivered to TWA, and Vultee sold its V-1A to American. In 1935, Fairchild offered a stretched

A DC-2 Breaks out of the Clouds – A slightly modified production version of the DC-1, the DC-2 was test flown on May 11, 1934, and began scheduled American Airlines service in December. Slightly over 200 were built and provided yeoman service to large and small carriers alike. Courtesy American Airlines

American Airlines Officials Launch New York-Chicago DC-3 Service, June 25, 1936 – C.R. Smith (gray suit/straw hat, left center) and other dignitaries and flight crew prepare to send off the *Flagship Illinois*, first dayplane DC-3. Introduced as The Douglas Sleeper Transport (DST), the fast, roomy airliner made all preceding passenger aircraft obsolete and would become known as "The Plane that Changed the World." Courtesy American Airlines

8-passenger version of its Model 71, called the Model 100, which began service with Pacific Alaska. The only significant rivals to the Boeing and Douglas transports were, however, from Lockheed, which had introduced its first commercial aircraft, the revolutionary Vega, in 1928. First among these was the Model 10 Electra, initially flown in February 1934. A trim, all-metal monoplane, with twin fins and seating for eight passengers, it was followed by the Model 14 Super Electra. Of the airliners in wide use, these two Lockheeds were the fastest of their day.

Meanwhile, several manufacturers applied their prewar efforts to the creation of large, over-water flying boats and amphibians of great range. Among these creations were the pace-setting Consolidated Commodore and the graceful Martin M-130, which gave Pan American Airways the means to open the Pacific to passenger travel. The firm of Russian émigré Igor Sikorsky, who is perhaps better known as the father of the helicopter, delivered his 40-passenger S-42 in 1934 that allowed Pan

Am to dominate the Caribbean and South American water routes. Boeing's huge 70-passenger B-314, which came on the scene in 1939, gave Juan Trippe's airline the ability to initiate transatlantic, scheduled service. Only one other giant flying boat was destined to enter U.S. service, the Vought-Sikorsky VS-44 of 1942; although late, one ship would fly on into the early 1970s.

In June 1938, Douglas flew a large, four-engined, land-based transport, with three fins and a tricycle landing gear. This DC-4, later relabeled DC-4E (E = Experimental), was capable of transporting 42 passengers, but was deemed too large by the airlines that had requested it. In an unusual step, Douglas reworked the aircraft into the smaller DC-4, which enjoyed great service during World War II as the military C-54. The same year, 1940, Boeing pioneered the pressurized cabin with its four-engined B-307 Stratoliner, which was based largely on the company's B-17 Flying Fortress bomber. The fast Lockheed Model 18 Lode-

A Speedy Airliner – Successful with the Vega and Orion, Lockheed turned its attention to a larger transport; capable of hauling 8-10 passengers, the model 10 was faster than either the Boeing 247 or the Douglas DC-2/DC-3. Chicago and Southern's Model 10B Lockheed Electra over the Mississippi River. Courtesy Delta Airlines

Winter Operations – This remarkable photograph of diverse American Airlines fleet elements gathered in the snow was shot in Winter 1934-1935. Aircraft pictured are: Stinson Model U (top left), Ford 5-At Tri-Motor (bottom left), Stinson Model U (top center), Stinson Model A (middle center), Curtiss CO-32 Condor II (bottom center), Douglas DC-2 (top/bottom right). Courtesy American Airlines

November 22, 1935 – Alameda, California. Pre-departure ceremonies before Pan Am's *China Clipper*, a Martin M-130 flying boat, leaves on the first transpacific airmail flight from San Francisco to Manila. Courtesy Pan American World Airways

Mainliner *Lake Ontario* – Scaled down from the experimental Douglas DC-4E, the DC-4 became familiar to millions as the C-54 Skymaster military transport of World War II. Hundreds were employed by the postwar airlines, including United. Courtesy United Air Lines

November 29, 1935 – The *China Clipper* is moored to Pan Am's landing stage in Manila Bay after completing the first transpacific airmail flight, and is surrounded by well-wishers. The Manila Hotel is in the background. Courtesy Pan American World Airways

star entered service with Mid-Continent Air Lines in March 1940 and, like the Model 14, probably achieved greater fame as a wartime light bomber with Allied air forces.

PASSENGER AIRLINERS, 1932-1945

Name	Year of Initial Service	Seating
Consolidated 20	1932	9
Stinson Model U	1932	12
Boeing Monomail	1933	6
Boeing 247	1933	10
Clark-G.A.-43	1933	10
Boeing 247D	1934	10
Curtiss T-32 Condor II	1934	14
Douglas DC-2	1934	18
Lockheed Model 10	1934	10
Sikorsky S-42	1934	32
Stinson SR	1934	5
Vultee V-1A	1934	8

Martin M-130	1935	36
Stinson Model A	1935	8
Douglas DC-3	1936	21
Sikorsky S-43	1936	12
Lockheed Model 14	1937	14
Grumman G-21	1938	9
Boeing 314	1939	74
Beechcraft Model 18	1940	9
Boeing 307	1940	33
Lockheed Model 18	1940	14
Boeing 314A	1941	74
Vought-Sikorsky VS-44	1942	47
Curtiss C-46	1945	36
Douglas DC-4	1945	44

The Ultimate Piston Douglas – Designed for transcontinental and intercontinental operations, the DC-7 series were the final piston airliners developed by Douglas. Some 330 of three variants were built, including the Continental Airlines DC-7B *City of Chicago*, shown here. Courtesy Continental Airlines

Following World War II, many Douglas DC-3s and DC-4s, together with Curtiss C-46 Commandos, were declared surplus by the military and formed the basis for expansion or creation of a number of American airlines. While looking at Douglas, we might mention that the availability of increasingly more powerful engines allowed that firm to stretch and pressurize the basic DC-4 into the DC-6, -6A, and -6B, with over 500 delivered between 1947 and 1955. Substitution of a turbo-compound Pratt & Whitney power plant allowed Douglas to produce the DC-7 and DC-7B as well as its final, piston-engined model, the long-range DC-7C Seven Seas of 1955. This was the first American airliner capable of transporting a full load of passengers nonstop across the Atlantic.

Douglas rivals, Lockheed and Boeing, were not quiet during the war years. In January 1943, the former flew the remarkably advanced L-049 Constellation. This triple-finned beauty would become longer, more capacious and powerful, and even more glamorous as some 850 were built in four additional variants over the next fifteen years. Largest of the immediate postwar airliners, Boeing's Model 377 Stratocruiser was also based, like the B-307, on a bomber, the B-29 Superfortress. It featured two pressurized decks (and is chiefly remembered for the usual bar downstairs) and could seat 100 passengers on transatlantic routes; despite its advanced engineering, only 55 were built. Another manufacturer, Convair, built the best, early-postwar, short-haul transport, the pressurized CV-240. It was followed by the CV-340 and CV-440, and all three are still around today as the turboprop-equipped Convair CV-580, -600, or -640.

Double-Decked Giants – Two American Overseas Airlines Boeing 377s at West Germany's Rhein-Main Airport ca. 1949. The Stratocruiser, employing the wings, engines, landing gear, and tail unit of the B-29 bomber, was the ultimate in airliner luxury in its day, but is now primarily remembered for its lower deck cocktail bar. Courtesy American Airlines

A Triple-Tailed Beauty – The Lockheed Constellation first flew in 1943 and was produced in five major versions, each more glamorous than the last. This L-749A, *Star of Delaware*, was TWA's final piston-engined airliner. Courtesy Trans World Airlines

Somewhat similar to the Convairs, and designed for the same market, were the Martin 2-0-2 and 4-0-4.

One of the most interesting developments on the postwar airliner scene was the introduction of turboprop engines. In this connection, we should remember the Vickers Viscount, the first passenger aircraft so equipped and the first British airliner to crack the U.S. market. In service with such carriers as Capital and United, the Viscount was extremely popular and allowed travelers fast and quiet passage, with a smooth ride and panoramic windows. During the late 1950s, Fokker, which had been largely quiet on the American scene since the early 1930s, introduced its DC-3 replacement, the F-27 Friendship. For a time, this popular, high-wing monoplane was built in America by Fairchild (later, and briefly, the Fairchild-Hiller Corporation) and in its stretched version was marketed as the FH-227. Now built and distributed exclusively by Fokker, over 1,000 of these turboprops have been built since their introduction and many continue to see service around the world, including the United States where Air Wisconsin was taking delivery as late as 1985.

The development of new technology, further government stimulus, the inspiration of some gifted individuals, and the fact that many people had been exposed to air travel after Pearl Harbor led to an increased demand for air transport in the period following World War II. Not only had people become interested in flying between major or trunk cities, but desire was expressed for service to local communities. As a result, many airlines began to offer local service exclusively while major carriers often included stops in smaller towns. By the middle 1950s, America's airlines were transporting many times more people than they had a quarter of a century earlier. Perhaps it was fitting then that they take a quantum leap forward into the jet age.

The honor of flying the first commercial jetliner goes to the British. Unfortunately for them, their Comet I failed structurally while in service and the ball was passed to the U.S. builder, Boeing. On July 15, 1954, that firm flew its Model 367-80, a swept-wing, company-funded prototype of a new breed of "big jet." Backed by huge USAF orders for tanker variants, Boeing offered an enlarged civil version, which it called the 707. Within months, America's larger airlines were lined up in a row, seeking the new aircraft, discarding their propeller equipment (much of it in excellent condition) to smaller carriers as the new jetliners were obtained. On October 28, 1958, Pan American World Airways opened the United States commercial jet era with 707 service to Europe.

PASSENGER AIRLINERS, 1946-1958

Name	Year of Initial Service	Seating
Fairchild F-24W	1946	4
Lockheed L-049	1946	60
Douglas DC-6	1947	60
Grumman G-73	1947	12
Lockheed L-749	1947	81
Martin 2-0-2	1947	36
Boeing 377	1948	112
Convair CV-240	1948	40
DeHavilland-Canada DHC-2	1948	8
DeHavilland DH-104	1950	19
Douglas DC-6B	1951	95
Lockheed L-1049A	1951	71
Martin 4-0-4	1951	40
Convair CV-340	1952	44
DeHavilland-Canada DHC-3	1952	11

Douglas DC-7	1953	99
Lockheed L-1049C	1953	71
Cessna 180	1954	5
Douglas DC-7B	1955	99
Fokker F-27	1955	52
Lockheed L-1049G	1955	66
Vickers Viscount 700	1955	75
Convair CV-440	1956	52
Douglas DC-7C	1956	110
DeHavilland DH-114	1957	20
Lockheed L-1649A	1957	74
Boeing 707	1958	202

The Boeing 707 and its variants – the 707-320 and 720 – were a tough act to challenge, but Douglas did so in 1955 by creating a similar four-engined aircraft with slightly less sweep in the wings. Like the Boeing, the Douglas DC-8 was improved and made more powerful and a total of 556 were built before production ended in 1972. Convair also attempted to enter the jetliner marketplace. Its CV-880 and CV-990A were faster than either the 707 or DC-8, though of smaller capacity. Neither could find a market as the result of competition and technical difficulties, and the resulting financial loss forced Convair out of the airliner-manufacturing business. Meanwhile, overseas, the French SNCASE (later Áerospatiale) won a government contract for a short-haul jet, which it flew in May 1955 as the Caravelle. Novel in slinging its two engines in pods at the rear of the fuselage, the Caravelle managed to find American customers and in the process set the stage for competing U.S. jetliners, the Douglas DC-9 and Boeing 727. The twin-engined DC-9 became the pride of both major – and local – service U.S. carriers in the 1960s and its refined variant, the DC-9 Super Eighty, is today one of the hottest items on airline shopping lists. On the other hand, the Boeing 727, a tri-motor similar in appearance, was sold in greater quantities than any other jetliner in history and has only recently been retired by its manufacturer in favor of the more advanced 757. Completing its family of aircraft begun with the 707 and 727, Boeing also introduced its short-haul 737, which, in its "Dash-300" version, is still popular.

The future appeared unlimited for commercial air transport growth in the 1960s. Forecasts promised steadily increasing markets and airlines believed they would require considerably more capacity than they had.

Jet and Prop-Jet – Shown with a company DC-9 is one of Ozark's Fairchild-Hiller FH-227s, a stretched Fokker F-27 Friendship. Introduced by the Dutch builder as a DC-3 replacement in 1958, some 1,000 F-27s (including 78 FH-227s) have been built since, making it the world's most widely sold turboprop airliner. Courtesy Ozark Airlines

America's First Jetliner – Born of a corporate gamble, the 707 was the world's largest and fastest passenger airliner when introduced. The first jet service by any U.S. carrier began on October 26, 1958, when the Pan American World Airways Clipper *America*, shown here, departed New York for Paris. Courtesy Pan American World Airways

USAir currently operates 15 Boeing 737-300s with 25 more on order. Courtesy USAir

A Hot Ticket – Known alternately as the Super 80, MD-80, or Dash 80, the DC-9-80 series relies for its popularity and quiet, full efficiency on the new Pratt & Whitney refan engine. Courtesy Frontier Airlines

World's Best-Selling Turbine-Powered Airliner – Designed as a medium/short haul trijet, the Boeing 727 has overtaken the DC-3 as the world's most widely employed airliner. With over 1,800 sold, it became the world's most widely purchased jetliner and the first to amass 1,000 orders without benefit of military contracts. Entering service in 1964, the 727 has been employed by a variety of domestic carriers, including Piedmont Airlines, which placed its first into operation on March 15, 1967. Courtesy Piedmont Airlines

Miniskirts and a Jumbojet – The first wide-bodied jetliner and still the world's largest commercial transport, the Boeing 747 has been manufactured in several versions, including passenger, freight, and "Combi." Pan American World Airways inaugurated Boeing 747-100 New York-London service on January 22, 1970, a fact celebrated by members of the flight crew in this photograph. Courtesy Pan American World Airways

The European Airbus – Working together under the label Airbus Industrie, the major airframe-component manufacturers of Western Europe introduced the fuel-efficient A300 in 1974. Equipped with U.S. engines, the medium/short haul airliner finally entered the American market in 1978 with Eastern Airlines. Pan Am began airbus operations in 1984 while Continental Airlines has recently placed it in service. Courtesy Airbus Industrie

At the same time, service at the other end of the air-transport spectrum was increasing as small airlines, initially called scheduled air taxis and then commuters, sprang up to feed traffic from small towns to larger communities. As a result of these perceived and actual service demands, manufacturers and airlines went forward with the acquisition of new and improved equipment.

Boeing, in 1966, elected to proceed with the design and construction of the first wide-bodied jetliner; indeed, this decision was a gigantic gamble calling for an investment considerably larger than the entire net worth of that company. Once a special manufacturing plant large enough to accommodate the project was finished, the 747 was born. Far larger than any other airliner had ever been, the 747, quickly nicknamed Jumbojet, was equipped with (actually depended upon) new, large turbofan engines of significantly increased thrust. Once in service, the 747 opened a new era in medium- and long-haul air transport through its ability to handle hundreds of passengers and/or tons of freight.

Boeing was followed in the wide-bodied arena by trijets from McDonnell-Douglas and Lockheed. The former built a popular (though seemingly accident-prone) aircraft, the DC-10, while the latter built a technically advanced transport, the L-1011 TriStar. Both are slightly smaller than the 747, stikingly similar in appearance, and capable of flying hundreds of passengers over long and medium distances.

PASSENGER AIRLINERS, 1959-1972

Name	Year of Initial Service	Seating
Convair CV-540	1959	52
Lockheed L-188	1959	99
Douglas DC-8-10	1959	179
Beechcraft Model 58	1960	5
Convair CV-880	1960	124
Douglas DC-8-30	1960	179
Piper PA-23	1960	6
Áerospatiale Caravell	1961	70
Douglas DC-8-50	1961	179
Cessna 185	1962	6
Convair CV-990A	1962	159
Boeing 727-100	1964	94
Convair CV-580	1964	48
Piper PA-31	1964	8
Áerospatiale Nord 262	1965	29
Beechcraft B80	1965	11
BAe (BAC) One-Eleven	1965	89
Cessna 206	1965	5
Convair CV-600	1965	56
Convair CV-640	1965	56
Douglas DC-9-10	1965	90
Piper PA-32	1965	7
DeHavilland-Canada DHC-6	1966	20
Nihon YS-11	1966	60
Britten-Norman BN-2	1967	9
Cessna 402	1967	9
Fokker F-28	1967	85
McDonnell-Douglas DC-8-61	1967	259
McDonnell-Douglas DC-8-62	1967	201
McDonnell-Douglas DC-9-30	1967	110
Beechcraft B99	1968	15
Boeing 737-200	1968	115
Cessna 207	1968	7
McDonnell-Douglas DC-8-63	1968	259
Boeing 747-100	1970	452
McDonnell-Douglas DC-10-10	1970	250

Piper PA-34	1971	6
Britten-Norman BN-2A	1972	17
GAF N-2	1972	17
Lockheed L-1011-1	1972	256
McDonnell-Douglas DC-10-30	1972	380
McDonnell-Douglas DC-10-40	1972	380

After 1970, the American "widebodies" were challenged by the Europeans, whose consortium-built Airbus Industrie A300 addressed a medium- and short-haul market seemingly ignored by the U.S. builders. In 1978, Eastern Airlines began flying the A300 and in 1984, Pan American joined in as it awaited delivery of a pair of smaller derivatives, the A310 and A320. Responding to the European effort, as well as to the need for advanced, more fuel-efficient airliners, Boeing late in the 1970s began construction of its twins, the 767 and 757. The former is a twin-aisle widebody while the latter is a single-aisle "narrowbody"; both mount two powerful, but quiet and fuel-saving, underwing engines and are just entering service.

Super-Efficient Boeing 767 – The first completely new Boeing design since the 747, the 767, launched in 1978, features an advance technology wing and quiet, fuel-efficient engines. Aimed at the medium/long-haul market and currently available in three variants, the two-aisle twin of the Boeing 757 entered service in September 1982 and on February 1, 1985, became the first twin-jet airliner to fly the transatlantic route in scheduled passenger service. Shown here is one of Delta Air Lines' ships. Courtesy Delta Air Lines

Executive Transport Turned Commuterliner – Developed by the late Ed Swearingen as a commercial version of his successful Merlin, the first Metro entered regional service in 1973. The Metro I has been followed by the Metro II (pictured here in Air Midwest livery) and the current Metro III model. With over 250 sold, Fairchild has placed its clean-lined 19 passenger airliner in service with some 44 carriers worldwide. Courtesy Air Midwest

In 1978, the U.S. Congress passed the Airline Deregulation Act, which largely took the government out of the economic regulation of air commerce, a position it had occupied since the 1930s. Consequently, new and old operators were free to establish their own routes and fares. In pursuit of greater profits in an exceedingly chancy industry, many elected to abandon service to smaller communities and concentrate on larger "hubs." The vacuum created allowed smaller operators, commuters, and air taxis to expand their roles, some significantly. These soon required new aircraft to meet the demands of providing transportation to variously sized cities. As a result, earlier local-service aircraft such as the Beech 18 and DeHavilland Heron have been joined by a host of newer, often foreign, designs. Among these aircraft are: the Beech 99 and 1900, the DeHavilland-Canada STOL (short take-off and landing) DHC-6 Twin Otter, DHC-7 (Dash 7), and DHC-8 (Dash 8), the CASA C-212 Aviocar, the Dornier Do-228, the Embraer EMB-110 Bandierante and EMB-120 Brasilia, the British Aerospace Models 146, 748, and Jetstream 31, the Áerospatiale Nord 262/Mohawk 298, the Fairchild-Swearingen Metro, the Fokker F-27 Friendship, F-28 Fellowship, and soon the F-100, the Nihon YS-11, the Piper Navajo, Navajo Chieftain, T-1020/T-1040, the Cessna 208 Caravan and 404 Titan, the SAAB SF-340, and the Shorts

330/360. As the appearance of the Aeritalia/Áerospatiale ATR-42 demonstrates, the arrival of new "commuter-liners" on the American scene has become something of a common event in the 1980s. It is probably accurate to say that the battle for market supremacy in this arena is as intense today as anything experienced by builders since Congress separated the airlines from the aircraft manufacturers in 1934.

PASSENGER AIRLINERS, 1973-1986

Name	Year of Initial Service	Seating
CASA C-212	1973	28
Fairchild Metro	1973	19
Piper PA-31-325	1973	10
Shorts S-25	1974	22
Fairchild Metro II	1975	19
McDonnell-Douglas DC-9-50	1975	139
Cessna 404	1976	9
Shorts 330	1976	30
Áerospatiale Mohawk 298	1978	29
Airbus Industrie A-300	1978	375
DeHavilland-Canada DHC-7	1978	50
BAe 748-2B	1979	48
Embraer EMB-110P	1979	19
Grumman/Gulfstream G-159-1C	1979	37
Lockheed L-1011-500	1979	330
McDonnell-Douglas DC-9-81	1980	172
McDonnell-Douglas DC-10-15	1981	380
Piper T-1020/T-1040	1981	9
Beechcraft C99	1982	19
Boeing 767-200	1982	290
Fairchild Metro III	1982	19
Shorts 360	1982	36
Beechcraft B1900	1983	19
Boeing 757	1983	200
Aeritalia/Áerospatiale ATR-42	1986	50

Canadian Stol-Liner — A pressurized, high wing $7.5 million 50-passenger airliner in the DeHavilland-Canada DHC-7 (Dash 7). With advanced STOL (short takeoff and landing) capabilities and an easily recognizable "T" tail, the small airliner has proven quite popular since its introduction in early 1975. Pictured here is a recent model in operation with Hawaiian Airlines. Courtesy DeHavilland Canada

Bandit from Brazil — Named for 17th Century colonizers of western Brazil, the Embraer EMB-110 Bandeirante was the first indigenous South American transport sold to U.S. commuter airlines. A 19-passenger, unpressurized turboprop, the $1.9 million plane was introduced in the U.S. by Aeromech Airlines of Clarksburg, West Virginia, in 1980. Since then, the Bandeirante has gained wide acceptance and production has exceeded 450. Courtesy Angelo C. Konhoulis

A Small Jetliner for Large Regionals—Transporting 111 passengers, the British Aerospace (HS) 146 is a fuel-efficient, pressurized, short-haul jetliner designed to offer low operating cost and capability from short, semi-prepared airfields. The 146 began service in the United States in late June 1983. Here passengers board Pacific Southwest Airlines' (PSA) inaugural Oakland to Burbank, California, flight, June 20, 1984. Courtesy British Aerospace

A Gaggle of Commuter Birds—Airliners of Atlantic Southeast Airlines parked on the company's Atlanta ramp in July 1986. The planes, all foreign-made, are (left to right): Shorts 360 (half), Embraer EMB-120 Brasilia, and two DeHavilland Canada DHC-7s (the nose of an EMB-110 Bandeirante appears under the tail of the DASH-7 furthest to the right), and, in the foreground, another Brasilia, a type ASA launched into U.S. service in 1985. Courtesy Walter C. White

PURPOSE/ARRANGEMENT

There have been a number of illustrated, coffee-table volumes on commercial aircraft published of late, many calling themselves "encyclopedias," and most having originated overseas. These works, usually arranged alphabetically by manufacturer and model number, have generally stressed worldwide developments primarily for the years since World War II. They have often included all manner of general-aviation, fixed- and rotary-wing aircraft in addition to airline transports and have given text at least equal standing with photographs.

The book at hand stresses history and grew out of an in-house work originally designed as a supplemental tool for students in the aviation curriculum at Salem College, West Virginia. Its purpose is to provide an easily usable and indexed photo guide to a significant number of large and small, domestic and foreign-built, air transports delivered to U.S. carriers between 1926 and 1986. The basic criteria for a type's inclusion here is its use in the delivery of passengers over routes—short, medium, or long—within this country and overseas. To that end, we include 143 examples only of fixed-wing, passenger-capable planes from the past sixty years. These are arranged chronologically, by year of first U.S. airline service (usually a year or so after test flight, but in the case of several examples—primarily foreign types, e.g., Vickers Viscount—considerably longer). With some exceptions, derivatives, though introduced later, are discussed with original entries. Each aircraft is illustrated, in so far as possible, in the livery of various American airlines, including:
Aero Corporation of California

Aeromech Airlines
Afro-Latin Airways
Air East Airlines
Air Florida Commuter
Air Midwest*
Air New England
Air North
Air Texas
Air U.S.
Air Wisconsin*
AirPac Airlines*
Alaska Airlines*
Alaska Star Airlines
All-American Aviation
Allegheny Airlines
Allen Aviation
Aloha Airlines*
Altair Airlines
America West Airlines*
AmericAir
American Airlines*
American Airways
American Overseas Airlines
Antilles Air Boats
Apache Airlines
Arizona Airlines
Arrow Air*
Aspen Airways*
Atlantic Gulf Airlines
Atlantic Southeast Airlines*
AVAir*
Aztec Airways
Bar Harbor Airlines*
Boeing Air Transport
Braniff International Airways/Braniff, Inc.
Brockway Air*
Canadian Colonial Airways
Capital Airlines
Caribair

Cascade Airways*
Catalina Air Lines
Catalina Seaplanes*
Central American Airways
Chalk's International Airline*
Challenger Airlines
Chicago & Southern Air Lines
Colgan Airways*
Continental Airlines*
Cumberland Airlines*
Delta Air Lines*
Eastern Air Transport
Eastern Airlines*
Eastern Atlantis Express*
Eastern Metro Express*
Empire Airlines*
Fischer Bros. Aviation*
Florida Airways
Fort Yukon Air Service
Freedom Airlines
Frontier Airlines*
Golden Gate Airlines
Golden Pacific Airlines*
Grand Canyon Airlines*
Hawaiian Airlines*
Hood Airlines
Imperial Airlines*
Inter-Island Airways
Interior Airlines
Island Airlines*
Islander Airways
Jet Aire Airlines*
Jet America*
Jetstream International Airlines*
Johnson Flying Service
Lake Central Airlines
Long Island Airways
McGee Airways
Mall Airways*

Marco Island Airways
Metro Airlines*
Mid-Pacific Airlines*
Midstate Airlines*
Mohawk Airlines
Monarch Air Lines
Muse Air*
National Air Transport
National Airlines*
National Commuter Airlines
NewAir
New York Air*
New York, Rio and Buenos Aires Line
Northeast Airlines
Nothwest Airways
Northwest Orient Airlines*
Overseas National Airways
Ozark Airlines*
Pacific Air Transport
Pacific-Alaska Airways
Pacific Seaboard Airlines
Pacific Southwest Airlines (PSA)*
Pan American World Airways*
Pennsylvania Airlines*
Pennsylvania Central Airlines
Piedmont Airlines*
Pilgrim Airlines*
Pocono Airlines*
PRINAIR*
Provincetown-Boston Airline (PBA)*
Ransome Airlines*
Reeve Aleutian Airways*
Republic Express*
Resort Airlines/TWA Express*
Rio Airways*
Robinson Airlines
Rocky Mountain Airways*
Ryan Air Service*
San Juan Airlines*

Scenic Airlines*
Shawnee Airlines
Simmons Airlines*
SkyWest Airlines*
Slocum Air
Southeast Airlines
Southern Air Transport
Suburban Airlines*
Sunworld International Airlines*
Susquehanna Airlines*
Swifte Air
TAG Airlines
Texas Air Transport
Texas International Airlines
TransAir*
Trans-Central Airlines
Transcontinental Air Transport
Transcontinental & Western Air Lines
Trans-Island Airways
Trans-World Airlines*
Tri-State Airlines

United Airlines*
Universal Airlines
USAir*
Valley Air Lines
Volunteer/Air Vol
Western Air Express
Western Airlines*
Wien Air Alaska
Wings Airways*
Wings West Airlines*
Wright Airlines*

*Denotes those in service as of January 1986

Although the emphasis is on photographic depiction, basic descriptions, statistics, and selected carrier-service listing are included for each airliner. While aimed primarily at general readers, the work may also prove of interest to students of all ages, teachers, airline officials and employees, travel agents, aviation journalists and historians, model makers, librarians, airport services personnel, and all kinds of flight personnel, actual and armchair.

ACKNOWLEDGMENTS

This work could not have been completed without the help of many people directly involved with building or operating the aircraft described or in the preservation of their history. For their assistance with details and/or photographs, their inspiration and cooperation, acknowledgment and thanks are due to:

R.E.G. Davies, Curator of Air Transport and Pete Suthard, Chief, Records Management Division, National Air and Space Museum; Richard G. Millstone, President, Clarksburg Travel Service; William Crutchly; Jackie B. Pate, Public Relations, Delta Air Lines; Robert M. Takis, Manager, Photographic Services, Corporate Communications, American Airlines; Ann Whyte, Manager, Public Relations, Pan American World Airways; Lynn McCloud, Manager, Editorial Services, USAir; Ann Saunders, Corporate Communications, Trans World Airlines; Michael A. Cinelli, Manager, Public Relations, Continental Airlines; Glenn Parsons, Director, Public Relations, Eastern Airlines; Charles Novak, Manager, Corporate Communications, United Airlines; Kristi Hansman, Sales Representative, Provincetown-Boston Airline; May Ann Leffler, Marketing Department, ComAir; Robert Freeman, Director of Stations, Colgan Airways; Jim Woolsey and Lisa Henderson, *Air Transport World*; Rob Dondero, International Sales Representative, Scenic Airlines; Fred Claire and David Tuttle, Los Angeles Dodgers; Frederick Armstrong, Acting Director, West Virginia Department of Archives and History; John Gedraitis, Public Relations, Beech Aircraft Corporation; Valerie A. Young, Executive Assistant, Áerospatiale Aircraft Corporation; Andrea Rosse, Public Relations Director, CASA, Inc.; Susan D. Tweedy, Public Relations, The DeHavilland Aircraft of Canada, Ltd.; Allison R. Ward, Marketing Support, Gulfstream Aerospace Corporation; Richard G. Koenig, Manager, Marketing Media, Grumman Aerospace

Corporation; Jack Isabel, Manager of News and Information, Western Region Public Affairs, General Dynamics; Ove Dahlen, Regional Director, Airline Sales, Saab-Fairchild International; Emily Neff, Photo Archivist, West Virginia Department of Culture and History; Anne Millbrooke, Corporate Archivist, United Technologies; Al Woldin, Regional Manager, Airline Sales, Fairchild Aircraft Corporation; Stan Cohen; Monica Lee, Manager of Administration, Short Brothers (USA), Inc.; Alice M. Muller, Vice-President Administration, Embraer Aircraft Corporation; Robert M. Hawk, Director of Public Affairs, Fokker Aircraft USA, Inc.; Robert Sheridan Jonas, Vice-President, Jonas Aircraft and Arms Company, Inc.

Anonymous individuals in the following organizations also supplied detail and/or photographs:

Air Midwest
Air South
Air Wisconsin
Airbus Industrie
Alaska Airlines
Aloha Airlines
America West Airlines
Boeing Commercial Airplane Company
Braniff, Inc.
Cascade Airways
Chicago Museum of Science and Industry
Chicago White Sox
Eleutherian Mills Historical Library
Federal Express
Fokker BV
Ford Motor Company
Frontier Airlines
Henry Ford Museum
Lockheed
Meseba Airlines
Midstate Airlines
Northwest Orient Airlines
Ozark Airlines
Philippine Airlines
Piedmont Airlines
PRINAIR
Ransome Airlines
Reeve Aleutian Airways
Rockwell International
Southwest Airlines
Standard Oil of California
Teledyne Ryan Aeronautical Library
U.S. Air Force
U.S. Federal Aviation Administration
U.S. Forest Service
U.S. National Archives
U.S. Navy
United Technologies
Western Airlines
Wien Air Alaska

Special appreciation is reserved for my colleagues at Salem College and KCI Aviation, without whose backing and aid this project could not have been completed. Dr. Ronald E. Ohl and Board of Trustee member Angelo C. Koukoulis, himself well known in the aviation community, generously supported and encouraged me to proceed. A number of the students in the local chapter of Alpha Etha Rho fraternity, as well as others in the Salem College Aviation Program, provided miscellaneous assistance. At KCI Aviation, Charles A. Koukoulis, CEO, and Dale Squire, Flight Instructor and Salem College Liaison, afforded me technical insight, airline operating data, and coordination of contacts and correspondence. Thanks to Amy Ragsdale and Steve Smith for their proofreading and editing assistance.

A special wave from the cockpit is sent to Robert E. Garrard of Bethesda, Maryland. A noted aviation photographer, many of his shots are employed here and add immeasurably to the dramatic impact. Also, S.C. Dean Gary McAllister, who spent countless hours helping me refine the manuscript, is deserving of that special appreciation really best known between friends.

Finally, warmest remembrances are held of the many hours during which my wife, Dennie, actively assisted—or just plain tolerated—me in the preparation of this work. Like many of those which preceded it, this outing has gone smoothly largely because of her involvement.

Myron J. Smith, Jr.
Salem, West Virginia
March 1, 1986

AIRCRAFT CATALOG *(by page)*

■ FORD-STOUT Series 2-AT to 4-AT Tri-Motor

First Service: 1925-1926

Type/Purpose: Single-engined, commercial, short/medium-haul transport (2-AT)
Tri-Motor, commercial, short/medium-haul transport (4-AT)

Number of Seats: 2 crew, 8 passengers (2-AT)/
2 crew, 10-11 passengers (4-AT)

Dimensions: Length: 46 feet (2-AT)/ 49.10 feet (4-AT)
Height: 13 feet
Wingspan: 58 feet (2-AT)/ 74 feet (4-AT)
Gross weight (pounds): 6,000 (2-AT)/ 10,000 (4-AT)

Engines: 1 Liberty (2-AT)/ 3 Wright J-4,-5, or 6−9 Whirlwind radial (4-AT)

Performance: Maximum range: 400 miles (2-AT)/
500+ miles (4-AT)
Service ceiling: 15,000 feet (2-AT)/18,000 feet (4-AT)
Maximum speed: 120−128 mph
Maximum cruising speed: 100 mph

Initial Test Flight: 1924 (2-AT)/ June 11, 1926 (4-AT)

Initial U.S. Operator Service: Ford Motor Company (private express), April 3, 1925 (2-AT)/Ford Motor Company, August 26, 1926 (4-AT)

Remarks: One of the, if not *the*, most important U.S. airliners prior to the introduction of the Boeing 247, the Ford Tri-Motor was originally conceived as entrepreneur Bill Stout's single-engined, 8-passenger 2-AT (AT = air transport) Air Pullman of 1924. Powered by a single Liberty engine, Stout's aircraft was the nation's first all-metal airliner, with a distinctive corrugated, sheet-aluminum skin covering its tubular-aluminum framework. Shortly after passage of the Kelly Act in 1925, Henry Ford was persuaded to take an interest in aviation and became Stout's backer, inviting the Stout Metal Airplane Company to relocate in Dearborn, Michigan. Ford's company airline began a private Detroit-Chicago express service on April 3 and a second Detroit-Cleveland operation on July 31, the same day it purchased the Stout concern. Meanwhile, watching the conversion by Anthony Fokker of his F-VIIA into the F-VIIA/3M, Ford employees found it a relatively simple matter to modify the 2-AT into a tri-motor. The prototype 3-AT, with a blunt nose, open cockpit, and unique power-plant layout, was destroyed in a $500,000 fire at the Dear-

born plant. It was quickly replaced with a second design, the 4-AT, also based on the 2-AT and having all three engines at the same level. Able to carry 11 passengers, the extremely rugged "Tin Goose" would quickly gain fame for its ability to land heavy loads on very small fields. Like the 2-AT, no 4-AT ever had a structural failure in flight. The aircraft was robust, uncomplicated, unheated, very noisy, and easily maintained, and if it had a failure, it was a need for additional power to meet the challenge of the Fokker F-10A. Production models of this 4-AT were somewhat larger than either the 2-AT or the Tri-Motor prototype, were more streamlined, moved the pilot and copilot inside the cabin, and required right-side cabin entry in contrast to later airliners. Series 4-AT-A through -F production came to 78 aircraft: 14 As, 39 Bs, 1 C, 3 Ds, 24 Es, and 1 F; the As and a few Bs had exhaust manifolds running up through their wings. Several 4-ATs soldier on long after their obsolescence, with at least one serving into the 1950s with the famous forest-fire-fighting Johnson Flying Service of Missoula, Montana. The world's record for continuous airline service with a single aircraft model also belongs to the 4-AT; from 1926 to the mid-1970s, Island Airlines flew 2 Bs over a 10-mile route from Port Clinton, Ohio to the Bass Islands in Lake Erie.

Selected List of U.S. Operating Airlines: Colonial Western Airways; Florida Airways; Ford Motor Company; Island Airlines; Johnson Flying Service; Maddux Air Lines; Rapid Air Lines ■

Florida Airways launched passenger service with these three Stout 2-ATs (the closest named *Miss Miami*, the one in the center *Miss St. Petersburg*, and the farthest unknown) on June 1, 1926; the pioneer airline was, however, soon thereafter forced to discontinue service when two of the three aircraft were lost. SI #A46893-J

Cabin of Ford Tri-Motor in 1929. Note that the radio operator sat in the front seat. Courtesy Pan American World Airways

Flight deck of a Pan Am Ford Tri-Motor. Courtesy Pan American World Airways

This Ford Tri-motor, shown at Idaho's Moose Creek landing field in 1962, was flown by Johnson Flying Service of Missoula, Montana. Courtesy U.S. Forest Service.

■ CURTISS LARK

First Service: 1926

Number of Seats: 1 pilot, 2 passengers

Dimensions: Length: 21 feet
    Height: 11 feet
    Wingspan: 31 feet
    Gross weight (pounds): 2,708

Engines: 1 Wright J-4 Whirlwind radial

Performance: Maximum range: 380 miles
    Service ceiling: 10,000 feet
    Maximum cruising speed: 97 mph

Initial Test Flight: late 1925 or early 1926

Initial U.S. Operator Service: Colonial Air Transport,
    June 18, 1926

Remarks: Only three of these fabric-covered biplanes were constructed, with two going to Colonial Air Transport and one to Florida Airways. The Lark not only possessed a Wright Whirlwind engine but was built with interchangeable wing panels, allowing for a longer wingspan on occasion. Employed primarily for mail operations, the aircraft could, on slow days, carry a maximum of two passengers in its forward cockpit.

Selected List of U.S. Operating Airlines: Colonial Air Transport; Florida Airways ■

With its long lower wing and Wright J-4 Whirlwind engine, this Curtiss lark of Colonial Air Transport, photographed at Boston Airport, flew the first service over C.A.M. No. 1 on July 1, 1926. Courtesy American Airlines

■ DOUGLAS M Series

First Service: 1926

Type/Purpose: Single-engined, commercial, mail/passenger
    transport

Number of Seats: 1 pilot, 2 passengers

Dimensions: Length: 29 feet (M-1 to 3)/28.11 feet (M-4)
    Height: 10.1 feet
    Wingspan: 40 feet (M-1 to 3)/44.6 feet (M-4)
    Gross weight (pounds): 4,968

Engines: 1 Liberty 12

Performance: Maximum range: 650-700 miles
    Service ceiling: 12,000 feet
    Maximum speed: 140 mph
    Maximum cruising speed: 110 mph

Initial Test Flight: July 6, 1925

Initial U.S. Operator Service: Western Air Express,
    April 17, 1926

Remarks: Based on the Douglas 0-2 U.S. Army observation planes, the Douglas DAM-1 was developed to succeed the DeHavilland DH-4 in U.S. airmail operations. The 5 biplane M-2s delivered to Western Air Express (WAE) in spring 1926 were slightly modified so as to be passenger/cargo convertible. Within a month of their arrival, Western launched America's first sustained passenger service between the California coast and Salt Lake City. For $60 per head, up to two passengers could be squeezed aboard the M-2 on folding chairs in the forward mail hold, giving the airline an extra profit over that derived from the U.S. Mail. WAE transported 209 customers in this uncomfortable fashion in 1926. Western later ordered another M-2 and operated the original DAM-1, brought up to M-2 standard and called the M-1. In March 1926, the U.S. Air Mail Service ordered 10 improved M-3s, following later in the year with an order for 40 M-4s, the most numerous of the M series. The M-4 could transport one passenger in place of a mail load, and featured night-flying equipment and a radio. Following the demise of the Post Office airmail operation, National Air Transport joined Western in flying the M series, total production of which was completed at 60 planes.

Selected List of U.S. Operating Airlines: National Air Transport; U.S. Air Mail Service; Western Air Express ■

The Douglas M-2 of famed Western Air Express pilot Fred Kelly. Courtesy McDonnell-Douglas

The Douglas M-3 was an improved version of the M-2 and was operated by the U.S. Air Mail Service. Courtesy McDonnell-Douglas

The M-2 developed for Western Air Express could transport 2 passengers and marked the beginning for Douglas as a major aircraft manufacturer. This unit (C-150) was restored to flying condition prior to its delivery to the National Air and Space Museum. Courtesy James P. Woolsey

Following the demise of the U.S. Air Mail Service in 1927, National Air Express joined Western Air Express in flying the Douglas M-4, the most numerous of the M series. SI #86-12050

■ FOKKER Model 4 Universal

First Service: 1926

Type/Purpose: Single-engined, commercial, short/medium-haul transport

Number of Seats: 2 crew, 5-6 passengers

Dimensions: Length: 33.6 feet
Height: 8.6 feet
Wingspan: 47.9 feet
Gross weight (pounds): 4,300

Engines: 1 Wright J-5 or 1 Wright J-6-9 Whirlwind radial

Performance: Maximum range: 525-700 miles
Service ceiling: 11,000-14,200 feet
Maximum speed: 118-130 mph
Maximum cruising speed: 100-105 mph

Initial Test Flight: Fall 1925

Initial U.S. Operator Service: Colonial Air Transport, May 1926

Remarks: Designed by Robert Noorduyn, the Model 4 Universal was one of the first modern, cantilevered, high-wing, monoplane designs to appear on the U.S. commercial air transport scene and the first aircraft bearing the Fokker name to be designed entirely in America. Produced by the Fokker Aircraft Corporation/Atlantic Aircraft Corporation, the Model 4 was similar in structure and appearance to contemporary Dutch-built Fokkers and had a welded, steel-tube fuselage and tail and a plywood-skinned, wood-frame wing with strut bracing. In its original form, the aircraft had an open cockpit ahead of the wing; later, the cockpit was enclosed and the pilot was moved to the left, allowing another person to sit in the cockpit in a fold-down seat, probably less comfortable than the individual, staggered seats in the passenger cabin. A unique feature of the Model 4's control system was the provision of double-rudder controls, but only one stick for the use of the two pilots. The wheel undercarriage was interchangeable with skis or floats. Fokker built 45 Model 4s.

Selected List of U.S. Operating Airlines: Aero Corporation of California; California Airways; Canadian Colonial Airways; Colonial Air Transport; Continental Air Express; Dominion Airways; Northwest Airways; Pacific Air Transport; Reynolds Airways; St. Tammany Gulf Coast Airways; Standard Air Lines ■

This Fokker Model 4 Universal was employed by the Aero Corporation of California during the mid-1920s. Courtesy Trans World Airlines

A Colonial Air Transport Fokker Model 4 Universal photographed at Buffalo, New York, in 1926. Note the plane's open cockpit. SI #743712

■ FOKKER F-VIIA / F-VIIA-3M

First Service: 1926

Type/Purpose: Single-engined, commercial, short/medium-haul trasport (F-VIIA)/
Tri-motor, commercial, short/medium-haul transport (F-VIIA-3M)

Number of Seats: 2 crew, 7-8 passengers

Dimensions: Length: 49.2 feet
Height: 12.5 feet
Wingspan: 63.3 feet
Gross weight (pounds): 7,650 (F-VIIA)/
9,000 (F-VIIA-3M)

Engines: 1 Bristol Jupiter radial (F-VIIA)/
3 Wright J-4 Whirlwind radial (F-VIIA-3M)

Performance: Maximum range: 560 miles
Service ceiling: 12,500 feet
Maximum speed: 122 mph
Maximum cruising speed: 100 miles

Initial Test Flight: September 4, 1925 (F-VIIA)

Initial U.S. Operator Service: Standard Air Lines, 1928 (F-VIIA)/Philadelphia Rapid Transit (PRT) Line, July 6, 1926 (F-VIIA-3M)

Remarks: The aircraft firm of Anthony Fokker designed the Fokker VIIA, high-wing, cabin monoplane in Holland and a number were exported to the United States, among other countries, for airline use. The least reliable feature of the sturdy aircraft was its single engine. While in America to plan possible participation in an endurance contest, Fokker wired Holland, ordering a tri-motor. The resulting F-VIIA-3M (3M = tri-motor) was personally demonstrated by Fokker in the 1925 Ford Reliability Tour. The tour was a great success for Fokker, whose firm soon received civil and military tri-motor orders. The original touring F-VIIA-3M was purchased by Edsel Ford for Commander Richard E. Byrd, who employed the aircraft to make the first overflights of the North Pole on May 9, 1926. The aircraft placed in service by the PRT Line were built in the Netherlands, assembled at Fokker's American plant, and delivered as American-made planes. As these foreign Fokkers were not designed for American conditions, Fokker's American factory turned its attention to an indigenous design, the F-10. A total of 25 Fokker F-VIIA-3Ms were assembled in the U.S.

Pan Am's 10-passenger Fokker F-VIIA/3m *General Machado* inaugurated the carrier's first scheduled passenger flight on January 16, 1928, a 60-min., 90-mile flight from Key West to Havana. Courtesy Pan American World Airways

Selected List of U.S. Operating Airlines: F-VIIA – Standard Air Lines; Universal Air Lines; *F-VIIA-3M* – Pan American Airways; PRT Line; Reynolds Airways; Western Air Express ■

Passengers board the *General Machado's* sistership *General New* in spring 1928. Courtesy Pan American World Airways

LAIRD LC-B/LC-R Commercial-Speedwing

First Service: 1926

Type/Purpose: Single-engined, commercial, short-haul transport

Number of Seats: 1 pilot, 2 passengers

Dimensions: Length: 22.9 feet
  Height: 8 feet
  Wingspan: 34 feet (LC-B)/28 feet (LC-R)
  Gross weight (pounds): 2,850 (LC-B)/2,914 (LC-R)

Engines: 1 Wright J-4 Whirlwind radial (LC-B)/
  1 Wright J-5 Whirlwind radial (LC-R200)/
  1 Wright J-6-9 Whirlwind radial (LC-R300)

Performance: Maximum range: 600–650 miles
  Service ceiling: 16,000 feet
  Maximum speed: 145 mph
  Maximum cruising speed: 120 mph

Initial Test Flight: 1926 (LC-B)/1928 (LC-R)

Initial U.S.Operator Service: Charles Dickenson,
  June 7, 1926

Remarks: Famous for the Swallow mail plane, E.M. ("Matty") Laird began building his LC (Laird Commercial) series in Wichita, Kansas, in 1924, moving his base to Chicago in 1926. In the Windy City, Laird began offering an improved LC, the Model B, which was more powerful and replaced the wood-wire fuselage of the preceding LC with one made from steel-clamped, aluminum tubing. In 1928, Laird began development of an improved and more appealing version, the LC-R, called Speedwing. The new aircraft was equipped with a Wright J-5 Whirlwind in its 200 version and Wright J-6-9 Whirlwind in its 300. Although the wings were clipped to six feet, the manufacture of the wooden wings and aluminum fuselage remained the same, as did the side-by-side seating for two passengers in the front cockpit. The most notable—and noticeable—feature of the new Laird was the use of a wooden I-strut attached to both spars in each wing, in place of the more traditional N-struts. A total of 5 LC-R200s and 10 LC-R300s were built, although Laird constructed a number of one-only designs to order. Among these were several racing planes, including one that allowed Jimmy Doolittle to win the 1931 Bendix cross-country race. The final variant was the LC-RW300 of 1930, 2 of which were built each with a single Pratt & Whitney R-985 Wasp Jr. radial. Employed as both mail and passenger aircraft on occasion, the LCs saw only limited airline service, including that with Charles Dickenson, a short-lived carrier taken over by Northwest Airways in late 1926.

Selected List of U.S. Operating Airlines: Northwest Airways ■

Northwest Airways Laird LC-R Speedwing. Note the large wing I-strut. Courtesy Northwest Orient Airlines

■ RYAN M-1/M-2

First Service: 1926

Type/Purpose: Single-engined, commercial, mail/passenger transport

Number of Seats: 1 crew, 2 passengers (M-1)/1 crew, 4 passengers (M-2)

Dimensions: Length: 22 feet
Wingspan: 36 feet
Gross weight (pounds): 3,500

Engines: 1 Wright Whirlwind radial

Performances: Maximum range: 500+ miles
Service ceiling: 19,000 feet
Maximum speed: 135 mph
Maximum cruising speed: 115 mph

Initial Test Flight 1926

Initial U.S. Operator Service: Pacific Air Transport, September 15, 1926

Remarks: Early in 1926, T. Claude Ryan in California began building the first aircraft of his own design, the M-1. This high-wing monoplane with prominent bracing and tandem, open cockpits would be marketed to carry mail and a couple of passengers. Nine M-1s were delivered to customers while the tenth incorporated so many improvements that Ryan rechristened it M-2. Outwardly, it was difficult to tell an early M-2 from an M-1, except that the cockpit doors of the former were moved to the right side, and flange-and-web, I-beam spars were substituted for the original box spars. A total of 18 M-2s were constructed. The first M-2 was eventually converted into Ryan's personal runabout, a five-place, cabin model, which he called the *Bluebird.* The improvements on this lone plane soon led to an order for a larger variant, which was eventually built as the Brougham. Work was under way on that new aircraft when a young man from St. Louis appeared at the San Diego factory and, pleased by inspection of the *Bluebird* and Brougham plans, asked Ryan designer Donald Hall to construct a special-order aircraft for a long-distance flight. The young man's name was Charles A. Lindbergh and his Hall-designed airplane, *Spirit of St. Louis,* would become the most-famous Ryan airplane of all.

Selected List of U.S. Operating Airlines: Colorado Airways; Pacific Air Transport ■

Pacific Air Transport's Ryan M-1 in flight. Courtesy United Airlines

■ STINSON SB-1/SM-1 Detroiter

First Service: 1926

Type/Purpose: Single-engined, commercial, short/medium-haul transport

Number of Seats: 1 pilot, 4 passengers (SB-1)/1 pilot, 5 passengers (SM-1)

Dimensions: Length: 28.10 feet
   Height: 9 feet
   Wingspan: 35.10 feet (SB-1)/36 feet (SM-1)
   Gross weight (pounds): 2,900 (SB-1)/3,280 (SM-1)

Engines: 1 Wright J-4 Whirlwind radial (SB-1)/
   1 Wright J-5 Whirlwind radial (SM-1)

Performance: Maximum range: 600–700 miles
   Service ceiling: 13,500 feet
   Maximum speed: 118 mph
   Maximum cruising speed: 100 mph

Initial Test Flight: January 25, 1926 (SB-1)/1927 (SM-1)

Initial U.S. Operator Service: Florida Airways, September 1926 (SB-1)/Northwest Airways, July 1, 1927 (SM-1)

Remarks: Designed as a cabin monoplane by Edward A. Stinson and Frederick Verville, the first Detroiter (SB-1), named after the city in which it was built, placed the pilot inside the cabin and, in two other firsts, featured an electric starter and mechanical wheel brakes. With a welded steel-tube fuselage and tail and wooden wings, the SB-1 was fabric covered and retained a classic gap between the top of the fuselage and the bottom of the upper wing. Immediately successful, the SB-1, of which 22 were manufactured, could be operated as either a passenger or cargo/mail plane. Its production ended in June 1927. The Detroiter achieved its greatest success in its high-wing-monoplane configuration, the SM-1 to 6 series, of which 96 were built. The SB-1 provided the first proper airliners for Northwest Airways, while the SM-1 helped launch the services of Braniff. Overseas, 4 SM-1Fs operated the first regular airmail service in China. When SM-1 production ended in 1928, Stinson was turning its attention toward the generally unrecognized business market, although it would be back in the airliner game with the larger SM-6000 and SM Models U and A during the following decade.

A three-passenger Stinson SB-1 Detroiter, one of three which formed the initial fleet of Northwest Airways. Courtesy Northwest Orient Airlines

Selected List of U.S. Operating Airlines: Florida Airways; Northwest Airways; Patricia Airways; Paul R. Braniff, Inc.; Wayco Air Service; Wien Alaska Airways; Wyoming Air Service ■

Paul R. Braniff Inc.'s original Stinson SM-1 Detroiter was employed on the Tulsa-Oklahoma City Airline in 1928; the carrier was sold to the Universal Aviation Corporation in 1929. In 1930, Tom and Paul Braniff organized Braniff Airways, later Braniff International Airways, later Braniff, Inc. SI #73-3667

■ BOEING Model 40/Model 40A

First Service: 1927

Type/Purpose: Single-engined, commercial, mail/passenger transport

Number of Seats: 1 pilot, 2 passengers (40A)/1 pilot, 4 passengers (40B/40C)

Dimensions: Length: 33.3 feet
Height: 12.4 feet
Wingspan: 44.2 feet
Gross weight (pounds): 6,000 (40A)/6,079 (40B/40C)

Engines: Pratt & Whitney Wasp radial (40A)
Pratt & Whitney Hornet radial (40B/40C)

Performance: Maximum range: 535–650 miles
Service ceiling: 16,100 feet
Maximum speed: 137.7 mph
Maximum cruising speed: 105 mph (40A)/
110–125 mph (40B/40C)

Initial Test Flight: July 7, 1925 (40)/May 20, 1927 (40A)/
October 5, 1929 (40B-4)

Initial U.S. Operator Service: Boeing Air Transport,
July 1, 1927 (40A)
Varney Air Lines, September 15, 1929 (40B-4)

Remarks: When government-oriented transcontinental airmail routes were handed over to private operators in 1926 to 1927, Boeing submitted the low bid for the key leg from San Francisco to Chicago. A new subsidiary, Boeing Air Transport, was formed and the Seattle factory completed a Liberty-engine-equipped aircraft, the Model 40. This prototype was reworked into the Model 40A, of which two dozen were built between January and June 1927. Unlike most of the competing airplane types used for mail service, the 40A had space for two passengers in a small cabin ahead of the pilot's open cockpit, in which, incidentally, a radio was added as a standard feature for the first time. As originally figured, the 40A could carry 1,200 pounds of mail in addition to its human cargo. When the Hornet engine became available in 1928, 19 surviving 40As were so equipped and the plane was redesignated Model 40B. In mid-1928, Boeing began to turn out the Model 40C, 11 of which were built, 10 with Wasp and 1 with Pratt & Whitney radials and all with cabins for four passengers. A year later, the final production model, an improved 40B called the 40B-4 became available. It featured four-passenger seating, space for 1,000 pounds of mail, improved cowling rings, radio, and steerable tail wheels and was the most numerous of the 40 series with 38 constructed. The success of Boeing's 82 Model 40s led the company to build the Model 80 and thus enter the airliner business it had come to dominate by the 1980s. Two Model 40s still survive, one in the Chicago Museum of Science and Industry and the other in the Henry Ford Museum, Dearborn, Michigan.

Selected List of U.S. Operating Airlines: Boeing Air Transport; National Park Airways; Pacific Air Transport; Varney Air Lines; Western Air Express ■

Boeing 40B-4 in Universal Air Lines markings. Courtesy American Airlines

A Boeing 40A of Boeing Air Transport seen flying mail and four passengers over its San Francisco-Chicago route in 1930. Courtesy United Airlines

■ FAIRCHILD FC-2/FC-2W

First Service: 1927

Type/Purpose: Single-engined, commercial, utility transport

Number of Seats: 1 pilot, 4 passengers (FC-2)/1 pilot,
6 passengers (FC-2W)

Dimensions: Length: 50 feet (FC-2)/33 feet (FC-2W)
Height: 9.6 feet (FC-2)/9.4 feet (FC-2W)
Wingspan: 44 feet (FC-2)/50 feet (FC-2W)
Gross weight (pounds): 3,600 (FC-2)/ 5,500 (FC-2W)

Engines: 1 Wright J-5 Whirlwind radial (FC-2)/
1 Pratt & Whitney R-1340 Wasp radial (FC-2W)

Performance: Maximum range: 700 miles
Service ceiling: 11,500 feet – 15,000 feet
Maximum speed: 122 mph – 127 mph
Maximum cruising speed: 104 mph – 115 mph

Initial Test Flight: June 20, 1927 (FC-2)/fall 1927 (FC-2W)

Initial U.S. Operator Service: Pan American Airways,
October 19, 1927 (FC-2)/Pan American Grace Airways
(PANAGRA), May 17, 1929 (FC-2W)

Remarks: A distinctive, high-wing monoplane built in both
the U.S.A. and Canada, the Fairchild FC series was widely
employed by private, bush, airline, and military pilots and
concerns. A total of 161 FC-2s were built and Cy Caldwell,
with one of these, flew the first private-enterprise international airmail on behalf of Pan Am from Key West to
Havana. The FC-2W was a stretched version of the FC-2
with a six-foot-longer wingspan and an engine that allowed
the aircraft twice the power of its predecessor. A total of 50
FC-2Ws were manufactured and with different engines
and slight modifications to the airframe, it was also sold
under the model designations 41, 42, and 51. As with the
FC-2, the FC-2W was widely employed in the Arctic with
skis or twin floats.

Selected List of U.S. Operating Airlines: FC-2 – Canadian
Colonial Airways; Clifford Ball Airlines; Colonial Western
Airways; Curtiss Flying Service; Pan American Airways;
Pan American Grace Airways (PANAGRA); West Indian
Aerial Express; *FC-2W* – Canadian Colonial Airways; In-
terstate Airlines; Pan American Grace Airways (PAN-
AGRA) ■

Shown in the cockpit of his Fairchild FC-2, *La Nina*, Cy Caldwell prepares to launch the first
U.S. private-enterprise international airmail service, Key West to Havana, on behalf of Pan
American Airways in October 1927. Courtesy Pan American World Airways

An excellent profile of a Fairchild FC-2W of the kind introduced by Pan American-Grace Airways (PANANGRA) on May 17, 1929. SI #49624A

A Fairchild FC-2W of Canadian Colonial Airways, a carrier which became a part of Colonial Airways in 1929. Courtesy American Airlines

Robert C. Reeve and Fairchild 51 on Valdez mudflats in 1936. Note landing gear. Courtesy Bob Reeve Collection, Reeve Aleutian Airways

■ SIKORSKY S-36

First Service: 1927

Type/Purpose: Twin-engined, route-proving amphibian

Number of Seats: 2 crew, 7 passengers

Dimensions: Length: 34 feet
    Height: 13.1 feet
    Wingspan: 71 feet
    Gross weight (pounds): 6,000

Engines: 2 Wright J-5 Whirlwind radials

Performance: Maximum range: 200 miles
    Service ceiling: 12,000 feet
    Maximum cruising speed: 90 mph

Initial Test Flight: 1927

Initial U.S. Operator Service: Pan American Airways, 1927

Remarks: Entered not for the number built, but for its significance: the S-36 was the first practical Sikorsky amphibian. Fully serviceable, it provided important experience for both its manufacturer and fledgling Pan American Airways and led to Sikorsky's first completely successful American-made aircraft, the S-38. Each of the five S-36s constructed was different in wingspan, cabin, cockpit, floats, nacelles, fins, and rudders with about the only commonality, aside from the twin tails, being the Wright J-5 power plant. The first U.S. Navy purchase of a Sikorsky airplane was an experimental, patrol version of the S-36, the XPS-1. ■

Pan Am took delivery of this Sikorsky S-36, *The Dawn,* on December 7, 1927. Courtesy Pan American World Airways

■ WACO Model 9/Model 10

First Service: 1927

Type/Purpose: Single-engined, commercial, short/medium-haul transport

Number of Seats: 1 pilot, 2 passengers

Dimensions: Length: 23.6 feet
Height: 7 feet
Wingspan: 30.7 feet
Gross weight (pounds): 2,025-2,400

Engines: 1 Curtiss OX-5 radial (Model 9)/
1 Wright J-5 Whirlwind radial (Model 10)

Performance: Maximum range: 400-500 miles
Service ceiling: 12,000 feet
Maximum speed: 97-126 mph
Maximum cruising speed: 84-90 mph

Initial Test Flight: 1925 (Model 9)/ 1927 (Model 10)

Initial U.S. Operator Service: Clifford Ball, April 21, 1927

Remarks: Highly versatile, the WACO Model 9 possessed a traditional straight-wing-biplane configuration, being one of the first production designs to feature welded, steel-tube construction for fuselage and tail. Capable of transporting mail, express, or up to two passengers in its forward cockpit, the aircraft could accommodate a large variety of power plants, although it normally had a war surplus Curtiss OX-5. The popular Model 10, introduced in 1927, was a refined version of the fabric-covered Model 9, with perhaps the most recognizable initial difference between the two versions appearing in their landing-gear design. Employed by business, sport, mail, airline, bush, and other operators, a new Model 10 could be purchased in fall 1927 for $2,385. The only regressive feature of the aircraft, as several passengers learned when leaks occurred, was the positioning of its radiator under the center section of the upper wing. In an effort to increase sales in 1928 and beyond, WACO Chief Test Pilot Charles Meyers was allowed to try a different wing design and a more powerful Wright engine. The resulting ATO Taperwing won a variety of air races, became a company production model (with variants), and increased WACO business. A total of 1,350 Model 9s and 10s were constructed, including between 55 and 60 Taperwings.

Selected List of U.S. Operating Airlines: Clifford Ball; Northwest Airways; Texas Flying Service; Woodley Airways ■

Texas Flying Service (a division of Southern Air Transport) operated a variety of small aircraft in 1928-1929, including at least two WACO Model 10 (third from right and far right). Courtesy American Airlines

A special-purpose version of the WACO Taperwing was this single-seat JYM equipped with a Wright J-6-7 Whirlwind radial. Northwest Airways employed three on mail routes. Courtesy Northwest Orient Airlines

■ BACH 3-CT Series 2-9 Air Yacht

First Service: 1928

Type/Purpose: Tri-motor, commercial, short-haul transport

Number of Seats: 2 pilots, 8-10 passengers

Dimensions: Length: 36.1-36.10 feet
    Wingspan: 52-58.5 feet
    Gross weight (pounds): 6,400-8,000

Engines: 1 Wright J-5 Whirlwind radial/
    2 Ryan-Siemens SH-12 radials (3-CT-2)/
    1 Pratt & Whitney Wasp/
    2 Ryan-Siemens SH-12 radials (3-CT- 3)/
    1 Pratt & Whitney Wasp/
    2 Wright Comet radials (3-CT-5)/
    1 Pratt & Whitney Hornet/
    2 Wright Comet radials (3-CT-6)/
    1 Pratt & Whitney Hornet/ 2 Wright J-5 Whirlwind
    radials (3-CT-8)/
    1 Pratt & Whitney Wasp/ 2 Wright J-6 or J-7 Whirlwind
    radials (3-CT-9)

Performance: Maximum range: 500-600 miles
    Service ceiling: 16,000-20,190 feet
    Maximum speed: 135-162 mph
    Maximum cruising speed: 100-136 mph

Initial Test Flight: 1927

Initial U.S. Operator Service: West Coast Air Transport,
    March 5, 1928

Remarks: The Bach airliners were noted for their engine "intermix," meaning different types of power plants were employed in hopes of keeping the plane aloft during difficulties. Designed by Californian Mort Bach, the Air Yacht was the only U.S.-certified civil transport made entirely of wood and was perhaps the quietest airliner of its day. The wing struts, looking something like those pioneered by Bellanca, ran from the lower longerons via the engine nacelles to the upper longerons. Bach built some 21 3-CTs between 1928 and these proved popular with Western feeder-lines from 1929 through 1934.

Selected List of U.S. Operating Airlines: Gilpin Airline; Pickwick Airways; Union Air Lines; West Coast Air Transport ■

This Bach 3-CT-6 was introduced by West Coast Air Transport on March 5, 1928, and was employed on routes from San Francisco to Seattle.
SI #A482036

■ BOEING Model 80/Model 80A

First Service: 1928

Type/Purpose: Trimotor, commercial, short/medium-haul transport

Number of Seats: 3 crew, 12-19 passengers

Dimensions: Length: 54.11 feet (80)/ 56.6 feet (80A)
Height: 15.3 feet
Wingspan (upper): 80 feet
Gross weight (pounds): 15,276 (80)/ 17,500 (80A)

Engines: 3 Pratt & Whitney R-1340 Wasp radials (80)/
3 Pratt & Whitney R-1860 Hornet raidals (80A)

Performance: Maximum range: 545 miles (80)/
460 miles (80A)
Service ceiling: 14,000 feet
Maximum speed: 128 mph (80)/ 138.7 mph (80A)
Maximum cruising speed: 115 mph (80)/
125 mph (80A)

Initial Test Flight: July 27, 1928

Initial U.S. Operator Service: Boeing Air Transport,
October 28, 1928 (80)

Remarks: The tri-motor, single-tail Model 80 was an expanded version of the successful Boeing 40A. This biplane introduced three-abreast seating making a shorter cabin possible; when launched in 1928 on the Chicago-San Francisco route of Boeing Air Transport, a predecessor of United Airlines, the winged contemporary of the Ford Tri-Motor and Fokker F-10 carried two pilots, a steward, and 3,800 pounds of payload, including 14 passengers, mail, express, and baggage. So successful were the four Model 80s that Boeing began work on a more powerful and slightly longer (18-19 passenger) variant, the Model 80A, which was certified in August 1929. Designed specifically for luxurious passenger transport, the aircraft, with its leather seats and veneer interior, quickly became known as the "Pullman of the Air." Ten 80As were built: eight passenger airliners, one open cockpit 80B, and one that became a deluxe oil company executive transport known as the Model 226. Eventually, several of the 80As were modified into 80A-1s, with engine cowlings, increased fuel capacity, and triple tail fins. All flew on with the United conglomerate until the introduction of the Boeing 247 in 1934. Two were later sold to Bob Reeve, who employed them for contract work with the U.S. Army as late as World War II.

Selected List of U.S. Operating Airlines: Boeing Air Transport; Reeve Aleutian Airways; United Air Lines ■

One of four Boeing Model 80s built for Boeing Air Transport in 1928; note the enclosed cockpit of early pattern engine cowlings. Courtesy United Airlines

Reeve Airways Boeing 80A at Merrill Field, Anchorage, Alaska, in 1942. Courtesy Bob Reeve Collection, Reeve Aleutian Airways

■ FOKKER F-10/F-10A Super Tri-motor

First Service: 1928

Type/Purpose: Tri-motor, commercial, short/medium-haul
transport

Number of Seats: 2 crew, 12 passenger (F-10)/ 3 crew,
14 passengers (F-10A)

Dimensions: Length: 50 feet (F-10)/ 50.7 feet (F-10A)
Height: 12.9 feet
Wingspan: 71 feet (F-10)/ 79.2 feet (F-10A)
Gross weight (pounds): 12,500 (F-10)/ 13,100 (F-10A)

Engines: 3 Pratt & Whitney Wasp radials

Performance: Maximum range: 900 miles (F-10)/
765 miles (F-10A)
Service ceiling: 15,420 – 18,000 feet
Maximum speed: 145 mph
Maximum cruising speed: 123 mph

Initial Test Flight: September 4, 1925

Initial U.S. Operator Service: Western Air Express,
May 26, 1928 (F-10)/
Western Air Express, November 13, 1928 (F-10A)

Remarks: The first Fokker trimotor completely designed in
the United States was the F-10. Assembled at Fokker's
American company, Atlantic Aircraft Corporation, the
plane employed Dutch-built, F-VIIA/B3 wings, a
U.S.-made Super Universal fuselage, and Wasp engines to
meet an initial requirement of Western Air Express. Seven
F-10s were built, of which four were delivered to WAE and
hence, by partial merger, to TWA, while two were converted to F-10A standard. The F-10A, built at a new Fokker
plant near Wheeling, West Virginia, introduced longer,
American-made wings and greater operating weight. Alto-
gether, some 60 of these improved models were constructed, a large run for its day. The commercial operation
of wooden-winged Fokker aircraft in the United States
came to an abrupt end following the March 31, 1931, crash
of a TWA F-10A, which killed all aboard including famed
Notre Dame football coach Knute Rockne. The accident
was blamed on wing failure and the resulting public out-
cry led the Aeronautics Branch of the Department of Commerce (sort of a predecessor to today's FAA) to ground all
Fokkers in American service. The aircraft were subsequently allowed to fly again, but only in nonpassenger
(primarily mail) service. Despite this finale, the Fokker
trimotors played an important role in the development of
U.S. air transport. Their success led to competition from
other three-engined, commercial airliners, notably those
of Bach, Stinson, Boeing, and Ford, and their failure forced
designers to develop successors that would include the
revolutionary Boeing 247 and the Douglas Commercials 1,
2, and 3.

Selected List of U.S. Operating Airlines: American Airways;
Colonial Air Transport; New York Airways; Pacific Air
Transport; Pan American Airways; Standard Air Lines;
Transamerican Air Lines; Transcontinental and Western
Air Lines; Universal Air Lines; Western Air Express; West
Coast Air Transport ■

American Airways became the largest Fokker F-10/F-10A operator with a fleet of 29. Courtesy
American Airlines

Pan Am was an important Fokker F-10 operator acquiring a fleet of twelve during its rapid expansion in 1929-1930. Courtesy Pan American World Airways

Launch customer for the Fokker F-10 was Western Air Express, which placed the trimotor into service on its Los Angeles-San Francisco route on May 26, 1928. Shown here under examination is N-5170—note the early service vehicle to the left of the plane's tail. Courtesy Western Airlines

■ FORD 5-AT Tri-Motor

First Service: 1928

Type/Purpose: Tri-motor, commercial, short/medium-haul
   transport

Number of Seats: 2 crew, 14 passengers

Dimensions: Length: 50.3 feet
   Height: 13 feet
   Wingspan: 77.10 feet
   Gross weight (pounds): 13,500

Engines: 3 Pratt & Whitney Wasp C radials

Performance: Maximum range: 550 miles
   Service ceiling: 18,500 feet
   Maximum speed: 150 mph
   Maximum cruising speed: 122 mph

Initial U.S. Operator Service: Northwest Airways,
   September 1, 1928

Remarks: Knowing of the advantages of the Fokker F-10A, Transcontinental Air Transport (T.A.T.) advisor Charles A. Lindbergh recommended that the 4-AT be redesigned to allow it greater seating capacity and more power. Thus a 4-AT-B was taken in hand, given a larger wing and Wasp engines, and relabeled the 5-AT. Enlarged and more powerful, the "Tin Goose" or "Tin Lizzie" became even more popular, and although there was much selling back and forth between carriers, the aircraft, initially costing $55,000, went on to equip 95 airlines worldwide. Series A to E production included 3 As, 42 Bs, 51 Cs, 20 Ds with square-cornered entry doors, and an E covered from a B. Many of these had mail compartments outboard of the wing-mounted engines. In addition to inaugurating the colorful (if short-lived) T.A.T. air-rail service in 1929, the Ford Tri-Motor did much to introduce the concept of air travel (and safety) to the public; all of the country's major carriers employed the aircraft, with Pan Am at one time operating a fleet of 24 and Transcontinental and Western Air a similar number. A 5-AT was Democratic-candidate Franklin D. Roosevelt's campaign plane in 1932. The Ford Tri-Motor outlasted the Fokkers on U.S. airlines by a number of years even after production ended in 1932; indeed, the hearty aircraft did not surrender its front-line position until completely outclassed by the new Boeing 247 and Douglas DC-2 of the 1930s. For years thereafter, the aircraft was employed on secondary routes and in bush operations, where owners frequently changed the power plant. In

1976, Scenic Airlines refurbished two 5-ATs (one was Roosevelt's campaign plane) for sightseeing tours over Arizona's Grand Canyon. In a seven-day, cross-country flight in September 1985, one of those Scenic Airlines Fords recreated the flavor of flight in the days when the "Tin Goose" ruled the airways of America.

Selected List of U.S. Operating Airlines: American Airways; Colonial Air Transport; Curtiss Flying Service; Eastern Air Transport; Island Airlines; Johnson Flying Service; Maddux Air Lines; National Air Transport; Northwest Airways; Pacific Air Transport; Pan American Airways; Pan American Grace Airways (PANAGRA); Pennsylvania Air Lines; Pitcairn Aviation; Robertson Air Lines; Scenic Airlines; Southwest Air Fast Express; Stout Air Services/ Ford Motor Company Airlines; Transcontinental Air Transport/ Transcontinental and Western Air Lines ■

Winter shot of a Northwest Airways Ford 5-AT. Northwest was the 1926 launch customer for the improved Tri-Motor. Courtesy Northwest Orient Airlines

Transcontinental Air Transport's Ford 5-AT *City of Columbus* flew the westbound inaugural of that carrier's air-rail service, July 1929. Courtesy Trans World Airlines

Pilot Arthur C. Burns poses next to his TWA Ford 5-AT-B Tri-Motor at Kansas City, ca. 1932. Courtesy Trans World Airlines

A Pan-Am 5-AT revs up its three engines. Courtesy Pan American World Airways

An American Airways 5-AT in flight. The three engines offered safety and dependability, but made the cockpit and passenger compartment extremely noisy. It was not uncommon for travellers to suffer temporary hearing loss following a trimotor trip. Courtesy American Airlines

■ HAMILTON H Series Metalplane

First Service: 1928

Type/Purpose: Single-engined, commercial, mail/passenger transport

Number of Seats: 1 pilot, 7-8 passengers

Dimensions: Length: 34.8 feet
Height: 9.3 feet
Wingspan: 54.5 feet
Gross weight (pounds): 5,750

Engines: 1 Pratt & Whitney R-1340 Wasp radial (H-45)/
1 Pratt & Whitney R-1690 Hornet radial (H-47)

Performance: Maximum range: 675 miles
Service ceiling: 15,000 feet
Maximum speed: 138 mph
Maximum cruising speed: 115 mph

Initial Test Flight: 1928

Initial U.S. Operator Service: Northwest Airways,
June 7, 1928

Remarks: Designed by James S. McDonnell, the original Metalplane (M-43) featured a skin of Alclad corrugated duralumin, a Wright J-4 Whirlwind engine, and a thick cantilevered wing. Production aircraft, designed by John Ackerman and assembled in Milwaukee, had high-mounted wings and sturdy landing struts; these bore more than a little resemblance to the Ford Tri-Motor. The H-45 and H-47 were differentiated by their power plants and both were available with Hamilton metal floats instead of conventional wheeled landing gear. Although both had their wingspans lengthened in 1929, production totals were small and service with scheduled airlines limited.

Selected List of U.S. Operating Airlines: Coastal Air Lines; Isthmian Airways; Northwest Airways; Universal Air Lines; Wien Alaska Airways ■

A Hamilton Metalplane of Universal Airlines, which became a part of American Airways in January 1930. Courtesy American Airlines

An excellent closeup of Northwest Airways' Hamilton Metalplane. Lead and largest Hamilton customer, Northwest operated 8-9 Metalplanes, initially on its St. Paul to Chicago route, but later as far west as Seattle. Courtesy Northwest Orient Airlines

Selected List of U.S. Operating Airlines: Alaska-Washington Airways; American Airways; Braniff Airways; Continental Airlines; Hanford Tri-State Airlines; International Airlines; Midland Air Express; Nevada Airlines; Pan American Airways; Transcontinental and Western Airlines; Varney Speed Lines; Wedell-Williams Air Service; Western Air Express ■

■ LOCKHEED Vega

First Service: 1928

Type/Purpose: Single-engined, light, commercial transport

Number of Seats: 1 pilot, 4–6 passengers

Dimensions: Length: 28 feet
Height: 8.4 feet
Wingspan: 41 feet
Gross weight (pounds): 5,200

Engines: 1 Wright J-5 Whirlwind radial (Model 1)/
1 Wright J-6 Whirlwind radial (Model 2)/
1 Pratt & Whitney Wasp B radial (Model 5)/ 1 Pratt & Whitney Wasp C radial (Model 5B/Model DL-1)

Performance: Maximum range: 690–900 miles
Service ceiling: 20,000–22,000 feet
Maximum speed: 180 mph
Maximum cruising speed: 155 mph

Initial Test Flight: July 4, 1927

Initial U.S. Operator Service: International Airlines, September 17, 1928

Remarks: Designed by John K. Northrup and basic to an entire family of fast transports, the Vega had a streamlined fuselage (the two plywood halves of which were formed in a cement mold) below a single, cantilevered, stressed-skin plywood wing. The high-wing monoplane originally lacked an engine cowling and covers for its fixed landing gear, but, later, after being fitted with streamlined wheel covers and, more importantly, a NACA cowling, the Vega's cruising speed was increased by 20 mph. There were so many models, (1, 2, 5, 5B, DL-1) and feature variations and conversions that it became nearly impossible to define a basic or standard Vega. A number were even custom built. While serving with nearly three dozen U.S. domestic airlines in the late 1920s and early 1930s, these speedy aircraft are probably best remembered for their involvement in all kinds of record-breaking flights by explorers, speed merchants, and adventurers. For example, in June and July 1931, Wiley Post and Harold Gatty made the first around-the-world flight by a purely commercial transport in their *Winnie Mae*, the same aircraft in which Post made the premier, lone air-circumnavigation of the globe in 1933. Some 130 Vegas were built. Alaska-Washington Airways maintained the largest U.S. fleet with 7.

Following their record-breaking 1931 around-the-world flight, Wiley Post and Harold Gatty toured America showing off the famous Lockheed Model 5B Vega *Winnie Mae*, shown here at Wertz Field, Charleston, West Virginia. Courtesy West Virginia Dept. of Archives and History

Continental Airlines Lockheed Vega, a reproduction of its first commercial aircraft. Courtesy Continental Airlines

■ RYAN Brougham Series B-1 to B-7

First Service: 1928

Type/Purpose: Single-engined, commercial, short-haul transport

Number of Seats: 1 pilot, 4 passengers (B-1/B-3)/ 1 pilot, 5 passengers (B-5/B-7)

Dimensions: Length: 22 feet (B-1/B-3)/ 28.4 feet (B-5/B-7)
Height: 8.10 feet
Wingspan: 36 feet (B-1/B-3)/ 42.4 feet (B-5/B-7)
Gross weight (pounds): 3,500 (B-1/B-3)/ 4,000 (B-5/B-7)

Engines: 1 Wright J-5 Whirlwind radial (B-1)/ 1 Wright J-5 or J-6 Whirlwind radial (B-3)
1 Wright J-6 Whirlwind radial (B-5)/ 1 Pratt & Whitney C1 Wasp radial (B-7)

Performance: Maximum range: 500+ miles (B-1/B-3)/ 720 miles (B-5/B-7)
Service ceiling: 16,000 feet (B-1/B-3)/ 18,000 feet (B-5/B-7)
Maximum speed: 125 mph (B-1/B-3)/ 150 mph (B-5/B-7)
Maximum cruising speed: 115 mph (B-1/B-3)/ 120 mph (B-5/B-7)

Initial Test Flight: 1926 (B-1)/ 1928 (B-3/B-5)/ 1929 (B-7)

Initial U.S. Operator Service: Ryan Airlines, June 1928

Remarks: Stablemate to Lindbergh's famous New York-Paris plane, the Brougham would satisfy public demand for "a plane like Lindy's" and become Ryan's vehicle for commercial viablility. Based on the *Spirit of St. Louis* and the M-2, the B-1 was a four-place, single-engined, high-wing monoplane. Complete with the *Spirit's* distinctive spinner nose and burnished aluminum cowling, but with larger tail surfaces and a shorter wingspan, the B-1 was an immediate success and 150 were built by fall 1928. The B-3 featured increased baggage capacity, enlarged tail surfaces, a wider cabin, modified engine cowling, and better main landing-gear struts; 8 were manufactured in 1929. A total of 48 slightly stretched, five-place, and more powerful B-5s were built and were noted for their ability to take off in less than 300 feet. The last true Brougham type was the B-7, slightly stretched, more powerful, roomier, and more expensive than the B-5. Only 6 B-7s were built before Ryan succumbed to the Great Depression in 1932. Broughams remained popular for some years and were often em-ployed by smaller airlines, charter carriers, businessmen, and flying schools. Three surviving B-1s were rescued in 1955 and reworked to represent Lindbergh's famous plane in the Jimmy Stewart movie of *The Spirit of St. Louis.*

Selected List of U.S. Operating Airlines: Bowman Airways of Alaska; Embry-Riddle; National Airlines Air Taxi Service; Pickwick Latin American Airways; Pike's Peak Air Lines; Robertson Airplane Service; Ryan Airlines; Thompson Flying Service; Tri-State Airlines ■

Based upon Lindbergh's *The Spirit of St. Louis* and complete with its distinctive spinner nose and burnished aluminum cowling, the Ryan Brougham entered service in 1928 and remained popular with smaller carriers for several years. SI #A4069E

■ SIKORSKY S-38

First Service: 1928

Type/Purpose: Twin-engined, commercial amphibian

Number of Seats: 2 crew, 8 passengers

Dimensions: Length: 41 feet
    Height: 13.1 feet
    Wingspan: 71.8 feet
    Gross weight (pounds): 10,480

Engines: 2 Pratt & Whitney Wasp C radials (38A)/
    2 Pratt & Whitney Wasp SC1 radials (38B)

Performance: Maximum range: 500 miles
    Service ceiling: 16,000 feet
    Maximum speed: 105 mph

Initial Test Flight: June 25, 1928

Initial U.S. Operator Service: Pan American Airways,
    October 31, 1938

Remarks: Proclaimed in its day as both "the world's safest airplane" and "a collection of spare parts flying in formation," the S-38 was, as Igor Sikorsky put it, "the real originator of the Sikorsky Aircraft Company." Based upon the S-36, the amphibian, with its wood-frame hull and sesqui-wing, proved to be extremely versatile and one of the most successful of its type ever constructed. The S-38 not only filled the need for and requirements of a scheduled airliner, but was employed in route proving, business, and exploration (the latter most notably by Martin and Osa Johnson in Africa). A total of 111 S-38s were built, including the Model B of 1929, which featured more powerful forward-mounted engines and a sloping windshield. In 1931, Sikorsky built 20 single-engined, 4-5 passenger S-39s, which together with the success of the S-38 led Pan Am to seek a 40-passenger ship, the S-40.

Selected List of U.S. Operating Airlines: American Airways; Colonial Western Airways; Curtiss-Wright Flying Service; New York, Rio and Buenos Aires Airways; Northwest Airways; Pan American Airways; Western Air Express ■

Pan Am inaugurated Sikorsky S-38 service over certain of its Caribbean routes on October 31, 1928. Courtesy Pan American World Airways

American Airlines' predecessor company Colonial-Western Airways inaugurated a short-lived twice-daily service between Buffalo and Toronto on June 29, 1929, with three Sikorsky S-38s, including this example shown in American Airways livery. Courtesy American Airlines

Scheduled passenger service linking Honolulu with the outer Hawaiian Islands was begun by two Inter-Island Airways Sikorsky S-38s on November 11, 1929. Courtesy Hawaiian Airlines

■ STEARMAN C-3B/R Sport Commercial/Business Speedster

First Service: 1928

Type/Purpose: Single-engined, commercial, mail/passenger transport

Number of Seats: 1 pilot, 2 passengers

Dimensions: Length: 24 feet
Height: 8 feet
Wingspan: 35 feet
Gross weight (pounds): 2,650

Engines: 1 Wright J-5 Whirlwind radial (C-3B)/
1 Wright J-6-7 Whirlwind radial (C-3R)

Performance: Maximum range: 620 miles
Service ceiling: 18,000 feet
Maximum speed: 126 mph
Maximum cruising speed: 108 mph

Initial Test Flight: 1928 (C-3B)/ 1929 (C-3R)

Initial U.S. Operator Service: Varney Air Lines, 1928

Remarks: The C-3 series of 1927-1930 was Lloyd Stearman's major product until World War II when his Kaydet became more famous. One of the three original founders of the Travel Air Manufacturing Co. of Wichita (predecessor of Beech Aircraft), Stearman designed the 2000 to 4000 series Travel Airs before departing from the company in 1926 to form his own concern. The first plane the now-independent builder designed was the C-1 biplane, a three-seater with a two-seat front cockpit, steel-tube fuselage, overhanding top wing, and innovative wheel brakes. Similar in appearance to a Travel Air, the C-1 was a prototype and led to the C-2, a more powerful model with a relocated radiator and realigned push rods. A number of C-2s went to Varney Air Lines as mail planes. The C-3, which followed, featured increased power from a larger Wright engine and a higher price tag. A total of 185 C-2s and C-3s were manufactured, the majority of which were C-3Bs equipped with Wright J-5 Whirlwind radials. The principal variant of the C-3B was the C-3MB; 15 of these mail planes were manufactured, each with a 33-cubic-foot mail hold replacing the front cockpit. As these aircraft were phased out of mail operations, they were often converted into C-3Bs called "Specials." The C-3B went out of production in July 1929 and was replaced by a new model, the C-3R. This aircraft featured minor im-

provements, including a somewhat rounder fuselage, an engine drag ring, and larger tail surfaces. As the Depression deepened, orders for the C-3R became fewer and only 39 were constructed, production ending in October 1931. Although out of production, the C-3s flew on throughout the 1930s. Many were employed by business, charter, and air taxi operators while others were employed as crop dusters or flight trainers. A few remain in flying condition in the 1980s, all in the hands of antique airplane enthusiasts.

Selected List of U.S. Operating Airlines: American Airways; Interstate Airlines; National Parks Airways; Southern Air Transport; Transcontinental Air Transport; TWA; Universal Air Lines; Varney Air Lines; Western Air Express ■

TOP: The Stearman LT-1 was specifically developed for mail/passenger operations by Interstate Airlines, which operated three on a Chicago to Atlanta route in 1928. When Interstate became a part of American Airways in January 1930, at least one LT-1 went along as part of the deal and was probably retired in 1934. Courtesy American Airlines

BOTTOM: Equipped with a Wright J-6-7 Whirlwind radial (here hidden by the engine drag ring) and moveable tail wheel, this Stearman C-3R or 4-CM1 was one of eight operated by American Airways, all of which were retired in 1934. Courtesy American Airlines

■ BELLANCA CH Series

First Service: 1929

Type/Purpose: Single-engined, commercial, short-haul transport

Number of Seats: 1 pilot, 5–7 passengers

Dimensions: Length: 27.9 feet (300/400)/ 40.8 feet (30/31)
Height: 8.4 feet
Wingspan: 46.4 feet (300/400)/ 50.6 feet (30/31)
Gross weight (pounds): 3,700 (300/400)/ 5,600 (30/31)

Engines: 1 Wright J-5 Whirlwind radial or 1 Wright J-6-9 Whirlwind radial (300)/
1 Pratt & Whitney Wasp S3H1 radial (400/30/31)

Performance: Maximum range: 800 miles (300/400)/ 600–1,000 miles (30/31)
Service ceiling: 13,000 feet (300/400)/ 25,000 feet (30/31)
Maximum speed: 128 mph (300/400)/ 180 mph (30/31)
Maximum cruising speed: 110 mph (300/400)/ 180 mph (30/31)

Initial Test Flight: 1928 (300)

Initial U.S. Operator Service: New York-Asbury Park Air Lines, August 1929 (300)

Remarks: Italian-immigrant designer Guiseppe M. Bellanca's first commercial success was the CH series, high-wing, cabin monoplanes, Pacemaker and Skyrocket. These two types were based on the WB-1 of 1925, built while Bellanca was an employee of the Wright Aeronautical Corporation. In addition to establishing the high-wing-monoplane configuration as something of a standard in aircraft production, the SB-1 incorporated three other features that would become Bellanca trademarks: a distinctive "hump" fuselage, tapered wing tips with square ends, and most importantly, wide fairings on the "bow-legged" main landing gear, which could be considered as auxiliary airfoils, contributing to total lift. The performance of the WB-2 *Columbia*, which followed Lingbergh across the Atlantic, allowed Bellanca to open his own manufacturing concern and to build his first commercial aircraft, the CH-200 of 1928. From it was developed the CH-300, which first flew in late 1928 or early 1929; a five-seater, its freighter version, the PM-300 was the first of the line to be labeled Pacemaker. Approximately 36 CH-300s were eventually built. A more powerful and slightly modified variant of the popular 300 was certified in April 1930 as the CH-400 Skyrocket; some 50 of these were constructed. Both the Pacemaker and Skyrocket were similar in size and outline to contemporary competitors, such as the Stinson Detroiter, the Ryan Brougham, and the Travel Air 5000/6000. Unlike some concerns, Bellanca did not fold during the Depression and the firm continued to turn out improved, CH-style monoplanes throughout the 1930s. It was during these years that the CH designation was dropped in favor of the single letters E, F, and J with the old 300s and 400s becoming Models 30 and 31. Not counting the WB-1 and -2 prototypes nor the special planes developed for distance flyers, the dozens of CH series aircraft produced saw excellent utility, charter, and commuter service and earned a reputation as rugged transport, which could go anywhere "with anything that would go through the door."

Selected List of U.S. Operating Airlines: Chicago and Southern Airways; Colorado-Utah Airways; Cordova Air Service; Marine Airways; New York-Asbury Park Air Lines; Pacific Seaboard Air Lines; Pollack Flying Service; Star Air Lines ■

The Bellanca CH-300, an example of which is shown here, was first introduced by New York-Asbury Park Air Line in August 1929. SI #815422

■ FAIRCHILD Model 71

First Service: 1929

Type/Purpose: Single-engined, commercial, utility transport

Number of Seats: 1 pilot, 6-7 passengers

Dimensions: Length: 33 feet
    Height: 9.4 feet
    Wingspan: 50.2 feet
    Gross weight (pounds): 5,500

Engines: 1 Pratt & Whitney R-1340 Wasp radial

Performance: Maximum range: 650 miles
    Service ceiling: 15,500 feet
    Maximum speed: 135 mph
    Maximum cruising speed: 110 mph

Initial Test Flight: 1928

Initial U.S. Operator Service: Pan American Grace Airways
(PANAGRA), May 17, 1929

Remarks: The Fairchild Model 71 was essentially a cleaned-up version of the FC-2W; slightly modified, it went through seven variants, 71A to 71E. A total of 142 Model 71s were constructed in the U.S.A. and Canada, seeing service with both bush operators and small- to medium-sized airlines. Passenger/cargo convertible, the aircraft's landing gear could be switched from wheels to floats or skis. In 1929, Fairchild extensively reconfigured a Model 71 into a Model 72; this did not enter production, and company emphasis was shifted to the Model 100 Pilgrim.

Selected List of U.S. Operating Airlines: Interstate Airlines; Marine Airways; Pacific Alaska Airways; Pan American Airways; Pan American Grace Airways (PANAGRA); Reeve Aleutian Airways; Universal Air Lines ■

Reeve Airways Fairchild 71 at Northway Field, near Nabesna, Alaska, in 1941. Morrison-Knudsen, Courtesy Bob Reeve Collection, Reeve Aleutian Airways

Pan Am made extensive use of its Fairchild Model 71s in Latin America. Courtesy Pan American World Airways

■ FOKKER Model 8 Super Universal

First Service: 1929

Type/Purpose: Single-engined, commercial, short/medium-haul transport

Number of Seats: 2 crew, 7 passengers

Dimensions: Length: 36.11 feet
   Height: 9.1 feet
   Wingspan: 50.8 feet
   Gross weight (pounds): 5,500

Engines: 1 Pratt & Whitney Wasp radial

Performance: Maximum range: 420 miles
   Service ceiling: 18,000 feet
   Maximum speed: 128-138 mph
   Maximum cruising speed: 118 mph

Initial Test Flight: Fall 1927

Initial U.S. Operator Service: Western Air Express
   August 31, 1929

Remarks: Originally known as the Universal Special, the Fokker Model 8 was a stretched and strengthened version of the Model 4 Universal. It possessed a more powerful engine than its predecessor, as well as a longer fuselage, straight-tapered, cantilevered wings, an enclosed cockpit, and seating for 6 to 7 passengers. The spidery landing-gear arrangement of the Universal was superceded by single, streamlined struts with shock absorbers, but like the Model 4, the Super Universal's undercarriage was interchangeable with floats or skis. Among the features on certain Model 8s were reverse-slope windscreens and Townend rings encircling the power plants. A total of 123 Super Universals were constructed and, in addition to their widespread use with U.S. civil operators, several were also acquired for transport duty by the U.S. Navy. Popular in Canada and the Far East, 14 of the total were built by Canadian-Vickers under license while 47 more were similarly manufactured by the Nakajima Aircraft Company for use by Japan Air Transport, Manchurian Airlines, and the Japanese Army Air Force. Three similar aircraft were built in Holland and were known as the Fokker F-XI.

Selected List of U.S. Operating Airlines: American Airways; National Parks Airways; St. Tammany Gulf Coast Airways; Standard Air Lines; Texas Air Transport; Western Air Express; Universal Air Lines ■

TOP: Western Air Express Fokker Super Universal on the Denver-El Paso Route. Courtesy Western Airlines

MIDDLE: A Fokker Model 8 Super Universal of American Airways. Note the wing landing lights and the Townend ring around the Pratt & Whitney Wasp engine. Courtesy American Airlines

BOTTOM: Fokker Super Universal of Texas Air Transport, a short-lived carrier which merged with Gulf Air Lines in 1928 to form Southern Air Transport. Courtesy American Airlines

■ FOKKER F-14

First Service: 1929

Type/Purpose: Single-engined, commercial, short/medium-haul transport

Number of Seats: 1 pilot, 7-9 passengers

Dimensions: Length: 43.4 feet
Height: 12.4 feet
Wingspan: 59.5 feet
Gross weight (pounds): 7,200

Engines: 1 Pratt & Whitney Hornet A radial

Performance: Maximum range: 730 miles
Service ceiling: 18,000 feet
Maximum speed: 137 mph
Maximum cruising speed: 115 mph

Initial Test Flight: Spring 1929

Initial U.S. Operator Service: Western Air Express, December 12, 1929

Remarks: Apparently a retrograde design, the F-14 was the last civil Fokker built in the United States prior to the short-lived Fairchild (Fairchild-Hiller) F-27/FH-227 run of the late 1950s and early 1960s. The aircraft was designed to meet a Western Air Express requirement for a replacement for its Douglas mail planes, a request that specified a six-passenger cabin. Attempting to create both a passenger airliner and a fast mail plane, Fokker delivered a parasol-wing, cabin monoplane, which incorporated a separate mail/express compartment located ahead of the cabin. In something of a throwback in design, an open cockpit was located far aft atop the steel-tube fuselage (the top of which was made of corrugated duralumin) behind the wing, which was positioned above the fuselage. To reach his high perch, the pilot was forced to climb upward via three toeholds in the left side of the fuselage. The manufacturer was extremely displeased with the F-14 and attempted to modify it (F-14A) by lowering the wing atop the fuselage and moving the pilot into a cabin before the wing. Neither the F-14 nor the F-14A were popular with America's commercial operators and all but 4 of the 35 built were sold to either the U.S. Army Air Corps (C-14) or to Canadian airlines. Western Air Express and, later, Trancontinental and Western Air operated 4 aircraft in California-Utah service between 1930 and 1933.

Selected List of U.S. Operating Airlines: TWA; Western Air Express ■

One of four Western Air Express Fokker F-14s photographed at its Alhambra base. Courtesy Trans World Airlines

Unlike most other Fokker Transports, the F-14, shown here in Western Air Express livery, was a parasol monoplane. Courtesy Western Airlines

■ LOENING C-2 Air Yacht

First Service: 1929

Type/Purpose: Single-engined, commercial, amphibian

Number of Seats: 2 crew, 6 passengers

Dimensions: Length: 34 feet
   Height: 13.2 feet (wheels down)
   Wingspan: 46 feet
   Gross weight (pounds): 5,900

Engines: 1 Wright R-1750 Cyclone radial

Performance: Maximum range: 400 miles
   Service ceiling: 12,500 feet
   Maximum speed: 130 mph
   Maximum cruising speed: 120 mph

Initial Test Flight: 1928

Initial U.S. Operator Service: Air Ferry, Ltd., 1929

Remarks: Originally an open-cockpit military seaplane, the conversion of the Loening to a commercial model involved the installation of a passenger cabin and a different power plant. The aircraft, which blended a conventional aircraft fuselage to a single, main pontoon common to contemporary naval floatplanes, was built in only small numbers by the Loening Aeronautical Engineering Corporation, a division of the Keystone Aircraft Corporation, Bristol, Pennsylvania. Air Yachts were employed by only a few carriers and were largely restricted to inland lakes or bays; several were also employed by private operators. Total cost of a new 1929 C-2 was $27,900.

Selected List of U.S. Operating Airlines: Air Ferry, Ltd.; Gorst Air Transport; Western Air Express ■

Western's second Loening C-2 demonstrates its amphibious capability. Courtesy Trans World Airlines

Western Air Express operated two Loening C-2 amphibians on service to Avalon Harbor, Catalina. Here NC135-H is shown on the water. SI #86-12048

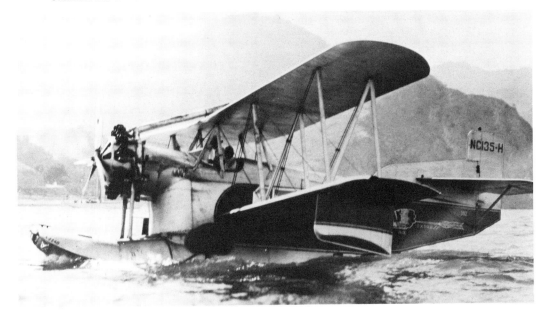

■ TRAVEL AIR 6000 Series

First Service: 1929

Type/Purpose: Single-engined, commercial, short/medium-haul transport

Number of Seats: 1 pilot, 5-7 passengers

Dimensions: Length: 30.10 feet (6000/B-6000)/
    31.2 feet (A-6000)
    Height: 9.3 feet
    Wingspan: 46.6 feet (6000)/ 54.5 feet (A-6000)/
    48.7 feet (B-6000)
    Gross weight (pounds): 4,100 (6000)/ 5,250 (A-6000/
    4,230 (B-6000)

Engines: 1 Wright J-5 Whirlwind radial (6000)/
    1 Pratt & Whitney Wasp radial (A-6000)/
    1 Wright J-6-9 Whirlwind radial (B-6000)

Performance: Maximum range: 560 miles (6000)/
    680   miles
    (A-6000)/ 550 miles (B-6000)
    Service ceiling: 12,000 feet (6000)/
    18,000 feet (A-6000)/ 16,000 feet (B-6000)
    Maximum speed: 120 mph (6000)/ 140 mph (A-6000)/
    130 mph (B-6000)
    Maximum cruising speed: 102 mph (6000)/
    120 mph (A-6000)/ 110 mph (B-6000)

Initial Test Flight: 1928

Initial U.S. Operator Service: National Air Transport, spring 1929

Remarks: A contemporary of the Ryan Brougham and Bellanca CH series, the large Travel Airs were often regarded as the best in their power and price range and thus saw much airline service in addition to private, charter, and bush operation. The high-wing, cabin monoplane, pushed on biplane-oriented Walter Beech by his partner Clyde V. Cessna, was introduced by National Air Transport in 1927 as the five-place, mail and passenger Model 5000. The Model 6000, which followed, was essentially a stretched Model 5000 with the rear seats and entrance door behind the wing and provision for a copilot. A slightly lengthened 6000, the Model A-6000 with a more powerful Pratt & Whitney engine, was introduced in 1929, but only 25 Model 6000s and A-6000s were built. The most popular variant in the Travel Air, cabin series was the B-6000, equipped with a Wright J-6-9 Whirlwind and in-troduced just before the Stock Market Crash. A total of 55 B-6000s were built. As the year turned, Travel Air was acquired by the Curtiss Aeroplane and Motor Company, which continued to produce the 6000 as the Curtiss-Wright Travel Air Sedan 6-B. Able to carry heavy loads and take off from short fields, this six-place model was produced in very small quantity. The Travel Airs remained popular, particularly with business operators and in the far West; although many were initially sold to corporate owners, a large number were later resold as bush transports. As late as 1947, 33 Model 6000s remained on the U.S. civil aircraft register.

Selected List of U.S. Operating Airlines: Bristol Bay Air Service; Cape Cod Airway; Clarksburg Airways; Clifford Ball Air Line; Continental Airways; Delta Air Services; Maddux Air Lines; National Air Transport; Northwest Airways; Paul B. Braniff, Inc.; Pittsburgh Airways; Reed Airline; Southern Air Transport; Universal Air Lines; Woodley Airways ■

A Southern Air Transport Travel Air B-6000 over a southwestern mission in 1929. Courtesy American Airlines

Delta's Travel Air 6000 on the ground. The large cabin Travel Airs were called "limousines of the air." Courtesy Delta Airlines

Delta Travel Air 6000 on the ground. This 90-mph aircraft was used to launch Delta's first passenger flight on June 17, 1929. Courtesy Delta Airlines

■ CONSOLIDATED Model 16
Commodore

First Service: 1930

Type/Purpose: Twin-engined, flying boat, commercial transport

Number of Seats: 3 crew, 18–22 passengers

Dimensions: Length: 61.8 feet
Height: 15.6 feet
Wingspan: 100 feet
Gross weight (pounds): 17,600

Engines: 2 Pratt & Whitney R-1860 Hornet B radials

Performance: Maximum range: 1,000 miles
Service ceiling: 11,250 feet
Maximum speed: 128 mph
Maximum cruising speed: 108 mph

Initial Test Flight: September 28, 1928

Initial U.S. Operator Service: New York, Rio and Buenos Aires Line, February 18, 1930

Remarks: A high-wing flying boat originally designed to support NYRBAL's effort to crack Pan Am's hold on the South American market, the Commodore was, unlike its contemporary Sikorsky amphibious competitors, a long-range aircraft; as the nation's first successful commercial flying boat, the plane would have great influence on later civil and military designs. Growing out of a design for the U.S. Navy, the all-metal Commodore, *Buenos Aires*, was christened at Anacostia by Mrs. Herbert Hoover on October 2, 1929. A survey flight quickly disproved the suitability of the plane's open cockpit and so cockpit enclosures were fitted to all subsequent aircraft. When Pan Am assumed control of NYRBA in September 1930, it purchased the 10 Commodores on hand and took direct delivery from Consolidated of the remaining 4 as they came off the production line. These flew the Miami-Rio route until 1935 when some were sold and the rest stationed at Miami as trainers. A couple survived until 1945 and one was sold that year to Bahama Airways, which operated it on a scheduled route between the Outer Islands and Bahama until later in 1965.

Selected List of U.S. Operating Airlines: Chamberlain Air Lines; New York Rio and Buenos Aires Line; Pan American Airways ■

The Third Consolidated Commodore *Havana* flies over the Statue of Liberty prior to its delivery to the New York, Rio and Buenos Aires line. Courtesy General Dynamics Corp., Convair Division

Pan Am acquired several Consolidated Commodores when it took over NYRBA line in 1930. Courtesy Pan Amercian World Airways

Lift-off of a Pan American Consolidated Commodore. The aircraft remained in frontline service to 1935. Courtesy Pan American World Airways

■ CONSOLIDATED Model 17/ Model 20 Fleetster

First Service: 1930

Type/Purpose: Single-engined, commercial short/medium-haul transport

Number of Seats: 2 pilots, 6–8 passengers (17)/ 1 pilot, 7-9 passengers (20)

Dimensions: Length: 31.9 feet (17)/ 33.9 feet (20)
  Height: 9.2 feet (17)/ 12 feet (20)
  Wingspan: 45 feet (17)/ 50 feet (20)
  Gross weight (pounds): 5,300 (17)/ 6,800 (20)

Engines: 1 Pratt & Whitney Hornet B radial

Performance: Maximum range: 750 miles (17)/
  800 miles (20)
  Service ceiling: 19,000 feet (17)/ 18,000 feet (20)
  Maximum speed: 180 mph (17)/ 174 (20)
  Maximum cruising speed: 153 mph (17)/ 160 mph (20)

Initial Test Flight: October 1929 (17)/ June 1932 (20)

Initial U.S. Operator Service: New York, Rio and Buenos Aires Line, January 1930 (17)/ Trans Continental and Western Air Lines, October 1932 (20)

Remarks: A contemporary of the Lockheed Vega, which it closely resembled, the Consolidated Fleetster was the first American all-metal, monocoque-fuselage, civil transport and was specifically designed to support NYRBA feeder operations in South America. Named after Rueben H. Fleet, president of Consolidated Aircraft Corporation, more powerful variants of the basic Model 17 included the 17-2C and 17-AF. The conventional, high-wing Model 17 did not sell well early in the Depression, so Consolidated sought to widen its market by introducing a variant, the Model 20. This aircraft adopted a parasol wing, made provision for one pilot aft the wing in an open cockpit, and like the Model 17 could be operated in mixed-passenger/cargo or all-cargo configuration. A final variant was the Model 20A, which matched the 20's parasol wing with the longer wings, modified undercarriage, and other improvements of the Model 17-AF.

Selected List of U.S. Operating Airlines: Model 17—Ludington Line; New York, Rio and Buenos Aires Line; Pacific-Alaska Airways; Pacific International Airways; Pan American Airways; *Model 20*—Transcontinental and Western Air Lines ■

TOP RIGHT: A pair of ski-equipped Pacific-Alaska Airways Consolidated Model Fleetsters. Formed by merger of three small independent carriers in 1932, Pacific Alaska became the Alaska Division of Pan Am in May 1941. Courtesy Pan American World Airways

TOP LEFT: A Pacific-Alaska Airways ski-equipped Model 17 Fleetster photographed in the snow of the middle 1930s. Courtesy Pan American World Airways

BOTTOM: Clearly exhibiting its open pilot cockpit and parasol-wing, NCI3209 was one of seven red and silver Model 20 Fleetsters which began Transcontinental and Western Air Service in 1932. Courtesy Trans World Airlines

■ CURTISS CO Model 18 Condor I

First Service: 1930

Type/Purpose: Twin-engined, commercial, medium-haul transport

Number of Seats: 3 crew, 18 passengers

Dimensions: Length: 57.1 feet
Wingspan: 91.8 feet
Gross weight (pounds): 17,378

Engines: 2 Curtiss GV-1570 Conqueror pistons

Performance: Maximum range: 500 miles
Service ceiling: 20,000 feet
Maximum cruising speed: 188 mph

Initial Test Flight: July 21, 1929

Initial U.S. Operator Service: Transcontinental Air Transport, 1930

Remarks: A modification of the Curtiss B-2 Condor U.S. Army bomber, the Model 18 was developed to meet the needs of airlines requiring greater seating capacity on their increasingly longer routes. Only six were built; the first three aircraft were essentially modified military aircraft, while the second three were more extensively planned, with shorter fuselages and other refinements. Complete with a box-like cabin and a biplane tail with twin rudders, the Condor I's high-cambered, wooden wings (fabric covered as was the fuselage) affected its speed. Three Model 18s were leased to T.A.T., which tested them on its routes, but eventually elected not to purchase. These were returned to the Curtiss factory at St. Louis where their tail sections, along with the engine nacelles, were reworked in order to stabilize oscillating flight characteristics. The six remained unsold until January 1931 when they were purchased by Eastern Air Transport (largely owned by the Curtiss-Wright Corporation) and placed into service. All were replaced by Douglas DC-2s in 1934 and four of them were sold to Clarence D. Chamberlain, who employed them in aerial exhibitions during the middle 1930s.

Selected List of U.S. Operating Airlines: Eastern Air Transport; T.A.T. ■

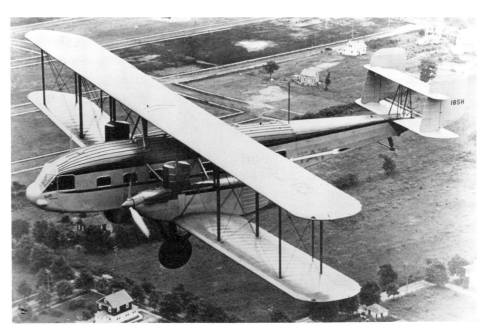

One of three Curtiss Condor I's leased to Transcontinental Air Transport, which tested the 18-passenger aircraft over its routes, but elected not to purchase. Courtesy Trans World Airlines
Eastern Air Transport introduced Curtiss CO Condor I service on December 10, 1930. SI #7817220

■ CURTISS Model 55 Kingbird

First Service: 1930

Type/Purpose: Twin-engined, commercial, short-haul transport

Number of Seats: 1 pilot, 7 passengers

Dimensions: Length: 34.9 feet
　　Height: 10 feet
　　Wingspan: 54.6 feet
　　Gross weight (pounds): 5,870

Engines: 2 Wright J-6-9 Whirlwind radials

Performance: Maximum range: 450 miles
　　Service ceiling: 12,000 feet
　　Maximum speed: 228 mph
　　Maximum cruising speed: 115 mph

Initial Test Flight: May 1929

Initial U.S. Operator Service: Eastern Air Transport, December 10, 1930

Remarks: Basically an upward-scaled, twin-engined version of the Curtiss Model 56 Thrush, the Kingbird had a very short fuselage nose—so short that the propellers of the inboard-mounted engines overlapped it. This feature was designed to reduce asymmetric-thrust problems in the event of engine failure. A total of 16 Model 55s were constructed, including 14 employed by Eastern Air Transport (largely owned by the Curtiss-Wright Corporation). The aircraft remained in Eastern service for several years, but were largely overshadowed by Curtiss Condor I's. All had been sold into private hands by the middle 1930s. ■

Beginning in 1930, Eastern Air Transport briefly employed 14 of these Curtiss Model 55 Kingbirds. SI #86-12046

■ FOKKER F-32

First Service: 1930

Type/Purpose: Four-engined, commercial, medium-haul transport

Number of Seats: 2-3 crew, 32 passengers (day)/
　　2-3 crew, 16 berthed passengers (night)

Dimensions: Length: 69.10-73 feet
　　Height: 16.6 feet
　　Wingspan: 99 feet
　　Gross weight (pounds): 22,500-24,250

Engines: 4 Pratt & Whitney Wasp radials or 4 Pratt & Whitney Hornet radials

Performance: Maximum range: 850 miles
　　Service ceiling: 13,000-18,000 feet
　　Maximum speed: 157 mph
　　Maximum cruising speed: 123 mph

Initial Test Flight: September 27, 1929

Initial U.S. Operator Service: Western Air Express, April 1, 1930

Remarks: The F-32 was the largest, most costly ($110,000), and least successful land-based transport of its era; the "32" in its number was employed as the result of a WAE request for a designation that indicated seating capacity. The aircraft offered a number of firsts to an, as yet, mostly nonflying American public. A trailblazer in passenger comfort, the F-32 used balsa wood in the fuselage for soundproofing and featured reclining seats and reading lights. The pilots enjoyed excellent instrumentation and good visibility. The power plants of America's first four-engined airliner were mounted in two underwing pods, each holding one push and one pull engine; cooling of the rear engine of each pair produced unsolved problems. The aircraft also introduced an engine fire-extinguishing system and various streamlining methods, e.g., "spats," were tried on the undercarriage. An expensive aircraft to operate ($1.25 per mile), only 2 of the 10 Fokkers manufactured were actually put into carrier service, both with WAE (and later TWA) on the San Francisco-Los Angeles route between April 1, 1930 and June 15, 1931. Subsequently, one F-32 was converted into a gas station on Los Angeles' Wilshire Boulevard where it remained until 1938. Another was dismantled at Wheeling, West Virginia, and was remodeled into a house trailer, which was destroyed in the Ohio River flood of January 1937. ■

The Western Air Express Fokker F-32 began operations in the Los Angeles-San Francisco route on April 1, 1930. Courtesy Western Airlines

America's first four-engined airliner, the Fokker F-32; note the underwing engine pods with their Pratt & Whitney engines in push-pull arrangement. Courtesy Trans World Airlines

■ STINSON SM-6000/ Model U

First Service: 1930

Type/Purpose: Trimotor, commercial, short/medium-haul transport

Number of Seats: 2 crew, 6 passengers (6000)/ 2 crew, 12 passengers (U)

Dimensions: Length: 36.10 feet (6000)/ 38 feet (U)
Height: 12 feet
Wingspan: 60 feet
Gross weight (pounds): 8,500-9,200

Engines: 3 Lycoming R-680-5 pistons (6000)/ 3 Lycoming R-680-BA pistons (U)

Performance: Maximum range: 400 miles
Service ceiling: 16,000 feet
Maximum cruising speed: 158-162 mph

Initial Test Flight: 1930

Initial U.S. Operator Service: New York-Philadelphia-Washington (Ludington) Airways, September 1, 1930 (6000)/ American Airways, spring 1932 (U)

Remarks: Relatively unknown today, the Stinson SM-6000/Model U was developed for smaller carriers or feeder-line operations. A high-wing monoplane with poor flying qualities, the 6000 was also produced with minor changes as the SM-6000B. A total of 11 Model 6000s and 42 Model 6000Bs were built. The Stinson U was a stretched version of the SM-6000B, designed by Art Saxon. Twenty U's were constructed, of which 16 were delivered to American Airways and 1 to Trans-American Airlines. Equipped with a Wright R-760-E1, a single Model U-1 was produced and delivered to Eastern Air Transport.

Selected List of U.S. Operating Airlines: SM-6000 — New York-Philadelphia-Washington Airways; Rapid Air Lines; Western Air Express, *SM-6000B* — Boston-Maine/Central Vermont Airways; Century Air Lines; Century Pacific Air Lines; Chicago and Southern Air Lines; New York-Philadelphia-Washington Airways; Pennsylvania Airlines; Rapid Air Lines; Trans-American Airlines, *Model U* — American Airways; Columbia Airlines; Iliolo-Negro Air Express; Trans-American Airlines, *Model U-1* — Eastern Air Transport ■

Chicago & Southern Air Lines' Stinson SM-6000B. The 6000B, known also as the Model T, was the production version of the SM-6000A. Courtesy Delta Airlines

American Airways, with 24 Stinson SM-6000s, was the type's largest single operator. Courtesy American Airlines

The Stinson Model U of 1932 found an enthusiastic operator in American Airways. Courtesy American Airlines

Delta Air Lines acquired its first Stinson SM-6000B in 1934. Courtesy Delta Airlines

■ BUHL CA Airsedan

First Service: 1931

Type/Purpose: Single-engined, commercial, short-haul transport

Number of Seats: 1 pilot, 4-8 passengers

Dimensions: Length: 27.8 feet
Height: 8.10 feet
Wingspan: 42 feet (CA-5)/ 36 feet (CA-3)
Gross weight (pounds): 3,700 (CA-5)/ 3,200 (CA-3)

Engines: 1 Wright J-5 Whirlwind radial

Performance: Maximum range: 700-840 miles
Service ceiling: 13,500-16,000 feet
Maximum speed: 120-134 mph
Maximum cruising speed: 105-112 mph

Initial Test Flight: 1927

Initial U.S. Operator Service: Reed Airline, fall 1931

Remarks: Based on the three-seater Buhl Airster, the first U.S. aircraft awarded an Approved Type Certificate (ATC), the CA series – the numerical designation reflected seating and not model sequence – was noteworthy as an early attempt to place both crew and passengers inside a cabin, a practice not then widely followed in commercial-airplane manufacture. Possessed of odd strut arrangements, unusually wide landing-gear tread, and unique cabin windows, the Buhls' most noteworthy feature was their extremely short lower wing. The CAs, one of the few passenger aircraft to employ the sesqui-plane concept (a bridge between the biplane and the monoplane), were stretched into six- and eight-place machines (CA-6/ CA-8) and made more powerful as well as shrunk into smaller models (CA-3C Sport Airsedan). Several were equipped with skis or floats and sold in Canada. Something more than 50 Buhls were constructed before the Depression wiped out the aircraft's air taxi, airline, and executive market. ■

This float-equipped Buhl Airsedan served with the Cherry Red Airline in Saskatchewan during the 1930s. SI #75-14775

■ FAIRCHILD Model 100/100A/ 100B Pilgrim

First Service: 1931

Type/Purpose: Single-engined, commercial, short-haul transport

Number of Seats: 1-2 crew, 8 passengers

Dimensions: Length: 38 feet
Height: 12.3 feet
Wingspan: 57 feet
Gross weight (pounds): 6,500

Engines: 1 Pratt & Whitney Hornet B radial (Model 100/100A)/
1 Wright Cyclone R-1820-E radial (Model 100B)

Performance: Maximum range: 440 miles
Service ceiling: 15,000 feet
Maximum speed: 136 mph
Maximum cruising speed: 110 mph

Initial Test Flight: October 22, 1930 (Model 100)/
July 14, 1931 (Model 100A)/
November 25, 1931 (Model 100B)

Initial U.S. Operator Service: American Airways, 1931 (100A)/ 1932 (100B)

Remarks: Only one Model 100, the prototype, was built, featuring foldable fabric-covered wings of metal structure. The 100A, a development of the high-wing Model 100, boasted a redesigned cockpit, a lavatory, and extensive fuselage fairing for passenger luggage and the 100B was made more powerful with an increased fin area. A total of 27 Pilgrims were constructed.

Selected List of U.S. Operating Airlines: Alaskan Airways; American Airways; Pacific Alaska Airlines ■

Fairchild Pilgrim 100-A of American Airways, which flew all 16 of this version. Courtesy American Airlines

One of several former American Airlines Pilgrim 100s acquired by Alaska Airlines after 1934. Courtesy Alaska Airlines

■ LOCKHEED Model 9 Orion

First Service: 1931

Type/Purpose: Single-engined, commercial, mail/passenger transport

Number of Seats: 1 pilot, 6 passengers

Dimensions: Length: 27.6 feet
Height: 9.3 feet
Wingspan: 42.9 feet
Gross weight (pounds): 5,200 – 5,400

Engines: 1 Pratt & Whitney R-1340 Wasp C radial (9)/
1 Wright R-1820-E Cyclone radial (9B)/
1 Pratt & Whitney S1D1 Wasp radial (9D)/
1 Pratt & Whitney R-1340 Wasp C radial (9E)/
1 Wright R-1820 Cyclone radial (9F)

Performance: Maximum range: 750 miles
Service ceiling: 22,000 feet
Maximum speed: 210 mph
Maximum cruising speed: 180 mph

Initial Test Flight: Fall 1930

Initial U.S. Operator Service: Bowen Air Lines, May 1931

Remarks: Lockheed named its Vega follow-ups after heavenly constellations and thus it was that the Model 9 Orion appeared, last and most numerous in the company's family of speedy, low-wing monoplanes sometimes called "plywood bullets." A total of 35 Orions were manufactured with 5 more obtained through conversions of earlier-series aircraft. There were several versions differentiated largely by their power plants, with the Model 9 (18) and Model 9D (13) the most numerous. Employing the first wing flaps ever installed on a Lockheed airplane, the Orion could land at only 55 mph. Additionally, the Model 9 was probably the first transport aircraft to employ a fully retractable undercarriage, the main wheels of which retracted up sideways and into the wing. Seating for passengers was provided inside the front fuselage while the pilot sat in an open cockpit equipped with a sliding canopy for cold-weather flights. Before the government banned single-engined passenger transports from the major airlines, the Orion served with several carriers desiring speed over capacity. On a sad note, when Wiley Post retired the Vega *Minnie Mae*, he obtained TWA's third Orion and employed it to fly to Alaska with Will Rogers in 1935 on a trip that would end in death for both men.

Selected List of U.S. Operating Airlines: Air Express; American Airways; Bowen Air Lines; Continental Airways; Inland Airlines; New York-Philadelphia-Washington Airway; New York & Western Airlines; Northwest Airways; Pan American Airways; TWA; Varney Speed Lines; Wyoming Air Service ■

Varney Speed Lanes (a predecessor of today's Continental Airlines) employed Orions on a 1-hour, 55-minute flight scheduled between San Francisco and Los Angeles and, reportedly, offered to refund passengers one dollar for every minute the aircraft was behind schedule. Courtesy Continental Airlines

American Airways, like other Orion operators, employed several of its aircraft on mail/express flights only. Note the blocked windows. One carrier, Air Express, used Model 9Ds in a 1933-1934 transcontinental freight service with average times of 16-17 hours coast to coast. Courtesy American Airlines

■ NORTHROP Alpha/ Gamma/Delta

First Service: 1931

Type/Purpose: Single-engined, commercial, mail/passenger transport

Number of Seats: 1 pilot, 6 passengers (Alpha/Gamma)/ 1 pilot, 8 passengers (Delta)

Dimensions: Length: 28.5 feet (Alpha/Gamma)/ 33.1 feet (Delta)
Height: 9 feet (Alpha/Gamma)/ 10.1 feet (Delta)
Wingspan: 41.1 feet (Alpha/Gamma)/ 49.9 feet (Delta)
Gross weight (pounds): 4,500 (Alpha/Gamma)/ 7,350 (Delta)

Engines: 1 Pratt & Whitney R-1340-SC-1 Wasp radial (Alpha/Gamma)/ 1 Wright SR-1820-F2 Cyclone radial (Delta)

Performance: Maximum range: 600-1,650 miles
Service ceiling: 17,000-23,000 feet
Maximum speed: 177 mph (Alpha/Gamma)/ 219 mph (Delta)
Maximum cruising speed: 145 mph (Alpha/Gamma)/ 208 mph (Delta)

Initial Test Flight: April-May 1930 (Alpha)/ 1933, (Gamma/Delta)

Initial U.S. Operator Service: TWA, April 1931 (Alpha)

Remarks: Technically, the Alpha followed John K. Northrop's Lockheed Vega introduced a few years earlier. A low-wing monoplane of all-metal construction (one of the first all-metal aircraft), the Alpha benefited from two important construction techniques. The first was wing fillets (fairings) developed after research at the Guggenheim Aeronautical Laboratory of the California Institute of Technology and fitted at the juncture of the wing and fuselage to increase aerodynamic efficiency. The second was a revolutionary multicellular stressed-skin wing, which dramatically increased the aircraft's strength. In operational design, the Alpha was basically a mail plane modified to carry six passengers in the front half of the fuselage with the pilot occupying a single open cockpit aft the wing. The Alpha appeared in several variants with TWA operating 14 until 1935. The Gamma, of which 38 were constructed, was an extension of the Alpha designed for high-speed, express-delivery operations. TWA flew three Gammas, in the first of which Jack Frye set a new U.S. freight-transport record of 11 hours, 31 minutes on May 13-14, 1934. When not hauling cargo, the carrier's Gammas were employed in high-altitude research. Only one eight-passenger, long-range Delta was acquired by TWA.

Selected List of U.S. Operating Airlines: National Air Transport; TWA ■

The Northrop Alpha, two examples of which are shown here, was introduced by TWA in 1931. The plane was important for its various physical and design features, including a multicellular stressed-skin wing, later used on the Douglas DCs. Courtesy Trans World Airlines

TOP RIGHT: A Northrup Delta of TWA. Eleven were built for the carrier with the first entering service in September 1933. Courtesy Trans World Airlines

BOTTOM: This TWA Northrop Alpha is now on display at the National Air and Space Museum. Courtesy Trans World Airlines

TOP LEFT: Nine Northrop Gammas were built with the first entering TWA service in May 1934, the same month in which one machine, piloted by Jack Frye, crossed the country in a record 11 hours, 31 minutes. Courtesy Trans World Airlines

■ SIKORSKY S-40

First Service: 1931

Type/Purpose: Four-engined, commercial, amphibian/
flying boat

Number of Seats: 6 crew, 24—40 passengers

Dimensions: Length: 76.8 feet
Wingspan: 114 feet
Gross weight (pounds): 34,000—34,600

Engines: 4 Pratt & Whitney Hornet B-1 radials (S-40)/
4 Pratt & Whitney Hornet T2D-1 radials (S-40A)

Performance: Maximum range: 500-950 miles
Service ceiling: 12,000—12,500 feet
Maximum speed: 134—140 mph
Maximum cruising speed: 115—120 mph

Initial Test Flight: August 7, 1931

Initial U.S. Operator Service: Pan American Airways,
November 19, 1931

Remarks: The first economical and practical four-engined
luxury airliner in U.S. service, the amphibious Sikorsky
S-40 was basically an S-38 scaled upward into a four-
engined airplane of thrice the weight and power. Aside
from size, there was at least one other difference between
the S-38 and S-40; the latter did not have a lower wing as
designer Igor Sikorsky elected to place the outrigger floats
at the end of horizontal struts. Juan Trippe ordered the first
Sikorsky S-40 on December 29, 1929, and that airplane
was certified on October 17, 1931, shortly after being christened *American Clipper* by Mrs. Herbert Hoover in
Anacostia Naval Air Station ceremonies. Incidentally, that
christening began Pan Am's famous Clipper line of
airliners with the carrier obtaining a copyright on the word
clipper and from time to time enforcing its ownership in
court. Pan Am often employed the S-40 as a flying boat,
having found that removal of the big, main landing gear
and tail wheel considerably improved performance and
allowed an 1,800-pound-payload increase. The first S-40
service betweem Miami and Cristobal was flown, via
Cuba and Jamaica, by pilots Charles Lindbergh and Basil
Rowe, thereby opening Caribbean operations, which
lasted until 1935 when the three S-40s were modified into
S-40As. While the S-40s were being modified into pure flying boats, their place was taken by the more-advanced and
larger S-42. Nevertheless, the S-40s remained in service on

lesser routes throughout the 1930s and, during World War
II, served as training aircraft. The first two were withdrawn from operations in 1943 and the last in 1944. The
world's largest commercial aircraft when introduced, the
pioneering trio had enjoyed extraordinarily long careers. ■

The Pan Am Sikorsky S-40 *Southern Clipper.* Though built as an amphibian, the aircraft was
normally operated as a flying boat.

Passengers depart the Pan Am Sikorsky S-40 *Caribbean Clipper.* A giant of its day, the Sikorsky
could seat 40 passengers. Pan American World Airways

■ SIKORSKY S-41

First Service: 1931

Type/Purpose: Twin-engined, commercial amphibian

Number of Seats: 3 crew, 14-16 passengers

Dimensions: Length: 33 feet
  Height: 15.3 feet
  Wingspan: 78.9 feet
  Gross weight (pounds): 13,800

Engines: 2 Pratt & Whitney R-1860 Hornet B1 radials

Performance: Maximum range: 575-920 miles
  Service ceiling: 15,000 feet
  Maximum speed: 133 mph
  Maximum cruising speed: 105 mph

Initial Test Flight: Autumn 1930

Initial U.S. Operator Service: Pan American Airways,
  August 1, 1931

Remarks: Based upon the S-38, the seven S-41s constructed had new all-metal hulls of improved design; the hull was 4 inches wider and 3 feet longer than the S-38, allowing the S-41 to transport four more passengers than its predecessor. Additionally, the sesqui-wing of the S-38 was eliminated in favor of a lengthened, high-wing, monoplane configuration and more powerful engines improved economy of operation. Four of the amphibians were operated by the U.S. Navy with the three remaining ones flown by Pan Am in the Caribbean as well as on its Boston-Halifax route, FAM 12. One Pan Am S-41 was lost in Boston Harbor in September 1931. ■

Under contract with Boston-Maine Airways, Pan Am flew two Sikorsky S-41s on F.A.M. 12 between Bangor, Maine, and Canada in 1931. Courtesy Pan American World Airways

A U.S. Navy Sikorsky S-41. Courtesy the Boeing Company.

■ BOEING 200/221/221A Monomail

First Service: 1933

Type/Purpose: Single-engined, commercial, cargo/mail/passenger transport

Number of Seats: 1 pilot, 6 passengers

Dimensions: Length: 41.2 feet (200)/
     41.1 feet (221/221A)
Height: 16 feet
Wingspan: 59.1 feet
Gross weight (pounds): 8,000

Engines: 1 Pratt & Whitney Hornet B radial

Performance: Maximum range: 575 miles
Service ceiling: 14,700
Maximum speed: 158 mph
Maximum cruising speed: 135 mph

Initial Test Flight: May 6, 1930 (200)/
     August 18, 1930 (221)

Initial U.S. Operator Service: Boeing Air Transport/
United Air Lines, 1933

Remarks: Similar in general layout to the Northrop Alpha, the Boeing Monomail is entered here not because of the number in service, but because the airplane was one of the most revolutionary in commercial-aviation history. Designated initially as a mail and cargo airplane, it increased performance not by the addition of brute horsepower, but by structural and aerodynamic refinements. The traditional biplane design with drag-producing struts and wires was replaced by a single, smooth, all-metal low wing of clean cantilever construction. The wheels were retracted into the wing during flight, and the drag of the air-cooled engine was greatly reduced by enclosing it in a newly developed "anti-drag" cowling. A second Monomail (221) was built the same year as the first. By adding 8 inches to the fuselage length and reducing the size of the mail compartment, Boeing was able to insert a cabin for six passengers between the engine bay and mail hold. Both Monomails were revised for transcontinental mail and passenger service, becoming the 221A. The Monomail's greatest failure was its advanced design: it was too progressive for the then-current state of the art in power plant and propeller design. Indeed, its Hornet engine was the same that powered the Boeing Model 40B, and by the time variable-pitch propellers capable of allowing fullest use of engine power became available, the aircraft was already on the verge of being replaced by the newer multi-engine designs it had inspired, most notably the Boeing 247. Both Monomails finished their U.S.-commercial service with Inland Air Lines (formerly Wyoming Air Service); one crashed and the other was withdrawn from service.

Selected List of U.S. Operating Airlines: Boeing Air Transport; Inland Air Lines; United Air Lines ■

With retractable landing gear and a capacity for six passengers; NC 10225 was the second Monomail and served with Boeing Air Transport. SI #86-12047

■ BOEING 247/247D

First Service: 1933

Type/Purpose: Twin-engined, commercial, medium-haul transport

Number of Seats: 3 crew, 10 passengers

Dimensions: Length: 51.4 feet (247)/ 51.7 feet (247D)
Height: 15.5 feet (247)/ 12.1 feet (247D)
Wingspan: 74 feet
Gross weight (pounds): 12,650 (247)/ 13,650 (247D)

Engines: 2 Pratt & Whitney Wasp S1D1 radials (247)/ 2 Pratt & Whitney Wasp S1H1G radials (247D)

Performance: Maximum range: 485 miles (247)/ 745 miles (247D)
Service ceiling: 18,400 feet (247)/ 25,400 feet (247D)
Maximum speed: 182 mph (247)/ 200 mph (247D)
Maximum cruising speed: 155 mph (247)/ 189 mph (247D)

Initial Test Flight: February 8, 1933 (247) spring 1934 (247D)

Initial U.S. Operator Service: United Air Transport Corporation, March 30, 1933 (247)/ United Air Lines, October 1934 (247D)

Remarks: Based on the technology of its predecessor B-9 bomber and Monomail and remarkable for its reliance on not three but two engines, the Boeing 247 changed U.S.-airliner configuration, while offering a more handsome aircraft, which could travel faster than its earlier competitors. The 247 was a single-aisle, low-wing, all-metal, stressed-skin monoplane with fully retractable landing gear. The United group (United Airlines as of May 1934) ordered 59 B-247s in 1932 and by January 1934, 54 of the world's first modern airliners had been delivered. This was the largest single civil aircraft order for years to come and was made on the basis of paper studies—there was no prototype. In the process of this order, however, United tied up Boeing production for two years, forcing competing carriers to turn to the California firm of Douglas, which went on to build the DC-1,-2, and -3 in response. The superior qualities of the 247 were well known (including the soundproofed fuselage, the introduction of air conditioning for the cabin, automatic pilot, the first civil supercharge engines, and component interchangeability) and in effect gave Douglas a target to surpass. Boeing did not attempt to combat the DC-1/2, but updated its twin engine by introducing the somewhat more refined 247D with its Hamilton-Standard variable-pitch propellers, full NACA cowlings, fabric-covered movable tail surfaces, and upward-aft-sloped windscreens. A total of 75 Model 247s were built and all but 3 were eventually converted to 247D standard, with the last 247Ds delivered in September 1935. No match for the Douglas DC-2 in economics, passenger comfort, or performance, a 247D delivered from United Air Lines production and flown by Clyde Pangborn and Roscoe Turner came in second by less than an hour to a stock KLM DC-2 in the transport category of the 1934 11,333-mile, London-Australia MacRobertson Air Race. One of the most significant transport designs of all time, the 247 was flown by United until early in World War II.

Selected List of U.S. Operating Airlines: National Parks Airlines; Pennsylvania-Central Airlines; United Air Lines; Western Airlines; White Pass Airways; Wyoming Air Services; Zimmerly Airlines ■

THE BOEING 247 OF 1933. The first all-metal streamlined monoplane transport. Its basic design formula is still found in the best transport craft flying today. Known as the forerunner of all modern-type transport airplanes, it introduced control surface trim tabs, automatic pilot and de-icing equipment. It was the first twin-engine monoplane able to climb on one engine with a full load, and the first high-speed multi-engined transport to use supercharged engines of the type formerly confined to military planes. It made possible travel from coast to coast in America, in less than 20 hours with only seven intermediate stops. Through several versions, 75 of this model were built. Courtesy Boeing Company

■ CLARK (General Aviation) G.A.-43

First Service: 1933

Type/Purpose: Single-engined, commercial, short-haul transport

Number of Seats: 2 crew, 10 passengers

Dimensions: Length: 43.1 feet
　　Height: 12.6 feet
　　Wingspan: 53 feet
　　Gross weight (pounds): 8,750

Engines: 1 Wright Cyclone F1 radial

Performance: Maximum range: 850 miles
　　Service ceiling: 18,000 feet
　　Maximum speed: 195 mph
　　Maximum cruising speed: 162 mph

Initial Test Flight: May 22, 1932

Initial U.S. Operator Service: Western Air Express, 1933

Remarks: Almost unknown and unremembered, the G.A.-43 designed by Virginius Clark and manufactured by the General Aviation Manufacturing Corporation of Dundalk, Maryland, was among the first cantilevered-low-wing, all-metal, retractable-landing-gear airliners. Passengers were accommodated on individual leather-upholstered seats in a heated, roomy, and sound-insulated cabin also provided with a toilet. Extremely clean aerodynamically, only five aircraft were built, including the prototype, with one operated by Pan Am's subsidiary, SCADTA, in Columbia. Only one was operated in America, Western Air Express' between Cheyenne and Albuquerque in 1933. ■

In this familiar photograph, the Western Air Express Clark G. A.-43 is shown at Denver Municipal Airport in 1933. Courtesy Western Airlines

■ BELLANCA P-100/P-200 Air Bus

First Service: 1934

Type/Purpose: Single-engined, commercial, short-haul transport

Number of Seats: 2 pilots, 12–14 passengers

Dimensions: Length: 40.1 feet
Height: 10.4 feet
Wingspan: 65 feet
Gross weight (pounds): 9,500

Engines: 1 Curtiss Conqueror CV-1570 radial (P-100)/
1 Pratt & Whitney Hornet or 1 Wright Cyclone radial (P-200)

Performance: Maximum range: 700 miles
Service ceiling: 14,000 feet
Maximum speed: 145 mph
Maximum cruising speed: 122 mph

Initial Test Flight: May 1930

Initial U.S. Operator Service: New York/Suburban Air Lines, summer 1934

Remarks: Designed by Guiseppe Bellanca and based on his earlier Model J, the P-100 was noteworthy for its distinctive landing gear supports, which were expanded into airfoils that added 200 square feet of lifting area to the high wing. The P-100 matched the seating capacity of the larger Fokker and Ford Tri-Motors and cost only $2,500 less ($38,500); aerodynamics and cost aside, however, safety-minded, potential operators feared for the reliability of a large transport with only one engine. Finding no buyers in the Depression year of 1931, Bellanca changed the engine of the P-100 into the P-200 and attempted to sell the six aircraft he had built to civil operators under their new label. Only four could be unloaded to two carriers. Undaunted, the manufacturer was eventually able to push off his remaining units to the U.S. Army, which designated them C-97s. At least one P-200 was part of the West Virginia Air Tour Association in the early 1930s.

Selected List of U.S. Operating Airlines: Martz Airlines; New York/Suburban Air Lines ■

Photographed at Wertz Field, Charleston, on May 16, 1932, this Bellancha Air Bus (upper right in rear line) belonged to the West Virginia Air Tour Association. Courtesy West Virginia Dept. of Culture and History

■ CURTISS T-32 Condor II

First Service: 1934

Type/Purpose: Twin-engined, commercial, medium-haul transport

Number of Seats: 3 crew, 13 – 14 passengers

Dimensions: Length: 49 feet
Height: 16.4 feet
Wingspan: 82 feet
Gross weight (pounds): 17,500

Engines: 2 Wright SGR-1820-3 Cyclone radials

Performance: Maximum range: 716 miles
Service ceiling: 23,000 feet
Maximum speed: 190 mph
Maximum cruising speed: 155 mph

Initial Test Flight: January 30, 1933

Initial U.S. Operator Service: American Airways,
May 5, 1934

Remarks: Although it had certain similarities to the Condor I, the T- 32 (named for its 3,200-pound payload) was, in fact, a completely new design. Faster and possessed of a more portly fuselage than its namesake, the Condor II featured a single fin/rudder/tail assembly, wooden wings, neat engine cowlings, and the first electrically operated, semi-retractable, main landing gear. The fabric-covered T-32 was the last biplane airliner to be introduced by a major carrier in the Untied States; refined variants were offered as the AT-32A-E and a total of 45 of all versions were manufactured. Although American inaugurated "sleeper service" (12 bunks in specially soundproofed cabins), the carrier was soon forced to abandon its chunky aircraft in light of the availability to its competitors of speedier aircraft, such as the Boeing 247 and Douglas DC-2. The last T-32 was withdrawn from front-line U.S. service in 1936, but many flew on in various capacities with military and civil operators around the globe. Incidentally, the last operational T-32, a unit of the Peruvian Air Force, was not retired until 1956.

Selected List of U.S. Operating Airlines: American Airlines; Eastern Air Transport ■

An excellent profile of an American Airways Condor II, ca. 1934. The last biplane airliner to enter frontline U.S. service, it could serve as both a day plane and a night sleeper. Courtesy American Airlines

One of American's first sleeper T-32s, NC 12354 was destroyed in a fatal crash near Liberty, New York, in 1934. Courtesy American Airlines

■ DOUGLAS DC-1/DC-2

First Service: 1934

Type/Purpose: Twin-engined, commercial, medium-haul transport

Number of Seats: 3 crew, 12 passengers (DC-1)/ 3 crew, 14-18 passengers (DC-2)

Dimensions: Length: 59.11 feet (DC-1)/ 61.11 feet (DC-2)
Height: 16 feet (DC-1)/ 16.4 feet (DC-2)
Wingspan: 85 feet
Gross weight (pounds): 17,500 (DC-1)/ 18,500 (DC-2)

Engines: 2 Wright SGR-1820-3 Cyclone radials (DC-1)/
2 Wright SGR-1820-F3 Cyclone radials (DC-2)

Performance: Maximum range: 1,000 miles
Service ceiling: 23,600 feet
Maximum speed: 210 mph
Maximum cruising speed: 196-200 mph

Initial Test Flight: July 1, 1933 (DC-1)/ May 11, 1934 (DC-2)

Initial U.S. Operator Service: TWA, September 1933 (DC-1)/
TWA, May 18, 1934 (DC-2)

Remarks: With Boeing production facilities tied up for two years in building the superior Model 247 for United Air Lines, other carriers were forced to look elsewhere for advanced transports. Even before the first Boeing flew, TWA Operational Vice President Jack Frye prevailed upon Donald Douglas to come up with a competitive design. As the disadvantages of the 247 were known, Douglas was able to avoid these, as well as Frye's demand for a trimotor, and offered a prototype called the DC – Douglas Commercial – 1. Larger than the 247, the DC-1 employed many of the advances of the single-engined Northrop Alpha (Douglas had acquired Northrop in 1932) design in wing and fuselage, NACA cowlings, superior flaps, and other aerodynamic improvements, many based on research in the Guggenheim Aeronautical Laboratory wind tunnel at Cal Tech. Convinced of the soundness of the Douglas product, as well as the safety of its two-engined configuration, TWA accepted the DC-1 in September 1933. The aircraft was extensively tested during the first six months of 1934, during which time it set 11 U.S. and 8 international speed-distance records. So impressed were TWA officials that they elected to purchase 20 (later increased to 31) of a slightly stretched DC-1 labeled the DC-2. With larger engines, controllable-pitch propellers, flaps, and 14-passenger capacity, the

DC-2 entered service fourteen months after the Boeing 247 and immediately began snatching business away from it. The DC-2, of which 130 civil models were eventually built, far outclassed all previous airliners (including the 247, Ford Tri-Motor, Stinson Model A) in performance, economics, and passenger comfort. Incidentally, it was a standard KLM-manned DC-2 that won the transport division of the 1934 London-Australia MacRobertson Air Race and, in total speed, came in second only to a specially designed, British Comet racer. It is probably correct to say that had Boeing not been monopolized by United in production of the 247, there might never have been a DC-2 or its more illustrious successor, the DC-3. The last DC-2 was delivered in July 1937 and most of those with American airlines continued to serve until replaced by DC-3s during the late 1930s and early 1940s.

Selected List of U.S. Operating Airlines: American Airlines; Braniff Airways; Eastern Airlines; General Airlines; Pan American Airways; Pan American Grace Airways (PANAGRA); TWA ■

The Douglas DC-1 prototype photographed at Glendale, California, in summer 1933. Courtesy McDonnell Douglas

TOP LEFT: The Douglas DC-1 flies in TWA livery. Note the registration number. Courtesy McDonnell Douglas.

TOP RIGHT: Refueling a Douglas DC-2 of Transcontinental and Western Airlines. Courtesy Trans World Airlines

BOTTOM: The old and the new—an American Airlines DC-2 parked at Chicago Airport, ca 1934, as passengers prepare to board a company Ford 5-AT Tri-Motor (left). Courtesy American Airlines

■ LOCKHEED Model 10 Electra

First Service: 1934

Type/Purpose: Twin-engined, commercial, short-haul transport

Number of Seats: 3 crew, 8-10 passengers

Dimensions: Length: 38.7 feet
Height: 10.1 feet
Wingspan: 55 feet
Gross weight (pounds): 9,750

Engines: 2 Pratt & Whitney Wasp Junior SB radials (10A)/
2 Wright R-975-E3 Whirlwind radials (10B)/
2 Pratt & Whitney Wasp Junior SDC-1 radials (10C)/
2 Pratt & Whitney R-1340-SH1 Wasp radials (10E)

Performance: Maximum range: 810 miles
Service ceiling: 21,650 feet
Maximum speed: 202 mph
Maximum cruising speed: 180 mph

Initial Test Flight: February 23, 1934

Initial U.S. Operator Service: Northwest Airways,
August 11, 1934

Remarks: Spurred on by success with the Vega and Orion, the reorganized Lockheed Aircraft Corporation developed the Model 10 for fast airline operations, giving it distinctive twin fins and rudders. Its launch by Northwest Airways marked its arrival as the third (behind the Boeing 247 and DC-2) modern all-metal, low-wing, twin-engined airliner to enter U.S. carrier operations within a two year period. There were four main versions—A to C and E—and a total of 149 were manufactured before production ended in 1941. Unlike the builder's single-engined transports Vega through Orion, the Electra was of all-metal construction with a monocoque fuselage, and metal-skinned wing and tail surfaces. The interior of the wing covering was corrugated, the main wheels retracted into the engine nacelles, and the engine propellers were all constant-speed, two-blade models. A number of Model 10s were owned privately or by corporations and some were employed in spectacular long-distance flights, including: Jimmy Doolittle's record 1936 transcontinental flight of 5 hours 55 minutes; an Electra that sped film of the coronation of King George VI from Britain to America in May 1937; and one lost with Amelia Earhart while on a round-the-world flight in July 1937. The aircraft was employed by foreign carriers and those in the far North, including Pacific Alaska Airways, had Electras with nonretractable ski undercarriages. Later generations of commercial-transport aircraft benefited from the high-altitude research conducted by a specially equipped U.S. Army Electra designated XC-35.

Selected List of U.S. Operating Airlines: Boston-Maine/Northeast; Braniff Airways; Chicago and Southern Air Lines; Delta Air Lines; Eastern Airlines; Mid-Continent Airlines; Naples Airlines; National Airlines; Northwest Airways; Pacific Alaska Airways; Pan American Airways ■

Delta employed a Lockheed Model 10B as a training-survey aircraft once it was withdrawn from passenger service. Courtesy Delta Airlines

Delta Air Lines Lockheed Model 10B was equipped with 440 hp Wright R-975-E3 Whirlwind radial engines. Courtesy Delta Airlines

Designed primarily for the corporate market, the speedy six-passenger Lockheed Model 12A Electra Junior also found service with a number of airlines. Courtesy Lockheed-California Company, via James P. Woolsey

■ LOCKHEED Model 12A Electra Junior

First Service: 1934

Type/Purpose: Twin-engined, short-haul, commercial/ corporate transport

Number of Seats: 2 crew, 6 passengers

Dimensions: Length: 36.4 feet
    Height: 9.9 feet
    Wingspan: 49.6 feet
    Gross weight (pounds): 8,650

Engines: 2 Pratt & Whitney Wasp Junior R-985-SB2 radials

Performance: Maximum range: 950 miles
    Maximum speed: 225 mph
    Maximum cruising speed: 213 mph

Initial Test Flight: June 27, 1936

Initial U.S. Operator Service: Varney Air Transport, May 14, 1937

Remarks: The Electra Junior was a scaled-down version of the highly-successful Model 10 with seating for six instead of ten. The aircraft, by retaining the Electra's power plant, possessed greater performance, a Lockheed selling point as it approached the primary executive market. A total of 63 civil and 66 military examples were built and while most of the former were to serve with such corporations as the oil industry or with such government agencies as the Civil Aeronautics Administration, a number were taken by airlines wishing fast transport or feederline capabilities.

Selected List of U.S. Operating Airlines: Boston-Maine & Central Vermont Airlines ("Sky Baby"); Delta Air Corp.; Fischer Bros. Aviation; Florida Airmotive; Midwest Airways; Pacific Northern Airlines; Pan American Airways; Santa Maria Air Lines; Southwest Airways; Swift Air Service; TWA; United Air Lines; Varney Air Transport/Continental Air Lines; Western Air Express; Western Alaska Airlines ■

■ SIKORSKY S-42

First Service: 1934

Type/Purpose: Four-engined, commercial, flying-boat transport

Number of Seats: 5 crew, 32 passengers

Dimensions: Length: 52 feet
Height: 21.3 feet
Wingspan: 118 feet
Gross weight (pounds): 43,000

Engines: 4 Pratt & Whitney R-1690-S5D1-G Hornet radials

Performance: Maximum range: 750 miles
Service ceiling: 15,000 feet
Maximum speed: Maximum cruising speed: 140 mph

Initial Test Flight: March 1934

Initial U.S. Operator Service: Pan American Airways, August 16, 1934

Remarks: Designed in 1932 to meet Pan Am's requirement for an oceanic flyer to succeed its twin-boomed S-40, the Sikorsky S-42 was the world's most advanced flying boat when it appeared. Equipped with a very-high-aspect-ratio wing (10.3), it was the first Sikorsky to feature wing flaps (and excellent they were), an adjustable horizontal stabilizer, and variable-pitch propellers. With its superior hull design and the first use of flush riveting on a commercial airplane, the aircraft would take off in 35 seconds with a full load in a dead calm. During the summer of 1934, the first S-42, piloted by Charles A. Lindbergh, established or returned numerous flying-boat records to the United States. The need for refueling bases had forced Pan Am, with U.S.-government support, to negotiate a number of mid-ocean bases, but in November 1935, a PAA S-42 became the first airplane to inaugurate regular scheduled service across the Pacific to Hong Kong and New Zealand, and across the Atlantic to England and Portugal in 1937. The last of the first S-42 series was delivered in 1937 and employed as a survey plane for Mid- and North-Atlantic, route-proving runs. A total of 10 S-42s were built, the latter 7 being improved As or Bs with slightly greater wingspans, higher gross weights, and improved Pratt & Whitney Hornet S2E-G radials. While jettisoning fuel near Pago Pago on January 11, 1938, Pan Am's pioneering chief pilot, Edwin C. Musick, his crew, and *Clipper II* were lost in a midair explosion. One S-42 was destroyed by the Japanese at Manila on December 8, 1942, and another was lost at Manaos, Brazil, on July 27, 1943. The last 4 were scrapped on July 15, 1946. ■

The Sikorsky S-42 began scheduled Miami to Rio service on August 16, 1934. Courtesy Pan American World Airways

Travellers depart a Pan Am Sikorsky. Note the irregular passenger windows. Courtesy Pan American World Airways

Here, at Ford Island Naval Air Station in Hawaii, ca. 1936, is the first Sikorsky S-42B *Hong Kong Clipper*. Courtesy Pan American World Airlines.

Shown here on wheels which could be attached for taxiing purposes is the S-42 prototype and first production Sikorsky, NC-822M, later renamed *Brazilian Clipper*. Courtesy Pan American World Airways

■ STINSON Reliant SR Series

First Service: 1934

Type/Purpose: Single-engined, commercial, short-haul transport

Number of Seats: 1 pilot, 4–5 passengers

Dimensions: Length: 25-28 feet
    Height: 8.5 feet
    Wingspan: 40-42 feet
    Gross weight (pounds): 3,200-4,700

Engines: 1 Lycoming R-680-6 radial or 1 Wright R-760 Whirlwind radial or 1 Pratt & Whitney Wasp Junior radial

Performance: Maximum range: 400-600 miles
    Service ceiling: 15,000 feet
    Maximum speed: 147 mph
    Maximum cruising speed: 138 mph

Initial Test Flight: Spring 1933

Initial U.S. Operator Service: McGee Airways, 1934

Remarks: Sharing such common features as an all-metal cabin with a strut-braced, constant-chord, high-wing-monoplane configuration, the Stinson SR to SR-6 series of 1933 to 1935 were quite conventional in appearance, differing only in power plants or cabin comforts. Despite this, the aircraft were quite competitive with such rivals as the Bellanca CH-400 or the Fairchild F-24. The popular executive, private, and air-taxi plane underwent something of a design revolution with the SR-7 of 1936. That model introduced a double-tapered wing atop an SR-6 airframe; the new wing not only increased the aircraft's performance and sales, but gave the entire type a new name: "Gull Wing Stinson." The model continued to be updated through the SR-8, -9, and -10 and as was the case with the earlier Reliants, the major differences were again in power plants. Employed primarily by corporate and private owners, the SRs continued to be built even after Stinson was merged with Vultee and many saw liaison service with the U.S. military in World War II. After the war, the Reliant equipped many small carriers and bush operators worldwide.

Selected List of U.S. Operating Airlines: Alaska Airlines; All-American Aviation; American Airlines; McGee Airways; Northern Consolidated Airlines; Northwest Airways; Pollack Flying Service; Wien Alaska Airlines; Wyoming Air Service ■

Northwest Airlines employed its Stinson Reliant for light passenger, survey, and training duties. Courtesy Northwest Orient Airlines

Stinson SR of Alaska Airlines predecessor, McGee Airways. Courtesy Alaska Airlines

Like Northwest, American Airlines employed the Stinson Reliant on training and route survey work. Note the DC-3 to the plane's left. Courtesy American Airlines

USAir predecessor All-American Aviation operated a mail-pickup service with Stinson Reliants. Courtesy USAir

■ VULTEE V-1/V-1A

First Service: 1934

Type/Purpose: Single-engined, commercial, medium-haul transport

Number of Seats: 1 pilot, 8 passengers (V-1)/ 2 pilots, 8 passengers (V-1A)

Dimensions: Length: 35.6 feet (V-1)/ 37 feet (V-1A)
Height: 9.3 feet (V-1)/ 10.2 feet (V-1A)
Wingspan: 48 feet (V-1)/ 50 feet (V-1A)
Gross weight (pounds): 7,250 (V-1)/ 8,500 (V-1A)

Engines: 1 Wright R-1825-F2 radial (V-1)/
1 Wright R-1820-G2 radial (V-2)

Performance: Maximum range: 950–1,000 miles
Service ceiling: 20,012 feet
Maximum speed: 225 mph (V-1)/ 240 mph (V-1A)
Maximum cruising speed: 215 mph (V-1)/
217 mph (V-1A)

Initial Test Flight: February 19, 1933 (V-1)

Initial U.S. Operator Service: American Airlines, September 9, 1934 (V-1A)

Remarks: Designed by Gerald Vultee and a contemporary of the Northrop Delta, the V-1 was the last of the fast, high-performance, single-engined airliners adopted by front-line U.S. carriers during the 1930s. An all-metal, low-wing, cantilevered monoplane with a monocoque fuselage, two-spar wing, stressed-skin covering, an NACA cowling, and inward-retracting main undercarriage, the V-1 prototype featured an enclosed forward pilot cockpit with the pilot's seat on the left and a mail hold on the right. Slightly larger and heavier with improved performance from a larger engine, the 25 production V-1As carried two crew and had trailing-edge wing flaps. All 26 aircraft were constructed by the Aircraft Development Corporation at Glendale, California. With 20 V-1As to compliment its fleet of Curtiss T-32 Condor IIs, American Airlines was the largest operator, flying the clean Vultee into 1937. A number of V-1A variants were employed by corporate and military operators. Among these was one, the V-1A8, which Major James Doolittle flew nonstop across the country in 1935 in the record speed of 11 hours, 59 minutes. Another of the same type, called the *Lady Peace*, with long-range tanks, blanked-off windows, and a fuselage filled with 50,000 ping-pong balls (for flotation if forced down at sea), piloted by entertainer Harry Richman and crack Eastern pilot Henry T. "Dick" Merrill, made the first round-trip flight between New York and London in September 1936. At least seven former American Airlines planes found their way to Spain during the Civil War. A twin-engined version of the V-1A was planned, but in 1936, Vultee, seeing the days of the single-engined airliner to be limited, left the commercial market in favor of military-aircraft design.

Selected list of U.S. Operating Airlines: American Airlines; Bowen Air Lines; Canadian-Colonial Airways. ■

American Airlines operated ten of its Vultee V-1As on its Fort Worth-St. Louis-Chicago route. Courtesy American Airlines

■ MARTIN M-130

First Service: 1935

Type/Purpose: Four-engined, commercial, flying-boat transport

Number of Seats: 7-9 crew, 36 passengers (short haul)/ 7-9 crew, 18 passengers (long haul)

Dimensions: Length: 90.1 feet
Height: 24.7 feet
Wingspan: 130 feet
Gross weight (pounds): 51,000-52,252

Engines: 4 Pratt & Whitney Twin Wasp R-1830-S2A5G radials

Performance: Maximum range: 3,200 miles (passengers)/ 4,000 miles (mail)
Service ceiling: 8,000-10,000 feet
Maximum speed: 179181 mph
Maximum cruising speed: 157 mph

Initial Test Flight: December 30, 1934

Initial U.S. Operator Service: Pan American Airways, November 22, 1935

Remarks: Ordered by Pan Am in 1934, three Martin "Clippers" were built and are remembered as the first airplanes to carry passengers on scheduled transoceanic flights. A high-wing, monoplane flying boat, the Martin was noteworthy for its structural efficiency and the introduction of integral fuel tanks (within its hull). The passenger cabin, some 45 feet long, was compartmentalized with each of three cabins having settees convertible into bunks. Each ship cost $390,000 for airframe and engines, plus $40,000 for certain furnishings and extras. The M-130s' primary function was passenger and/or mail transport in the Pacific area and with Chief Pilot Edwin Musick at the controls, the *China Clipper* inaugurated transpacific Martin flight, November 22-December 6, 1935. The three flying boats caught the fancy of the American public and remained popular, even though the *Hawaii Clipper* was mysteriously lost on July 28, 1938. The two remaining boats, *China Clipper* and *Philippine Clipper*, were turned over to the U.S. Navy in 1942 for shuttle work in the Pacific and Caribbean. The *Philippine Clipper* was lost on January 21, 1943, but the *China Clipper* flew on until a landing accident at Port of Spain, Trinidad, on January 8, 1945, caused her destruction. ■

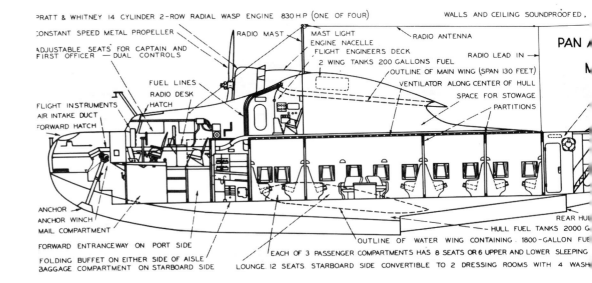

November 22, 1935 – Pan Am's Martin M-130 flying boat, *China Clipper*, leaves San Francisco for Manila via Honolulu, Midway, Wake and Guam carrying the first United States transpacific airmail. Courtesy Pan American World Airways

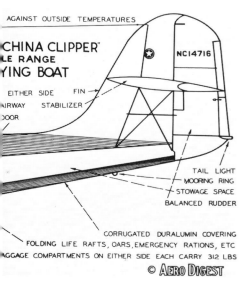

AGAINST OUTSIDE TEMPERATURES

"CHINA CLIPPER"
LE RANGE
YING BOAT

NC14716

EITHER SIDE — FIN
AIRWAY — STABILIZER
DOOR

TAIL LIGHT
MOORING RING
STOWAGE SPACE
BALANCED RUDDER

CORRUGATED DURALUMIN COVERING
FOLDING LIFE RAFTS, OARS, EMERGENCY RATIONS, ETC
AGGAGE COMPARTMENTS ON EITHER SIDE EACH CARRY 312 LBS

© AERO DIGEST

Courtesy Pan American World Airways

The Martin M-130 *Hawaii Clipper* on the water at Ford Island, Pearl Harbor, after completing the first leg of the first transpacific passenger flight, October 1936. Courtesy Pan American World Airways, via Stan Cohen

■ STINSON Model A Trimotor

First Service: 1935

Type/Purpose: Trimotor, commercial, short/medium-haul transport

Number of Seats: 2 crew, 8 passengers

Dimensions: Length: 36.1 feet
Height: 14.2 feet
Wingspan: 60 feet
Gross weight (pounds): 10,200

Engines: 3 Lycoming R-680-5 radials or 3 Pratt & Whitney S3H1 Wasp radials

Performance: Maximum range: 600 miles
Service ceiling: 16,500 feet
Maximum speed: 180 mph
Maximum cruising speed: 162 mph

Initial Test Flight: April 27, 1934

Initial U.S. Operator Service: Delta Air Corporation, July 1935

Remarks: A follow-up to the SM-6000/Model U, the Model A was a trimotor, low-wing monoplane designed to meet American Airways specifications for a nine-place feederliner. Of mostly fabric-covered, all-metal construction, the Model A had a single-spar, cantilevered wing, which was strut-braced to the top of the fuselage and possessed trailing-edge flaps. The main landing wheels were almost fully retractable into the engine nacelles, in the rear of which were located mail and baggage lockers. Reported as having the flight qualities of an iron bathtub, the Model A was withdrawn from Delta service in 1937 and American operations the following year. As the aircraft was retired by its original owners, other carriers, including some overseas, stepped in to acquire them. A total of 30 were manufactured.

Selected List of U.S. Operating Airlines: American Airlines; Central Airlines; Delta Air Lines ■

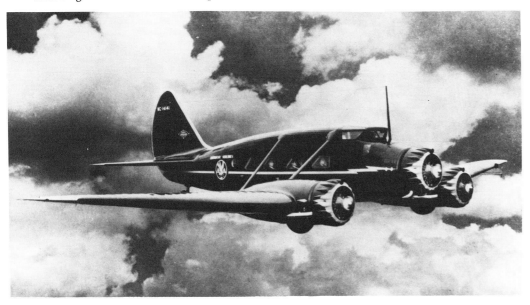

An excellent view of Delta's strut-braced Stinson Model A. Due to the builder's failure to meet American Airways' exact specifications, Delta Air Corporation became the trimotor's launch customer in July 1935. Courtesy Delta Airlines

American Airlines Stinson Model A's, like the one shown here, were sold to other carriers, including Australia's ANA. Courtesy American Airlines

■ DOUGLAS DST/DC-3/Super DC-3

First Service: 1936

Type/Purpose: Twin-engined, commercial, short/medium-range transport

Number of Seats: 3 crew, 14-31 passengers

Dimensions: Length: 64.5 feet (DST/DC-3)/ 64.8 feet (Super DC-3)
  Height: 16.11 feet (DST/DC-3)/ 17.11 feet (Super DC-3)
  Wingspan: 94.6 feet (DST/DC-3)/ 90 feet (Super DC-3)
  Gross weight (pounds): 25,000-36,800

Engines: 2 Wright GR-1820 Cyclone radials or 2 Pratt & Whitney R-1830 Twin Wasp radials

Performance: Maximum range: 1,200 nautical miles (DST)/
  1,300 nautical miles (DC-3)/
  1,900 nautical miles (Super DC-3)
  Service ceiling: 23,200 feet
  Maximum cruising speed: 167 knots (DST/DC-3)/
  218 knots (Super DC-3)

Initial Test Flight: December 17, 1935

Initial U.S. Operator Service: American Airlines,
  June 25, 1936 (DST)/
  American Airlines, September 18, 1936 (DC-3)/
  Capital Airlines, August 1, 1950 (Super DC-3)

Remarks: In continuous service for half a century by summer 1986, the Douglas DC-3 is *the* classic airliner; the most widely employed civil or military transport in history, it is still employed by 26 U.S. carriers and well deserves its title as "the plane that changed the world." The aircraft had its origin in a 1934 request from C.R. Smith to Donald Douglas for a sleeper transport that could replace the Curtiss Condor IIs American Airlines was then employing on its Boston-Dallas-Los Angeles route. Douglas was initially reluctant to proceed with the new design as his DC-2 was just becoming available; Smith's promise of firm business made the project feasible. American placed an initial order for 10 Douglas Sleeper Transports (DST), as the plane was initially known, in July 1935 and the prototype was test flown in December; it was certified on April 29, 1936, the day Smith took delivery of his first $110,000 aircraft.

Of cantilevered, low-wing, monoplane configuration with the stressed-skin, multicellular-wing construction of the DC-2, the all-metal DC-3 enjoys an almost circular monocoque fuselage (in cross section) with an internal cabin height sufficient to allow most passengers to stand upright in the single offset aisle. In fact, a stretch of its predecessor, the airliner was equipped with more powerful engines, a stronger undercarriage, an enlarged tail, and 16 sleeping berths. The first DC-3, the "day-plane" version of the DST, with seating for 21-24 passengers and four bunk windows deleted, was delivered to American on August 8, 1936. Quickly gaining wide acceptance, the DC-3 soon replaced the DST in Douglas order books (to say nothing of the DC-2) and, flying for both scheduled and nonscheduled carriers, had captured 95 percent of all U.S. airline traffic by 1938 and 90 percent of the world's by 1940. In the period 1936-1941, the U.S.-national-passenger mileage increased nearly 600 percent with most of that directly attributable to the adoption of the DC-3 as standard equipment by the nation's air carriers. Before World War II, 417 standard-model DC-3s were produced and were sold to America's airlines in this numerical order: American, 72; United, 39; Eastern, 35; Pan Am, 34; TWA, 29; Northwest, 12; and Braniff, 10. Following Pearl Harbor, 194 civil DC-3s were quickly impressed into U.S. military service; during the remainder of the conflict, another 10,238 were manufactured and were operated by U.S. and Allied forces as the C-47/Dakota. Following victory, thousands of the military models became surplus, were reconfigured to airliner status, and served to equip dozens of civil carriers. In 1949, Douglas sought to bring out a replacement, the Super DC-3 or DC-3S, by modernizing, stretching, and making more powerful the DC-3; in light of the increasing availability of newer equipment, however, few orders were received. Other than the original DST and the DC-3S stretch, there has been remarkably little change in the aircraft's airframe design. Over the past 50 years, however, the power plant has been altered frequently, including 13 variants of the Wright Cyclone, 11 of the Pratt & Whitney Twin Wasp, and even the installation of the Rolls Royce Dart of Pratt & Whitney turboprops. The search for an effective DC-3 replacement has been underway for at least the past 35 years, but only the Fokker F-27 Friendship has come close to filling the bill. Indeed, the DC-3 is as popular in certain quarters today as it was with the majors in the late thirties. Basler Flight Service of Oshkosh, Wisconsin, is currently refurbishing DC-3s for airline service, and offering them for sale at approximately $125,000—about $25,000 more than C.R. Smith paid for his first DST in 1936. No other airliner of its size can today be purchased for that amount, which in 1985 was roughly 15 percent of the cost of, say, a new Em-

braer EMB-110 Bandierante or a Beech C-99 commuterliner. Cost effectiveness and rugged dependability explain why an aircraft, which enjoys a proud place of display in the National Air and Space Museum, continues to have an impact on workaday airlines.

Selected List of U.S. Operating Airlines: Allegheny Airlines; All-American Aviation; American Airlines; Arizona Airways; Capital Airlines; Chicago and Southern Air Lines; Continental Airlines; Delta Air Lines; Eastern Airlines; Flying Tiger Line, Frontier Airlines; Hawaiian Airlines; Mohawk Airlines; Monarch Airlines; North American Airlines; North Central Airlines; Northeast Airlines; Northwest Orient Airlines; Ozark Airlines; Pacific Northern Airlines; Pan American Grace Airways (PANAGRA); Pan American World Airways; Pennsylvania-Central Airlines; Piedmont Airlines; Pilgrim Airlines; Southern Airways; Southwest Airways; TWA; United Airlines; Western Airlines; West Coast Airlines; (1984-1985): Aero-Dyne Airlines; Aero Virgin Islands; Audi Air; Baron Aviation Services; Basler Airlines; Bo-S-Aire Airlines; Caribbean Air Service (CASAIR); Caribbean Aviation Services; Century Airlines; Crystal Shamrock Airlines; Emery Worldwide; Florida Airmotive; Four Star Aviation; Harold's Air Service; Hogan Air; Lynbird International; Northern Airways; Provincetown-Boston Airline (PBA); Pro Air Services; Saber Aviation; Selair; Skyfreight; Skyfreighters Corporation; Summit Airlines; Trans-North Air; Virgin Air

DC-3 Celebration In honor of the fiftieth anniversary of history's best-known airliner, we present here an extra generous selection of DC-3 photographs.

American Airlines DST.
Courtesy American Airlines

LEFT: Delta Air Lines. Courtesy Delta Airlines

RIGHT: Frontier Airlines. Courtesy Frontier Airlines

Lake Central Airlines. Courtesy US Air

Mohawk Airlines. Courtesy US Air

Provincetown-Boston Airline (PBA). On March 1, 1985, PBA's *Old 36* (shown here on the far left in a photo taken at Barnstable Airport, near Hyannis, Mass., on November 13, 1984) recorded its 87,687th operational hour, making it commercial aviation's highest total-time aircraft ever. Courtesy Chris Sorensen via James P. Woolsey

■ SIKORSKY S-43

First Service: 1936

Type/Purpose: Twin-engined, commercial amphibian

Number of Seats: 2-3 crew, 16-17 passengers

Dimensions: Length: 52 feet
　　Height: 17.8 feet
　　Wingspan: 86 feet
　　Gross weight (pounds): 19,500

Engines: 2 Pratt & Whitney Wasp radials or 2 Pratt
　　& Whitney Hornet radials

Performance: Maximum range: 500-775 miles
　　Service ceiling: 20,012 feet
　　Maximum speed: 190 mph
　　Maximum cruising speed: 150-166 mph

Initial Test Flight: June 1, 1935

Initial U.S. Operator Service: Pan American Airways,
　　April 1936

Remarks: Known as the "Baby Clipper," the S-43 was a scaled-down, short-range successor to the S-42, which employed much of the technology formulated in the construction of its predecessors. Employed also as a flying boat, the amphibian in April 1936 set four world altitude records for its type over Stratford, Connecticut; the first, an altitude of 24,950 feet without payload, still stands. A total of 53 were constructed, of which 26 were sold to civil carriers, beginning with Inter-Island Airways on November 18, 1935 (the plane was disassembled in California and shipped to Hawaii by steamer). Pan American Airways maintained the largest commercial fleet for operations around the Caribbean and on the interior waterways of South America, as well as on the Seattle-Juneau run by its Northwest Division. The largest operator of the S-43 was the U.S. Navy, which labeled its ships JRS-1s; one JRS is preserved at the National Air and Space Museum. The U.S. Army flew 5 S-43s as X10A-8s. A number of the sleek amphibians were sold overseas and one went to Howard Hughes. Following World War II, S-43s served with Reeve Aleutian Airways (1950–1958), Alaska Airlines, Hawaiian Airlines and Avalon Air Transport.

Selected List of U.S. Operating Airlines: Alaska Airlines; Avalon Air Transport; Hawaiian Airlines; Inter-Island Airways; Pan American Airways; Reeve Aleutian Airways ■

Pan Am's Sikorsky S-43 was nicknamed the "Baby Clipper." Courtesy Pan American World Airways

Reeve Aleutian Airways operated a Sikorsky S-43 over its routes into the early 1960s. Courtesy Reeve Aleutian Airways

Inter-Island Airways' Sikorsky S-43, ca. 1935. Courtesy Hawaiian Airlines

■ LOCKHEED Model 14 Super Electra

First Service: 1937

Type/Purpose: Twin-engined, commercial, short/medium-haul transport

Number of Seats: 3 crew, 12 passengers

Dimensions: Length: 44.3 feet
Height: 11.1 feet
Wingspan: 65.6 feet
Gross weight (pounds): 17,500

Engines: 2 Pratt & Whitney S1E2G Hornet radials or
2 Wright GR-1820-F62 Cyclone radials or
2 Wright GR-1820-G3 Cyclone radials

Performance: Maximum range: 1,590 miles
Service ceiling: 21,500 feet
Maximum speed: 257 mph
Maximum cruising speed: 237 mph

Initial Test Flight: July 29, 1937

Initial U.S. Operator Service: Northwest Airlines,
September 1937

Remarks: Known as the Super Electra, Electra Senior, Old Boomerang, Sky Zephyr, or just "the 14," Lockheed's Model 14 followed the structural and aerodynamic concepts of the Model 10 Electra while introducing a number of new features. Intended to provide airlines passenger/cargo flexibility, the Super Electra had a deep elliptical-section, monocoque fuselage and freight holds under the flooring. Unlike the Electra, the Model 14 was a mid-wing monoplane that featured a new wing designed by Clarence L. "Kelly" Johnson to incorporate large-area, rolling Fowler flaps, "letter box" slots near the outer leading edges, and a compound taper on the trailing edges. It was the first airliner to introduce two-speed super-chargers and feathering airscrews. Smaller in capacity than a DC-3, the aircraft was also less expensive, considerably faster and offered greater range. Three different variants were sold, each with a different pair of Pratt & Whitney engines. A Model 14 (in British registry) carried Neville Chamberlain to the Munich Conference in 1938, the same year Howard Hughes employed a Super Electra to establish a new around-the-world record of 3 days, 19 hours, 14 minutes. A total of 112 civil Super Electras were built in the United States before Pearl Harbor and all but a few were employed by airlines. Overseas, the Model 14 found service with various carriers and, under license, Japan built 119 as Type LO military transports and 121 as Ki-56s for the Japanese Army Air Force. The aircraft's greatest fame came during World War II when it was modified and produced as the Hudson (RAF) and A-28, A-29, AT-18 (USAAF), Allied patrol bomber and training aircraft.

Selected List of U.S. Operating Airlines: Continental Airlines; Mid-Continent Airlines; Northwest Airlines; United Air Lines ■

A Northwest Lockheed 14 draws a crowd. Courtesy Northwest Orient Airlines

Northwest Airlines introduced Lockheed 14 service in September 1937, calling its aircraft the *Sky Zephyr*. SI #86-12049

■ GRUMMAN G-21
Series A to G Goose

First Service: 1938

Type/Purpose: Twin-engined, commercial, short/medium-haul amphibian

Number of Seats: 1-2 crew, 7-10 passengers

Dimensions: Length: 38.4 feet
Height: 12 feet
Wingspan: 49-50.1 feet
Gross weight (pounds): 7,500-12,500

Engines: 2 Pratt & Whitney R-985 Twin Wasp Jr. radials
(G-21A/B)/
4 Avco Lycoming GSO-480-B2D6 pistons (G-21C/D)/
2 Pratt & Whitney of Canada PT6-A20 turboprops
(G-21E)/
2 Pratt & Whitney of Canada PT6-A27 turboprops
(G-21G)

Performance: Maximum range: 800-1,600 miles
Service ceiling: 20,000-22,000 feet
Maximum speed: 201 mph
Maximum cruising speed: 191 mph

Initial Test Flight: May 29, 1937

Remarks: The first civil design of today's huge Grumman Corporation, this middleweight amphibian was a high-wing, all-metal monoplane (with retractable wheels), which could compete with contemporary land planes and, indeed, could be configured as an amphibian, a flying boat, or a land plane. Its two-step hull was divided into six watertight compartments and entry for the pilots and passengers was through a two-section door on the left, behind the wing. Employing the float for which LeRoy Grumman was famous, fixed wing-tip floats, a modern air-foil, efficient flaps, and other refinements, the Goose was nearly as aerodynamically clean as, say, a Beech Model 18. The aircraft was widely purchased by the U.S. military for service in World War II and flew with the U.S. Navy, Army, and Coast Guard. Following the conflict, many of the 250 or so surviving G-21s entered the civil market where the absence of competing amphibians gave them a monopoly when their capability was required. In mid-1958, McKinnon Enterprises, Inc., of Sandy, Oregon, began a Goose conversion program for a number of A and B models. Their first product was the G-21C, made more powerful with 4 Avco Lycoming pistons. The Model D of 1960 was similar to the C, except for increased control surfaces and a 36-inch stretch of the bow with windows in it. Nine years later, the Model E appeared with Pratt & Whitney engines (with a Garrett power plant, one Model F was constructed for the Alaskan Fish and Wildlife Service). The Model G also appeared in 1969 with more powerful engines, an enlarged cabin, bigger doors, and a wet wing with 586-gallon fuel capacity. Originally costing $50,000, the G-21 was selling (when available) for upward of ten times that figure in the early 1980s. Interestingly enough, there were 72 G-21s on the U.S. civil register in 1980 (as compared to 50 in 1948) and, except for avionics and power plant, these were little changed from their original configuration.

Selected List of U.S. Operating Airlines: AirPac, Inc.; Alaska Coastal/Alaska Airlines; Alaska Island Air; Antilles Air Boats; Avalon Air Transport/Catalina Airlines; Chalk's International Airlines; Reeve Aleutian Airways; Westflight Aviation; (1984–1985): AirPac, Inc.; Air Transport Services; Alaska Airlines; Alaska Island Air; Catalina Seaplanes; Channel Flying; Kenmore Air; Westflight Aviation ■

Reeve Grumman Goose at an Aleutian airfield in 1972. Courtesy Reeve Aleutian Airways

■ BOEING 314/314A Clipper

First Service: 1939

Type/Purpose: Four-engined, commercial, flying-boat
   transport

Number of Seats: 6-10 crew, 74 passengers (day)/
   5-9 crew, 40 berthed passengers (night)

Dimensions: Length: 106 feet
   Height: 27.7 feet
   Wingspan: 152 feet
   Gross weight (pounds): 84,480

Engines: 4 Wright GR-2600-A2 Double Cyclone radials

Performance: Maximum range: 5,200 miles
   Service ceiling: 19,800 feet
   Maximum speed: 199 mph
   Maximum cruising speed: 184 mph

Initial Test Flight: June 7, 1938 (314)/ March 20, 1941 (314A)

Initial U.S. Operator Service: Pan American Airways,
   March 29, 1939 (transpacific)/
   June 28, 1939 (transatlantic)

Remarks: Designed by Wellwood E. Beall and derived (in part) from Boeing's XB-15 bomber, the Model 314 was one of the most luxurious airliners of all time. Pan Am signed an initial order for six on July 21, 1936, with options for six more. A high-wing monoplane, the Boeing was the first aircraft to incorporate a full cantilevered wing with no external struts or flying wires. Following difficulty with a single fin/rudder, the plane eventually was given three. Cockpits and crew spaces were located on the upper deck, while passenger accomodations were on the second, within the deep hull. Indeed, the giant flying boat was the first "wide-bodied" aircraft and with 12.5-foot cabins, the amount of cabin space per passenger was the highest on any airliner before or since. Hot meals were served on tables in a dining lounge and the storage of fuel in integral sea-wing tanks (pumped to feeder tanks in the wing) eliminated hull fuel storage thus allowing smoking in the passenger compartments. Pan Am picked up its option in 1939 and the six additional aircraft, with slight improvements and more powerful engines, were delivered in 1941 as 314As. During World War II, three were sold to Britain while the remaining nine served U.S. military interests, hauling high-priority cargo and passengers—including President Roosevelt—overseas. In mid-1942, one of the

British Boeings flew Winston Churchill to the U.S. and back to England in 27 hours. Made obsolete by long-legged land planes, all of the 314As had been lost in accidents or scrapped by 1951, except one. That plane was the ex-BOAC clipper, *Bristol* (the 1942 Churchill plane). Sold to a minister who hoped to fly to Russia and discuss peace with Stalin, it was sunk when a hurricane swept over its Baltimore Harbor berth that year.

An unidentified Pan Am Boeing 314 departs San Francisco Bay one day in 1939, with Alcatraz Island and the Bay Bridge on the horizon. Courtesy Stan Smith, via Stan Cohen

Boeing's third 314 was christened *Yankee Clipper* by Mrs. Franklin D. Roosevelt at New York on March 3, 1939; three weeks later, she flew a final survey of foreign bases, setting a world's record for the transportation of passengers across the Atlantic in a heavier-than-air craft, and on the return, informally inaugurated Atlantic air express. In May 1939, she flew the first airmail flight to Europe, completing the first scheduled round-trip airmail service over the Atlantic. Sold to the U.S. Navy in World War II, the *Yankee* crashed and was destroyed at Lisbon, Portugal, on February 22, 1943. Courtesy Pan American World Airways

Delivered to Pan Am's Pacific Division at San Francisco in March 1939, the second Boeing 314 was christened *California Clipper* on April 25. In July 1940, she established regular fortnightly mail service between Los Angeles and Auckland, New Zealand; she began scheduled service from San Francisco to Singapore in May 1941 and launched official transpacific air express in August. Courtesy Pan American World Airways

The fourth Boeing 314 was christened *Atlantic Clipper* at Baltimore on April 25, 1939; on June 17, she made the first formal passenger crossing of the Atlantic Ocean transporting 16 reporters and 2 Pan Am officials. Sold to the U.S. Navy during World War II, she ferried high-priority freight and passengers between the United States, Britain, and Portugal. Courtesy Pan American Airways

■ BEECHCRAFT Model 18

First Service: 1940

Type/Purpose: Twin-engined, commercial, commuter/regional, executive, air-taxi, utility transport

Number of Seats: 2 crew, 7-9 passengers

Dimensions: Length: 31.11 feet (A)/ 34.3 feet (S)/
34.2 feet (CT)/ 35.2 feet (H)
Height: 9.4 feet
Wingspan: 47.8 feet (A/S/CT)/ 49.8 feet (H)
Gross weight (pounds): 6,500 (A)/ 7,500 (S)/ 9,450 (CT)/
9,900 (H)

Engines: 2 Wright R-760-E2 (A)/
2 Pratt & Whitney Wasp Jr. (S)/
2 Continental R-9A (CT)/
2 Pratt & Whitney Wasp Jr. (H)

Performance: Maximum range: 668 miles (A)/
1,000 miles (S)/ 900 miles (CT)/ 1,400 miles (H)
Service ceiling: 20,000 feet (A)/ 27,500 feet (S)/
23,800 feet (CT)/ 21,400 feet (H)
Maximum speed: 202 mph (A)/ 240 mph (S/CT)/
236 mph (H)
Maximum cruising speed: 167 mph (A)/
224 mph (S/CT)/ 209 mph (H)

Initial Test Flight: January 15, 1937

Initial U.S. Operator Service: Wiggins Airways,
February 1940

Remarks: Designed by Walter Beech and Ted A. Wells as a corporate aircraft and bearing a striking resemblance to the Lockheed Model 10 Electra, the Beech 18 was a contemporary of the Douglas DC-3 and shared with its famous, if larger, cousin a simple and robust airframe construction and reliable power plant unstressed by even heavy loads. A conventional low-wing monoplane, the 18 went through thirty-two modifications during a continuous production life of more than thirty-two years. During that time, over 9,200 were built (or rebuilt) for civil and military operators, setting a twin-engined production record which, when finished on November 26, 1969, led to the plane's achievement of honors as the most versatile, noncombat aircraft of its type ever manufactured. More than 2,000 Beech 18s remain on the U.S. civil register, including a number modified during the 1960s by fuselage lengthening or the addition of turboprop engines. Many

airlines in this country and abroad began scheduled passenger service with the Model 18 and a few American carriers still employ the gallant old airplane in that capacity.

Selected List of U.S. Operating Airlines: Air Pac Airlines; American Flag Airlines; Aurora Air Service; Bard Air; Blackhawk Airways; Bo-S-Aire Airlines; Caribbean Aviation Services; Circle Rainbow Air; Connie Kalitta Services; DHL Airlines; Florida Airmotive; Four Star Aviation; General Aviation; Gull Air; Hawaiian Sky Tour; Hogan Air; North Continent Airlines; Panorama Air Tour; Pro Air Services; Saber Aviation; Sair Aviation; Semp Airways; SMB Stage Line; Transtar Air Cargo; Viking Express; Virgin Air; Walker's Cay Airline ■

The Robinson Airlines Beech 18 *Air Chief Niagara* at Ithaca Municipal Airport, May 1946. Founded in 1945, this pioneer regional changed its name to Mohawk Airlines in August 1952. Courtesy Beech Aircraft Corp.

A Beech 18 of Inland Air Lines ca. 1940. Formerly Wyoming Air Service (to April 1938), Inland was purchased by Western Airlines in October 1943. Courtesy Beech Aircraft Corp.

Texas Airlines Beech 18 revs up for departure. Courtesy Beech Aircraft Corp.

The Beech Super H18, shown here in flight over the Midwest, was manufactured after September 1963 and featured tricycle landing gear. Courtesy Beech Aircraft Corp., via James P. Woolsey

■ BOEING 307 Stratoliner

First Service: 1940

Type/Purpose: Four-engined, commercial transport

Number of Seats: 5 crew, 33 passengers

Dimensions: Length: 74.4 feet
　　Height: 20.9 feet
　　Wingspan: 107.3 feet
　　Gross weight (pounds): 42,000

Engines: 4 Wright GR-1820-97 Cyclone radials

Performance: Maximum range: 2,390 miles
　　Service ceiling: 23,800 feet
　　Maximum speed: 246 mph
　　Maximum cruising speed: 222 mph

Initial Test Flight: December 31, 1938

Initial U.S. Operator Service: Pan American Airways/
　　TWA, summer 1940

Remarks: A total of nine airliners were delivered on a 1937 order: three to PAA, five to TWA, and one to Howard Hughes for private use. The B-307 was the first four-engined, pressurized airliner built in America and originated as a transport counterpart to the B-17 Flying Fortress. Employing the bomber's wings, engines, and tail, the Stratoliner had a new fuselage, which was 3.6 feet greater in diameter and arranged for commercial purposes and was said to resemble a "dirigible with wings." Prior to Pearl Harbor, TWA's quintet recorded 4,522,500 accident-free miles of U.S. domestic service while PAA's three were employed in South America. All were pressed into World War II service, after which TWA flew its B-307s on Midwest routes until selling them to a French independent carrier in April 1951. Incidentally, those aircraft found their way to Southeast Asia where they provided diplomatic flights until 1974. ■

Boeing 307 of TWA; note the mechanic on the starboard side, who gives an idea of the aircraft's size. Courtesy Trans World Airlines

An excellent starboard profile of the Pan Am Boeing 307 Stratoliner *Clipper Flying Cloud*, which was placed into service during the summer of 1940. Courtesy Pan American World Airways

■ GRUMMAN G-44 Widgeon

First Service: 1940

Type/Purpose: Twin-engined, commercial/executive amphibian

Number of Seats: 1-2 crew, 4-5 passengers

Dimensions: Length: 31.1 feet
　　Height: 11.5 feet
　　Wingspan: 40 feet
　　Gross weight (pounds): 4,525 (G-44)/
　　5,500 (Super Widgeon)

Engines: 2 Ranger L-440C-5 radials (G-44)/
　　2 Continental W-670 radials or
　　2 Lycoming 0-435-A radials (G-44A)/
　　2 Lycoming R-680-E3 radials (Gannet Super Widgeon)/
　　2 Lycoming G0-480-B1D radials (McKinnon Super Widgeon)

Performance: Maximum range: 800 miles
　　Service ceiling: 20,000 feet
　　Maximum speed: 160-220 mph
　　Maximum cruising speed: 130-190 mph

Initial Test Flight: June 28, 1940 (G-44)/
　　August 8, 1944 (G-44A)

Remarks: Originally designed as a small private, executive amphibian, the Widgeon was, in fact, a scaled-down version of the G-21 Goose. A total of 32 civil models were constructed before World War II required additional production exclusively for the military. The G-44A, a refined variant with a modified hull, was introduced by Grumman in August 1944; in addition to those supplied to the government, approximately 50 of these were manufactured for the postwar civil market, bringing total Widgeon production to 286 machines. Following V-J Day, a number of G-44s were acquired by small U.S. airlines, particularly in Alaska. During the 1950s, some 70 G-44s, including a number formerly operated by the French Navy, were brought to the U.S., given new engines, retractable wingtip flats and other features, and were sold as the Gannet or McKinnon Super Widgeon. Few remain in service with American carriers.

Selected List of U.S. Operating Airlines: Gulkana Air Service; Interior Airlines; Peninsula Airways; Yute Air Alaska; Zap Airways ■

This Grumman Wigeon of Interior Airlines was photographed at Fairbanks, Alaska, in September 1968. Courtesy John P. Stewart, via Robert E. Garrard

■ LOCKHEED Model 18 Lodestar

First Service: 1940

Type/Purpose: Twin-engined, commercial, short/medium-haul transport

Number of Seats: 3 crew, 14 passengers

Dimensions: Length: 49.9 feet
   Height: 11.1 feet
   Wingspan: 65.6 feet
   Gross weight (pounds): 18,500

Engines: 2 Pratt & Whitney S1E2-G Hornet radials (18-07)/
   2 Pratt & Whitney SC3-G Twin Wasp radials (18-08)/
   2 Pratt & Whitney S1C3-G Twin Wasp radials (18-10)/
   2 Pratt & Whitney S4C4-G Twin Wasp radials (18-14)/
   2 Wright GR-1820-G102A Cyclone radials (18-40)/
   2 Wright GR-1820-G202A Cyclone radials (18-50)/
   2 Wright GR-1820-G205A Cyclone radials (18-56)

Performance: Maximum range: 1,890 miles
   Service ceiling: 21,500 feet
   Maximum speed: 272 mph
   Maximum cruising speed: 248 mph

Initial Test Flight: September 21, 1939

Western Air Lines' Lockheed Model 18 Lodestar. After Pearl Harbor, the pioneer carrier was left with only one Lodestar and three DC-3s to service its civilian route schedules, the remainder of the fleet being committed to war work. Courtesy Western Airlines

Initial U.S. Operator Service: Mid-Continent Airlines, March 1940

Remarks: An all-metal, mid-wing monoplane with an elliptical-section, monocoque fuselage, twin fins, and rudders, retractable undercarriage, and a three-piece wing fitted with built-in, leading-edge slots and Fowler flaps, the Model 18 was a stretched version of the Model 14 Super Electra, capable of transporting three more passengers. Indeed, the prototype was actually rebuilt from a Northwest Airways Model 14. Two more and similar conversions were made before the first production model flew on February 2, 1940. Lockheed offered seven main production models according to power plants and by the time production ceased in 1943, 625 Lodestars had been manufactured, including 325 U.S. Army Air Force C-60A troop transports. Over 100 civilian Model 18s were impressed into military service following Pearl Harbor, and the Vega Ventura bomber was a direct development of the Lodestar. The majority of military Lodestars were back in civilian service by the end of 1944 and several hundred remained on national aircraft registers around the world into the 1970s, employed primarily in executive or freight operations.

Selected List of U.S. Operating Airlines: Alaska Airlines; Alaska Star Airlines; Caribair; Catalina Air Transport; Continental Airlines; Mid-Continent Airlines; National Airlines; Pacific Alaska Airways; Pan American Airways; Pennsylvania Central Airways; Transocean Air Lines; United Airlines; Western Airlines ■

■ VOUGHT-SIKORSKY VS-44A

First Service: 1942

Type/Purpose: Four-engined, commercial flying boat

Number of Seats: 9 crew, 26-47 passengers

Dimensions: Length: 79.2 feet
    Height: 27.5 feet
    Wingspan: 124 feet
    Gross weight (pounds): 57,500

Engines: 4 Pratt & Whitney R-1830-S1C3G Twin Wasp
    radials

Performance: Maximum range: 3,598 miles
    Service ceiling: 18,996 feet
    Maximum cruising speed: 160 mph

Initial Test Flight: August 13, 1937 (SPBS-1)

Initial U.S. Operator Service: American Export Airlines,
    June 22, 1942

Remarks: The VS-44A originated as an unsuccessful bid by Sikorsky to build a flying boat (the XPSB-1 *Flying Dreadnought*) for the U.S. Navy. Following the combination of the Sikorsky firm with Chance Vought Aircraft in April 1939 (a union that lasted through December 1942), work was begun on turning the technically advanced but unaccepted military prototype into a commercial success. Seen as a major competitor to the Boeing Model 314, the VS-44A emerged as the last and ultimate Sikorsky flying boat. Three of the giant airliners were completed and all were purchased by American Export Airlines, which labeled them "Flying Aces" and extolled their comforts (full-length beds, minimum vibration, full galleys, lounges, dressing rooms, and smoking room) in its advertising. The first VS-44A was christened *Excalibur* by Mrs. Henry A. Wallace on January 17, 1942; soon thereafter, during crew familiarization flights, it crashed off Gander, Newfoundland. The two survivors operated successfully throughout World War II, proving to be the longest-legged aircraft in commercial service at that time and the only ones capable of flying commercially scheduled, nonstop transatlantic routes. Not only did the two launch nonstop flights along such wartime supply avenues as Bermuda-Trinidad-Puerto Rico-Africa, but established several records that held for a few years. Among these were the fastest nonstop Europe to America flight (July 1944) of 16 hours and 57 minutes and a nonstop transatlantic record 3,329 miles (October 1944) in

14 hours and 17 minutes. Surviving the Axis, the *Exeter* was lost in Argentina's Rio de la Plata in a bad night landing while on a charter flight in August 1947. The final VS-44A example, *Excambian*, served as a flying trading post in South America, from whence it was rescued by W.R. Probert. Repaired, it served with Avalon Air Transport from 1957 through 1967 when it passed to Charles Blair's Antilles Air Boats. Blair, who had been chief pilot when the VS-44A began regular AEA service in June 1942, flew *Excambian* until 1971. After its withdrawal from service, the giant rested ashore through 1977 when it was placed in storage at the Pensacola Naval Air Museum until 1981, the year it was moved to the Bradley Air Museum, Windsor Locks, Connecticut.

Selected List of U.S. Operating Airlines: American Export Airlines; Antilles Air Boats; Avalon Air Transport ■

TOP: The first Vought-Sikorsky VS-44A, *Excalibur*, was christened by Mrs. Henry A. Wallace on January 17, 1942, but was lost in a take-off accident that October. Courtesy United Technologies Corporation

BOTTOM: The Vought-Sikorsky VS-44A was the last and ultimate Sikorsky and a worthy competitor to the Boeing 314. Courtesy United Technologies Corporation

■ DOUGLAS DC-4

First Service: 1945

Type/Purpose: Four-engined, commercial, long-haul
transport

Number of Seats: 7 crew, 44-85 passengers

Dimensions: Length: 93.5 feet
Height: 27.6 feet
Wingspan: 117.6 feet
Gross weight (pounds): 73,800-82,500

Engines: 4 Pratt & Whitney Twin Wasp R-2000-2SD-BG
radials

Performance: Maximum range: 2,500-3,300 miles
Service ceiling: 22,300 feet
Maximum speed: 280 mph
Maximum cruising speed: 227 mph

Initial Test Flight: June 7, 1938 (DC-4E)/
February 14, 1942 (DC-4/C-54)

Initial U.S. Operator Service: American Export Airlines,
October 23-24, 1945 (transatlantic)/
American Airlines, March 7, 1946 (domestic)

Remarks: In the first instance of a cooperative reequipment
effort in the history of U.S. commercial aviation, Eastern,
American, Pan American, United, and TWA approached
Douglas in 1936 seeking a 40-passenger, pressurized, four-
engined transport. With $500,000 from those majors, the
manufacturer built the original DC-4 (later labeled DC-4E
(E = Experimental), triple-finned prototype – only to have
the potential customers find it too large for their needs. In a
move almost as dramatic as the five carriers' joint approach, Douglas scaled down its design into the single-
finned unpressurized DC-4A, the first commercial transport to incorporate the now-standard features of integral
fuel tanks in the wings and enclosed wheel wells. Orders
for 61 civilian models were accepted before Pearl Harbor
prevented further airline construction. Those completed
were joined by many hundreds of others in World War II
service as the military's C-54 Skymaster. Following their
conversion to commercial, standard, postwar planes (including the installation of porthole-shaped windows),
many surplus C-54/DC-4s found their way into the hands
of not only front-line carriers, but those of expanding,
charter or "non-sked" operators as well. Douglas also constructed 79 44-passenger civil DC-4s in 1946 and 1947, and

the aircraft was later reconfigured several times in an effort
to increase its capacity. By the early 1980s about 30 remained in the service of U.S. carriers, mostly small freight
or charter airlines.

Selected List of U.S. Operating Airlines: Alaska Airlines;
American Airlines; American Export Airlines; California
Central Airlines; Eastern Airlines; Northwest Orient Air-
lines; North American Airlines; Pacific Northern Airlines;
Pacific Southwest Airlines; Pan American World Airways;
Resort Airlines; Trans-Caribbean Airways; TWA; United
Airlines; (1984-1985): Aero Union Corporation; Biegert
Aviation; Bo-S-Aire Airlines; Florida Air Transport; Globe
Air; Pacific Air Express; Turks Air Limited ■

Servicing a TWA DC-4. The carrier's boss, Howard Hughes, preferred to sponsor the
Lockheed L-049 Constellation, but allowed purchase of several of these Douglas transports.
Courtesy Trans World Airlines

The single Douglas DC-4E shows its impressive size. It flew several experimental services for United Airlines in June 1939. Courtesy McDonnell Douglas

Ground crew check American Overseas Airlines Douglas DC-4 *Flagship Copenhagen*. An AOA Douglas made the first scheduled transatlantic (New York-Gander-England) flight on October 24, 1945. Courtesy American Airlines

Northwest Airlines Douglas DC-4 over Minnesota. Northwest became the nation's fourth transcontinental carrier on December 16, 1944. Courtesy Northwest Orient Airlines

Eastern Airlines introduced the Douglas DC-4 on its New York-Florida route in the spring of 1946. Courtesy Eastern Airlines

■ CURTISS C-46 Commando

First Service: 1946

Type/Purpose: Twin-engined, commercial, medium-haul cargo/passenger transport

Number of Seats: 4 crew, 36 passengers

Dimensions: Length: 76.4 feet
Height: 21.9 feet
Wingspan: 108 feet
Gross weight (pounds): 48,000

Engines: 2 Pratt & Whitney R-2800-51M1 Double Wasp radials

Performance: Maximum range: 1,800 miles
Service ceiling: 22,000 feet
Maximum speed: 269 mph
Maximum cruising speed: 195 mph

Initial Test Flight: March 26, 1940

Initial U.S. Operator Service: Began commercial service almost simultaneously with a number of non-sked operators in 1946-1947

Remarks: In 1937, Curtiss-Wright held discussions with several U.S. carriers concerning its manufacture of a pressurized twin-engined airliner larger than the DC-3. When test flown at St. Louis in 1940, the twin-finned 36-passenger CW-20 was the largest twin-engined aircraft in the world. Although no carrier orders were placed before Pearl Harbor, the U.S. Army Air Force saw the aircraft's potential as a transport and ordered it as the C-46 Commando. The prototype, subsequently fitted with a single fin/rudder and redesignated CW-20A, was turned over to the government, which sold it to the British in November 1941. Meanwhile, 25 C-46s were built (identical in most respects to the CW-20A except for cabin windows), followed by 1,491 C-46As, 1,410 C-46Ds, 17 C-46Es, and 234 C-46Fs for a total of 3,181. These planes could accommodate up to 8 tons of cargo or 40 troops on folding seats. After the war, hundreds of these transports were sold as surplus; its cargo capacity and ability to seat up to 62 passengers made the C-46 particularly attractive to the large number of nonscheduled and freight airlines that began to appear in 1946. Plans for a 36-seat CW-20E were abandoned after Eastern Airlines canceled its order. At the peak of its operation in the early 1960s, the C-46 served over 90 U.S. carriers; by the 1980s, only about 60 remained in American service, mostly with small freight and charter operators.

Selected List of U.S. Operating Airlines: Alaska Airlines; American Air Export & Import Company (AAXICO); Delta Air Lines; Flying Tiger Line, The; Northeast Airlines; Resort Airlines; Rich International Airways; Riddle Airlines; Slick Airways; Wien Air Alaska; (1984 – 1985): Astro Air Transport; Caribbean Air Service (CASAIR) ■

Curtiss C-46F of Northeast Airlines, which operated the transport in both cargo and passenger configurations. Courtesy Delta Airlines

Delta's C-46 flew primarily freight during the 1950s and 1960s. Courtesy Delta Airlines

■ FAIRCHILD F-24W

First Service: 1946

Type/Purpose: Single-engine, commercial/executive, short/medium-haul transport

Number of Seats: 1 pilot, 4 passengers

Dimensions: Length: 23.9 feet
Wingspan: 36.4 feet
Gross weight (pounds): 2,562

Engines: 1 Warner Super Scarab piston

Performance: Maximum range: 640 miles
Service ceiling: 15,000 feet
Maximum speed: 133 mph
Maximum cruising speed: 118 mph

Initial U.S. Operator Service: Robinson Airlines, 1946

Remarks: The Fairchild F-24W, which appeared in 1939, was a follow-up to the three-seat F-24C, one of America's first executive transports. Many hundreds of the F-24W were built for the U.S. Army Air Force, as the UC-61/61A communications aircraft during World War II and surplus military aircraft, together with postwar, Temco-built, civil F-24W-46s, began to equip smaller U.S. feeder-lines as early as 1946. Although none are in American scheduled or charter service today, several remain in civil use overseas.

Selected List of U.S. Operating Airlines: Mohawk Airlines; Robinson Airlines ■

Mohawk Airlines Fairchild F-24W, ca. 1950. Courtesy US Air

■ LOCKHEED L-049 Constellation

First Service: 1946

Type/Purpose: Four-engined, commercial, long-haul transport

Number of Seats: 4-5 crew, 43-60 passengers

Dimensions: Length: 95 feet
Height: 22.5 feet
Wingspan: 123 feet
Gross weight (pounds): 98,000

Engines: 4 Wright R-3350-C18 radials

Performance: Maximum range: 1,800 miles
Service ceiling: 25,000 feet
Maximum speed: 370 mph
Maximum cruising speed: 265 mph

Initial Test Flight: January 9, 1943

Initial U.S. Operator Service: TWA, Pan American, February 1946

Remarks: The Constellation originated with a TWA order for a 40-passenger airliner in 1939; however, before the prototype could be flown, World War II interrupted. When NX25600 became airborne in January 1943, it immediately became the first aircraft in a USAAF contract for 202, fast C-69 transports. The Constellation's aerodynamic design and powerful Wright engines made it much speedier than contemporary transport; indeed, the second production L-049 (piloted by Howard Hughes and Jack Frye) set a transcontinental Burbank-Washington speed record of 6 hours and 57 minutes on April 19, 1944. Only a few C-69s were delivered to the military before V-J Day and the Army canceled 180 of those it had on order. The remainder had their interiors converted to commercial standard and were delivered to carriers beginning in November 1945 (certification came in December). In addition to the 22 C-69 conversions, an additional 66 civil L-049s were built after the war. Both Pan Am and TWA launched commercial service with their pressurized Connies in February 1946.

Selected List of U.S. Operating Airlines: California-Hawaiian Airlines; Pan American Airways; TWA ■

The American Overseas Airlines Lockheed L-049 *Flagship Copenhagen* at La Guardia in 1946. Courtesy American Airlines

Employing its Lockheed L-049 Constellation, TWA opened the first postwar commercial America-Europe landplane service, flying New York-Paris on February 6, 1946. Courtesy Trans World Airlines

An impressive parade of Pan Am L-049s ca. 1946. Courtesy Pan American World Airlines

■ DOUGLAS DC-6/DC-6A/DC-6B

First Service: 1947

Type/Purpose: Four-engined, commercial, long-haul transport

Number of Seats: 3-5 crew, 56-60 passengers (DC-6)/ 3-5 crew, 69-195 passengers (DC-6B)

Dimensions: Length: 101 feet (DC-6)/ 112.3 feet (DC-6B)
Height: 29.3 feet
Wingspan: 118 feet (DC-6)/ 127.6 feet (DC-6B)
Gross weight (pounds): 95,200-107,000

Engines: 4 Pratt & Whitney R-2800-CA15 Double Wasp radials (DC-6)/
4 Pratt & Whitney R-2800-CB17 Double Wasp radials (DC-6A/DC-6B)

Performance: Maximum range: 2,750 miles (DC-6)/ 3,000 miles (DC-6A/DC-6B)
Service ceiling: 28,000 feet (DC-6)/ 22,000 feet (DC-6A/ 25,000 feet (DC-6B)
Maximum speed: 360 mph
Maximum cruising speed: 310-315 mph

Initial Test Flight: February 15, 1946 (DC-6)/ September 29, 1949 (DC-6A)/ February 2, 1951 (DC-6B)

Initial U.S. Operator Service: United Airlines, April 27, 1947 (DC-6)/ Slick Airways, April 20, 1951 (DC-6A)/ United Airlines, April 11, 1951 (DC-6B)

Remarks: Pressurized, the DC-6 was a postwar variant on the DC-4 offering the first stretch (80 inches) of the 4's basic fuselage. Promoted as the "ultimate in travel relaxation," the Douglas featured rectangular windows, lounges fore and aft of the cabin, and a buffet area in the middle of the plane. It offered one major technological advance, becoming the first airliner to employ the "hot wing," or heated, leading-edge anti-icing. A number of DC-6A cargo aircraft were built for Slick Airways and the U.S. military, but the next passenger model was the DC-6B. Stretched another 63 inches in the fuselage and with increased fuel capacity, the plane's gross weight rose and it had one-stop, trans-Atlantic range with a full tourist load. Indeed, the B's operating costs were so low that Tourist Class fares were introduced in 1952 using this aircraft, thereby opening air transportation to many who previously could not afford it. The DC-6Bs ordered by Pan Am employed track-mounted seats, allowing the first flexibility in interior arrangements wihin the same plane without factory modifications. A total of 175 DC-6s and 362 DC-6Bs were built and smaller carriers eagerly snatched up the highly economical plane as it became surplus to major airlines—even before production ended in 1958. A number remain in service in the 1980s.

Selected List of U.S. Operating Airlines: Alaska Airlines; American Airlines; Braniff International Airways; Delta Air Lines; National Airlines; Northwest Orient Airlines; North American Airlines; Rich International Airlines; Saturn Airways; Slick Airways; Trans-Continental Airlines; Trans Caribbean Airways; Trans World Airlines; United Airlines; Western Airlines; Zantop International Airlines; (1984-1985): Aero-Dyne Airlines; Caribbean Air Service (CASAIR); Challenge Air Transport; Florida Air Transport; Northern Air Cargo; Rich International Airways; Trans-Air Link; Trans-Continental Airlines; Turks Air Limited; Zantop International Airlines ■

An American Airlines DC-6 over New York City. American placed these Douglas transports in service on its New York-Chicago route in the spring of 1947. Courtesy American Airlines

United Airlines Douglas DC-6 *Mainliner Omaha.* United placed its DC-6 fleet into transcontinental service in April 1947. Courtesy United Airlines

■ GRUMMAN G-73 Mallard

First Service: 1947

Type/Purpose: Twin-engined, commercial, short/medium-haul amphibian

Number of Seats: 2 crew, 10-12 passengers

Dimensions: Length: 48.4 feet
Height: 18.9 feet
Wingspan: 66.8 feet
Gross weight (pounds): 12,750

Engines: 2 Pratt & Whitney R-1340-S3H1 Wasp radials

Performance: Maximum range: 730-1,380 miles
Service ceiling: 23,000 feet
Maximum speed: 215 mph
Maximum cruising speed: 180 mph

Initial Test Flight: April 30, 1946

Initial U.S. Operator Service: Air Commuting, Inc.,
June 9, 1947

Remarks: Based on experience with the G-21 Goose and designed for the airline market, the Grumman G-73 Mallard is a high-wing, cantilevered monoplane. All-metal, with a stressed-skin, two-step hull, it features an upswept tail unit, balancer floats, retractable, tricycle landing gear, and indented forward hull. Production was halted in 1951; the total built was 59, far fewer than the 250 expected of the market, which did not develop. Although the majority constructed saw extensive corporate and bush service, only a few came to be employed with scheduled carriers in the United States.

Selected List of U.S. Operating Airlines: Air Commuting, Inc.; Antilles Air Boats; Chalks International Airlines; Northern Consolidated Airways; Seagull Air Service; Swift Air Service; Trans-Catalina; Virgin Islands Seaplane Shuttle; Walker's Cay Airline ■

Previously owned by several U.S., U.K. and Canadian private and public concerns, Chalk's International acquired N73556 in March 1972. Painted in the carrier's distinctive blue and white livery, the G-73 Mallard *City of Miami* is shown here against the skyline of its namesake. Courtesy Grumman Aerospace Corporation

A closeup of the Grumman G-73 Mallard N2970 on the ramp at Miami shows the unique hull, cockpit, and tricycle landing gear of one of Chalk's International's amphibians. Courtesy Grumman Aerospace Corporation

◼ LOCKHEED Constellation Series L-649 to L-749A

First Service: 1947

Type/Purpose: Four-engined, commercial, long-haul transport

Number of Seats: 4-5 crew, 48-81 passengers

Dimensions: Length: 95 feet
Height: 22.5 feet
Wingspan: 123 feet
Gross weight (pounds): 107,000

Engines: 4 Wright R-3350-C18-BD1 radials (L-649)/
4 Wright GR-3350-749C-188D1 radials (L-749/L-749A)

Performance: Maximum range: 1,800 miles (L-649)/
2,500 miles (L-749)/ 2,800 miles (L-749A)
Service ceiling: 25,000 feet
Maximum speed: 370 mph
Maximum cruising speed: 265 mph (L-649)/
320 mph (L-749)/ 285 mph (L-749A)

Initial Test Flight: October 19, 1946 (L-649)

Initial U.S. Operator Service: Eastern Airlines (L-649)/
Pan American Airways, June 17, 1947 (L-749)

Remarks: The first true peacetime version of the Lockheed Constellation was the L-649; only 20 were manufactured and the more powerful airliner entered service with Eastern in May 1947. A few of these would later find their way into the hands of other operators such as Chicago and Southern. The L-749 variant became the most numerous of Constellations. Basically similar to the L-049, it featured increased fuel tankage in the wings, thus allowing nonstop (though not fully laden) transatlantic flights. In June 1947, the Pan Am *Clipper America* launched the first regularly scheduled around-the-world service. The L-749A model incorporated stronger landing gear, allowing higher operating weights. When Constellation production ceased in favor of the Super Constellation in 1951, a total of 113 L-749s/L-749As had been built.

Selected List of U.S. Operating Airlines: American Airlines; Chicago and Southern Air Lines; Delta Air Lines; Eastern Airlines; Northwest Orient Airlines; Pan American World Airways; TWA; Western Airlines ◼

Chicago and Southern Airlines' Lockheed L-649 *Ciudad Trujillo* was one of only 20 649s manufactured, most of which served with Eastern Airlines. Courtesy Delta Airlines

L749 A Constellation (Over Rickenbacker Causeway). Courtesy Eastern Airlines

Delta operated several "Connies" throughout the southeastern U.S. Courtesy Delta Airlines

■ MARTIN 2-O-2

First Service: 1947

Type/Purpose: Twin-engined, commercial, short/medium-haul transport

Number of Seats: 3 crew, 36 passengers

Dimensions: Length: 71 feet
Height: 28.5 feet
Wingspan: 93.3 feet
Gross weight (pounds): 42,700

Engines: 2 Pratt & Whitney R-2800-CA-18 Double Wasp radials

Performance: Maximum range: 635 miles
Service ceiling: 33,000 feet
Maximum speed: 312 mph
Maximum cruising speed: 280 mph

Initial Test Flight: November 22, 1946

Initial U.S. Operator Service: Northwest Airlines, November 15, 1947

Remarks: A low-wing, unpressurized monoplane designed for trunkline service as a DC-3 replacement, the Martin 2-0-2, the first U.S.-designed, twin-engined airliner to gain postwar certification, soon encountered trouble. When one was lost in 1948, an investigation revealed wing-structure weakness. Although essential modifications were made to the 31 existing aircraft, no more of this Convair 240 rival were built, the manufacturer and airlines preferring to concentrate on a replacement. Northwest Airlines was the only major American operator of this type, when it was new, but secondhand 2-0-2s served with several other carriers.

Selected List of U.S. Operating Airlines: Allegheny Airlines; California Central Airlines; Northwest Airlines; Pioneer Airlines; Southwest Airways; Transocean Airlines ■

Following the setback of a wing structural defect, all Martin 2-0-2s were grounded and modified into 2-0-2As. The pictured aircraft entered TWA service on September 1, 1950. Courtesy Trans World Airlines

Northwest Airlines launched the Martin 2-0-2 in November 1947 and, in the process, became the first U.S. carrier to fly a postwar twin-engined airliner. N93051 is shown here flying over the Jefferson Memorial, Washington, D.C. Courtesy Northwest Orient Airlines

■ BOEING 377 Stratocruiser

First Service: 1948

Type/Purpose: Four-engined, commercial transport

Number of Seats: 5 crew, 89-112 passengers

Dimensions: Length: 110.4 feet
Height: 38.3 feet
Wingspan: 141.3 feet
Gross weight (pounds): 83,500

Engines: 4 Pratt & Whitney R-4360-TSB3-G Wasp radials

Performance: Maximum range: 2,750-4,300 miles
Service ceiling: 33,000 feet
Maximum speed: 375 mph
Maximum cruising speed: 340 mph

Initial Test Flight: July 8, 1947

Initial U.S. Operator Service: Pan American World Airways,
September 7, 1948

Remarks: Originally a transport development of the Boeing B-29 Superfortress, the Stratocruiser employed a "double-bubble" two-deck fuselage plus the bomber's wings, engines, landing gear, and tail assembly. The largest and fastest airliner flying in 1948, the 70-ton giant transported its passengers in 6,600 cubic feet of "ambling room," which featured a forward family travel compartment and a lounge (with bar) on the lower level below the midship galley reached via a spiral staircase from the passenger cabin. More than any other commercial transport, this aircraft set the standard for long-range operations in the late 1940s. A total of 56 were constructed, from 1947 to 1949.

Selected List of U.S. Operating Airlines: American Overseas Airlines; Northwest Orient Airlines; Pan American World Airways; Transocean Airlines; United Airlines ■

At one time, Pan American was the largest B-377 operator with a fleet of 27, including the *Clipper Southern Cross* shown here. Courtesy Pan American World Airways

The Boeing 377 was popular with airline operators because of its great range. The man (lower right) walking away from this AOA Stratocruiser gives some idea of the plane's immense size. This example, *Flagship Great Britain*, would be renamed several times. Courtesy American Airlines

■ CONVAIR CV-240 Convairliner

First Service: 1948

Type/Purpose: Twin-engined, commercial, medium-haul transport

Number of Seats: 3 crew, 40 passengers

Dimensions: Length: 74.8 feet
Height: 26.11 feet
Wingspan: 91.9 feet
Gross weight (pounds): 41,790

Engines: 2 Pratt & Whitney R-2800-CA18 Double Wasp radials

Performance: Maximum range: 1,930 miles
Service ceiling: 24,900 feet
Maximum speed: 374 mph
Maximum cruising speed: 284 mph

Initial Test Flight: July 8, 1946 (Model 110)/ March 16, 1947 (Model 240)

Initial U.S. Operator Service: American Airlines, June 1, 1948

Remarks: Reacting to an American Airlines requirement, Consolidated Vultee Aircraft Corporation in 1945 developed its 30-passenger Model 110. Before the aircraft could be test flown, however, American let it be known that it was seeking a larger aircraft. Thus Consolidated brought out the Model 240, which employed the same power plant and overall configuration of the Model 110, but a slimmer-section fuselage, lengthened 3.8 feet, allowed the seating of 40 passengers. A total of 176 civil airliners followed, and after Consolidated Vultee became the Convair Division of General Dynamics Corporation in 1954, the CV-240 was better known in some circles as the Convairliner. This cantilevered, low-wing attempt at a DC-3 replacement saw wide initial service, with a few remaining in active service; many, however, have been reconfigured several times.

Selected List of U.S. Operating Airlines: American Airlines; Continental Airlines; Mohawk Airlines; Northeast Airlines; Pan American World Airways; Trans-Texas Airlines; Western Airlines; (1984-1985): Astro Air Transport; Combs Airways; Corporate Air; General Aviation; Providence Air; Trans-Florida Airlines ■

Continental Airlines CV-240. Courtesy Continental Airlines

Ozark was a major local service operator of the Convairliner, one of which is shown here at St. Louis, ca. 1958. Courtesy Ozark Airlines

Alaska Airlines Convair CV-240. Note the rear airstairs. Courtesy Alaska Airlines

■ DEHAVILLAND-CANADA DHC-2 Beaver

First Service: 1948

Type/Purpose: Single-engined, light, STOL transport

Number of Seats: 1 crew, 7-10 passengers

Dimensions: Length: 35.3 feet
Height: 9 feet
Wingspan: 48 feet
Gross weight (pounds): 5,370

Engines: 1 Pratt & Whitney Wasp Junior R-985-SB3-9 radial

Performance: Maximum range: 483-778 miles
Service ceiling: ?
Maximum speed: 163 mph
Maximum cruising speed: 135 mph

Initial Test Flight: August 16, 1947

Remarks: Originally designed to operate in the Canadian bush country, the 1,657 Beavers built represented the first in the DHC family of STOL (short-takeoff-and-landing) aircraft. Often fitted with twin floats or skis in place of landing wheels, the all-metal, high-wing monoplane gained rapid acceptance by small commuter and air-taxi operators and is currently in the inventory of many such U.S. carriers, especially in Alaska.

Selected List of U.S. Operating Airlines: (1984-1985): Alaska Air Guides; Alaska Bush Carrier; Alaska Island Airways; Alaska North Flying Service; Alaska Travel Air; Bellair; Bush Pilots Air Service; Chalk's International Airlines; Channel Flying; Chisum Flying Service of Alaska; Kenmore Air Harbor; Ketchikan Air Service; Ketchum Air Service; Lake Union Air Service; Seair Alaska Airlines; Tyee Airlines; Ward Air; Westflight Aviation; Wings of Alaska ■

De Havilland Canada's floatplane version of the DHC-2 Beaver over Toronto. Note the paddle on the starboard float—a handy item in bush operations. Courtesy De Havilland Canada

This wheeled DHC-2 Beaver of Wien Air Alaska was photographed at Fairbanks in September 1968. Note the Eskimo employee checking the plane's oil. Courtesy John P. Stewart, via Robert E. Garrard

The first DHC-2/T Turbo Beaver, in landplane configuration, flew initially on December 31, 1963. Courtesy De Havilland Canada

The first De Havilland DHC-2 Beaver flew on August 16, 1947. Courtesy De Havilland Canada

■ DEHAVILLAND DH-104 Dove

First Service: 1950

Type/Purpose: Twin-engined, commercial, short/medium-haul transport

Number of Seats: 1-2 pilots, 8 passengers

Dimensions: Length: 39.4 feet
Height: 13.4 feet
Wingspan: 57 feet
Gross weight (pounds): 8,950

Engines: 2 DeHavilland Gipsy Queen 70 Mk. 3 radials

Performance: Maximum range: 880 miles
Service ceiling: 18,500 feet
Maximum speed: 230 mph
Maximum cruising speed: 210 mph

Initial Test Flight: September 25, 1945

Initial U.S. Operator Service: Trans-National Airlines, 1950

Remarks: Designed to meet the wartime Brabazon Committee's specifications for a DH-89 Dragon Rapide replacement, the DH-104 Dove would become, until the advent of the Britten-Norman BN-2 Islander, the UK's most successful civil transport. A low-wing monoplane with cantilevered wings, retractable, tricycle landing gear, all-metal, stressed-skin fuselage, and a tall cockpit canopy, the Dove was the first British airliner to break into the American market, a feat accomplished as an executive transport. Available in several progressively advanced models, the DH-104 had become something of a common sight with U.S. regional carriers by the middle 1950s, usually appearing as a more powerful Mark 7A or Mark 8A. Production of the dove continued for 25 years with the last of 542 delivered in September 1967. In the early 1960s, the Riley Aeronautics Corporation of Ft. Lauderdale, Florida, began development of a modified Dove, the Riley 400; these were equipped with a swept tail fin, minor airframe changes, and two Lycoming 10-720 engines. A similar conversion, also in small numbers, was marketed into the late 1970s as the CJ600 of the Texas Airplane Manufacturing Company.

Selected List of U.S. Operating Airlines: Air East Airlines; Apache Airlines; Fischer Brothers Aviation; Midway Airlines; TAG Airlines; Trans National Airlines; (1984-1985): Hawaiian Air Tour Service ■

This PAC DH-104 Dove was captured while in flight over the southeastern U.S. sometime in the mid-1950s. SI #86-1652

■ LOCKHEED L-1049 Super Constellation

First Service: 1951

Type/Purpose: Four-engined, commercial, long-haul transport

Number of Seats: 4-5 flight crew, 71 passengers (L-1049A/-C/-E)/
4-5 flight crew, 66 passengers (L-1049G)

Dimensions: Length: 113.7 feet (L-1049A/-C/-E)/
116.2 feet (L-1049G)
Height: 24.9 feet
Wingspan: 123 feet
Gross weight (pounds): 120,000 (L-1049A/-C/-E)/
137,500 (L-1049G)

Engines: 4 Wright R-3350-956C-18CB-1 radials (L-1049A)/
4 Wright R-3350-DA1 radials (L-1049C/-E)/
4 Wright R-3350-DA3 radials (L-1049G)

Performance: Maximum range: 3,250 miles (L-1049A/-C/-E)/
4,600-5,400 miles (L-1049G)
Service ceiling: 25,000 feet
Maximum speed: 380 mph
Maximum cruising speed: 318 mph (L-1049A/-C/-E)/
328 mph (L-1049G)

Initial Test Flight: October 13, 1950 (L-1049A)/
February 17, 1953 (L-1049C)/
December 17, 1954 (L-1049G)

Initial U.S. Operator Service: Eastern Airlines, December 15, 1951 (L-1049A)/
TWA, October 19, 1953 (L-1049C)/
Northwest Orient Airlines, January 1955 (L-1049G)

Remarks: High seat-miles costs and the need to increase capacity caused Lockheed in 1949 to take an earlier model Constellation in hand for conversion into an improved aircraft, the L-1049. In one of the first and greatest examples of airframe stretching, the L-1049, which first flew in October 1950, was made more powerful, had an 18.4-foot-fuselage lengthening, and changed the previous circular openings to rectangular windows. The power available to the new variant did not, however, offset the increase in size and weight and thus only 24 were built and sold. After the L-1049B, a military model, the next civilian version was the L-1049C, of which 56 were manufactured. This aircraft introduced earlier piston engines with Wright Turbo-Com-pound models, which increased speed and allowed higher takeoff weights. To handle the extra weights, the wings were strengthened, thereby affording greater wing fuel-tankage. Ten airlines would operate the L-1049C. The L-1049D was a freighter, and only 18 detail-enhanced L-1049Es were constructed. The L-1049G, or "Super G," was essentially an L-1049C airframe married to larger engines; this model of the Super Constellation was intended for long-range operations and could be equipped with wing-tip fuel tanks. A total of 99 Super Gs were built and were followed by the final Super Constellation variant, the L-1049H. A passenger/cargo convertible model of the Super G, 53 of these versions were built, the last being delivered to The Flying Tiger Line in November 1958.

Selected List of U.S. Operating Airlines: Eastern Airlines; National Airlines; Northwest Orient Airlines; South Pacific Airlines; Trans-World Airlines ■

TOP: TWA Lockheed L-10496G "Super Connie." Notice the wing tip fuel tanks. Courtesy Trans World Airlines

BOTTOM: An Eastern Airlines Lockheed L-1049G photographed at Washington National Airport in June 1966. The person atop the airstairs gives an idea of the airliner's size. Courtesy John P. Stewart, via Robert E. Garrard

■ MARTIN 4-0-4

First Service: 1951

Type/Purpose: Twin-engined, commercial, short/medium-
haul transport

Number of Seats: 3 crew, 40 passengers

Dimensions: Length: 74.7 feet
Height: 28.5 feet
Wingspan: 93.3 feet
Gross weight (pounds): 44,900

Engines: 2 Pratt & Whitney R-2800-CB16 Double Wasp
radials

Performance: Maximum range: 2,600 miles
Service ceiling: 29,000 feet
Maximum speed: 312 mph
Maximum cruising speed: 280 mph

Initial Test Flight: October 21, 1950

Initial U.S. Operator Service: TWA, October 5, 1951

Remarks: Electing to abandon a 3-0-3 prototype, Martin
redesigned the wing of the 2-0-2, adding a pressurized
fuselage, stretched 3.3 feet, and other detail refinements,
including such innovations as air conditioning, a carry-on
luggage rack, and self-contained, aft loading stairs. When
production ended in 1953, 103 of these Convair CV-340
rivals had been delivered. The 4-0-4s changed hands several times as owners abandoned them in favor of newer
equipment; yet, as many as 14 remained in service into the
early 1980s.

Selected List of U.S. Operating Airlines: Eastern Airlines;
Mohawk Airlines; Pacific Air Lines; Piedmont Airlines;
Shawnee Airlines; Southern Airways; (1984-1985): Pro Air
Services; Provincetown-Boston Airlines ■

Ozark acquired a
number of Martin
4-0-4s by trading
several Convairliners
to Mohawk Airlines
in October 1964. Note the
rear airstairs. Courtesy
Ozark Airlines

MIDDLE: The crew of a TWA Martin 4-0-4 proudly departs after another
successful flight. TWA began service with the pressurized Martin in
October 1951 and at one time owned some 50 of the type. Courtesy Trans
World Airlines

BOTTOM: Eastern Airlines was a major and long time operator of the
Martin 4-0-4, starting with this example, N44OA. Although EAL employed
this type to launch its *Silver Falcon* service in January 1952, the falcon on
the tail was red. Courtesy Eastern Airlines

■ CONVAIR CV-340

First Service: 1952

Type/Purpose: Twin-engined, commercial, medium-haul transport

Number of Seats: 3 crew, 44 passengers

Dimensions: Length: 79.2 feet
Height: 28.2 feet
Wingspan: 105.4 feet
Gross weight (pounds): 47,000

Engines: 2 Pratt & Whitney R-2800-CB17 Double Wasp radials

Performance: Maximum range: 1,875 miles
Service ceiling: 24,900 feet
Maximum speed: 314 mph
Maximum cruising speed: 284 mph

Initial Test Flight: October 5, 1951

Initial U.S. Operator Service: United Airlines, November 16, 1952

Remarks: United Airlines, which had not flown the CV-240, was the first to order and employ the CV-340, a simple stretch of the Convairliner. To increase the size and power of its DC-3 replacement, Convair lengthened the fuselage 4.6 feet, increased wingspan to 105.9 feet, added more powerful engines, a different undercarriage, new flap arrangements, larger tires, and a new cabin interior. A total of 212 CV-340s were built.

Selected List of U.S. Operating Airlines: Braniff International Airways; Delta Air Lines; Hawaiian Airlines; Lake Central Airlines; National Airlines; North Central Airlines; Ozark Airlines; United Air Lines ■

Hawaiian Airlines Convair CV-340 ca. 1952. Formerly known as Inter-Island Airways, the carrier possessed a fleet of five 340s. Courtesy Hawaiian Airlines

Continental Airlines acquired a fleet of Convair CV-340s in the early 1950s, each equipped with a forward airstairs. Courtesy Continental Airlines

A Convair CV-340 of Delta Airlines, photographed at Atlanta in 1956. Courtesy Delta Air Lines

DEHAVILLAND-CANADA DHC-3 Otter

First Service: 1952

Type/Purpose: Single-engined, commercial, utility transport

Number of Seats: 1 pilot, 11 passengers

Dimensions: Length: 41.1 feet
Height: 12.6 feet
Wingspan: 58 feet
Gross weight (pounds): 8,000

Engines: 1 Pratt & Whitney R-1340-S1H1-G piston or
1 Pratt & Whitney R-1340-S3H1-G Twin Wasp radial
(DHC-3 standard)/
1 Pratt & Whitney of Canada PT6A-27 turboprop
(DHC-3 turbo)

Performance: Maximum range: 875 miles
Service ceiling: 18,000 feet
Maximum cruising speed: 132 mph

Initial Test Flight: December 12, 1951

Remarks: Based on the successful DHC-2 Beaver, the DHC-3 Otter is an all-metal, scaled-up version of the earlier aircraft designed for STOL (short-takeoff-and-landing) situations or floatplane operations. Of braced-high-wing configuration, the Otter remained in production until 1968; a total of 460 were built, including 66 for the RCAF and 227 for the U.S. military. In 1978, Cox Air Resources of Alberta developed a prototype conversion employing a turboprop engine, which increased speed to 150 mph and range to 1,045 miles.

Selected List of U.S. Operating Airlines: (1984-1985): Bush Pilots Air Service; 40-Mile Air; Herman's Air; Tyee Airlines; Westflight Aviation ■

TOP: This DHC-3 Otter shows the down position of the retractable wheels in its standard Edo floats. Courtesy De Havilland Canada

BOTTOM: This DHC-3 Otter, equipped with floats, clearly shows the design influence of its DHC-2 Beaver predecessor. Courtesy De Havilland Canada

■ DOUGLAS DC-7/DC-7B/ DC-7C Seven Seas

First Service: 1953

Type/Purpose: Four-engined, commercial, long-haul transport

Number of Seats: 3-5 crew, 99 passengers (7/7B)/ 3-5 crew, 110 passengers (7C)

Dimensions: Length: 100.7 feet (7)/ 108.11 feet (7B)/ 112.3 feet (7C)
Height: 28.7 feet (7/7B)/ 31.8 (7C)
Gross weight (pounds): 122,000 (7)/ 126,000 (7B)/ 143,000 (7C)

Engines: 4 Wright R-3350-988TC18EA-1 or -EA-4 Turbo-compound radials

Performance: Maximum range: 2,800 miles (7)/ 2,760 miles (7B)/ 4,250 miles (7C)
Service ceiling: 25,000 feet
Maximum cruising speed: 360 mph (7/7B)/ 355 mph (7C)

Initial Test Flight: May 18, 1953

Initial U.S. Operator Service: American Airlines, November 29, 1953 (7)/
Pan American World Airways, June 13, 1955 (7B)/
Pan American World Airways, June 1, 1956 (7C)

Remarks: The ultimate in Douglas propeller DCs, these were the final piston-engined improvements to the basic DC-4 and were designed for transcontinental and, later, intercontinental service. A total of 106 DC-7s, 109 -7Bs, and 121 -7Cs were constructed. When it appeared in late 1953, the DC-7 was the first U.S. commercial airliner able to operate nonstop, east-west transcontinental schedules against the prevailing winds and within eight hours, thereby negating the need for relief crews and intermediate stops. The DC-7C Seven Seas was designed to fly the North Atlantic nonstop, eliminating the usual Newfoundland refueling halt. To help it achieve this goal, it became the first passenger airplane since the Sikorsky S-42B to have fully stretched wings. The airliner's wing center section was extended five feet per side, with outer wings the same as those on the DC-7. This lengthening not only increased span, wing area, and aspect ratio, but provided more space for fuel tankage. A taller tail was added, the fuselage was stretched three feet, and greater seating

capacity was provided; the resultant aircraft became an excellent long-range competitor for the Lockheed Super Constellation. In operation, some reliability problems were encountered with the turbo-compound engines; however, the coming of the jetliner rendered the speedy cost effective DC-7s obsolete for front-line passenger carriage within months, although some operators converted their aircraft into DC-7F freighters. A few were flown by charter companies or corporations (e.g., the Chicago White Sox professional baseball team). Production ended in 1958.

Selected List of U.S. Operating Airlines: Braniff International Airways; Continental Airlines; Delta Air Lines; Eastern Airlines; National Airlines; Northwest Orient Airlines; Pan American World Airways; Riddle Airlines; Trans-World Airlines; United Airlines ■

United Airlines' DC-7 *Mainliner Fresno.* United ordered 25 of these Douglas transports on June 25, 1952, and placed the first in service on June 1, 1954. Courtesy United Airlines

Delta's DC-7. The Atlanta-based carrier placed its Douglas transports into Miami-Chicago operations on April 1, 1954. Courtesy Delta Airlines

Lift-off of the Pan Am DC-7C *Clipper Blue Jacket*, one of the long-range Douglas transports which helped to make possible regularly scheduled nonstop airline service over the North Atlantic. Courtesy Pan American World Airways

Northwest Orient Airlines placed the DC-7C on its transpacific routes on April 28, 1957. Courtesy Northwest Orient Airlines

■ CESSNA 180/185 Skywagon

First Service: 1954

Type/Purpose: Single-engine, utility transport or air taxi

Number of Seats: 1 pilot, 5-6 passengers

Dimensions: Length: 25.9 feet (180)/ 27 feet (185)
Height: 7.9 feet (180)/ 12.2 feet (185)
Wingspan: 35.10 feet
Gross weight (pounds): 2,800 (180)/ 3,320 (185)

Engines: 1 Continental 0-470-R piston (180)/
1 Continental I0-520-D piston (185)

Performance: Maximum range: 695-1,215 miles
Service ceiling: 19,600 feet (180)/ 16,400 feet (185)
Maximum speed: 148 kt (180)/ 141 kt (185)
Maximum cruising speed: 141 kt (180)/ 134 kt (185)

Initial Test Flight: 1953 (180)/ 1961 (185)

Remarks: Nearly 6,000 Cessna 180s and 3,500 185s have been delivered since the two aircraft entered production over two and three decades ago. Though more powerful, the 185 is essentially the same plane as the 180; however, it does have an improved wing, additional external bracing, and, most noticeable, a large dorsal fin. Each can carry its passengers in paired seats or, alternatively, the seats can be removed to permit an all-cargo configuration; the 185 can also handle an optional (detachable), under-fuselage cargo pack. Both aircraft have proven extremely popular with small operators and air taxis, due largely to their short-field capability and large capacity.

Selected List of U.S. Operating Airlines: (1984-1985): Alaska Air Charter; Alaska Island Airways; Alaska North Flying Service; Alaska Travel Air; Arctic Circle Air; Audi Air; Cape Smythe Air; Frontier Flying Service; Ketchum Air Service; Larry's Flying Service; Regal Air; Seair Alaska Airlines; Tyee Airlines; Ward Air; Westflight Aviation; Yute Air Alaska ■

This Cessna 180 Skywagon of Ft. Yukon Air Service was photographed at Fairbanks, Alaska, in September 1968. Courtesy John P. Stewart, via Robert E. Garrard

A Cessna 180 Skywagon of Long Island Airways, photographed at Long Beach, Calif., in September 1968. Courtesy John P. Stewart, via Robert E. Garrard

■ FOKKER F-27 FRIENDSHIP

First Service: 1955

Type/Purpose: Twin-engined, commercial, commuter/regional transport

Number of Seats: 2-4 crew, 46-52 passengers

Dimensions: Length: 77.3 feet
Height: 27.1 feet
Wingspan: 95.1 feet
Gross weight (pounds): 44,996

Engines: 2 Rolls-Royce Dart Mk 536-7R turboprops

Performance: Maximum range: 1,197 miles
Service ceiling: 29,500 feet
Maximum cruising speed: 298 mph

Initial Test Flight: November 24, 1955

Initial U.S. Operator Service: West Coast Airlines,
September 28, 1955

Remarks: Designed as a DC-3 replacement, the Friendship has come the closest of any transport to meeting that goal and in the process has become the world's most widely sold turboprop airliner. A cantilevered, high-wing monoplane, the F-27-100 basic model was subsequently made more powerful for the F-27-200. The aircraft was later modified for combination passenger and cargo service under the designations F-27-300 (F-27B) and -400. Meanwhile in 1956, Fokker concluded an agreement with the Fairchild Engine and Airplane Company (Fairchild-Hiller in 1964) to build the Friendship in North America, and it went on to build 205 Friendships in America (including 78 stretched FH-227s). The F-27-500 variant, which served as the model for Fairchild's FH-227, did not sell well under its original designation and Fokker thus proceeded to an improved version of the 200, the F-27-600, which features several of the improvements introduced in the 300/400. Sales of the Dutch-built F-27 have topped 500 units with the most recent American purchases of the $6.5 million pressurized aircraft going into service with Air Wisconsin in 1985.

Selected List of U.S. Operating Airlines: (1984-1985): Air Pac; Alaska Airlines; Britt Airways; Brockway Air; Connect Air; Horizon Air; Mesaba Airlines; Midstate Airlines; Mississippi Valley Airlines; Pacific Alaska Airlines; Pilgrim Airlines; Ransome Airlines; Suburban Airlines ■

One of six Midstate Airlines Fokker F-27s shown at the manufacturer's Dutch factory. Founded in 1964, Midstate provides scheduled service to points in eight midwestern states. Courtesy Midstate Airlines

One of two Fokker F-27 Friendships currently operated by Northwest Orient Air Link partner Mesaba Airlines, which is based at Minneapolis, Minn. Courtesy Fokker Aircraft U.S.A.

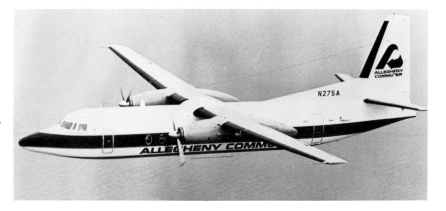

Suburban Airlines, founded in 1957 and a member of the Allegheny Commuter network since 1973, introduced the Fokker F-27 to its fleet in June 1984, on operations between Lancaster/Reading and Pittsburgh. Courtesy US Air

VICKERS VISCOUNT
Series 700 to 800

First Service: 1955

Type/Purpose: Four-engined, commercial, medium/short-haul transport

Number of Seats: 3-4 crew, 52-75 passengers

Dimensions: Length: 85.8 feet
Height: 26.9 feet
Wingspan: 93.8 feet
Gross weight (pounds): 72,500

Engines: 4 Rolls-Royce RDa.7/1 Mk 525 turboprops

Performance: Maximum range: 1,750 miles
Service ceiling: 25,000 feet
Maximum speed: ?
Maximum cruising speed: 350 mph

Initial Test Flight: August 20, 1952

Initial U.S. Operator Service: Capital Airlines, July 26, 1955 (700D)

Remarks: During World War II, a British body (The Brabazon Committee) made a series of recommendations aimed at getting the U.K. aircraft industry back into the civil-transport business following victory. Among the designs stemming from that committee's proceedings was this Vickers airliner, originally named Viceroy but renamed Viscount following India's independence. Originally flown as a 32-passenger plane (Model 630), the Viscount did not attract many purchasers until it was made more powerful and stretched into the 43-passenger Model 700. Following the Viscount's introduction on April 18, 1953, large numbers of orders were received, including a number from North America. The Viscount, which already had the mark of being the first turbine-powered airliner ever to carry fare-paying customers, would have the honor of being the first British transport ordered in large numbers by U.S. carriers. A low-wing, pressurized monoplane with wing-mounted engines, the Mark 700, which had been purchased in America by Capital Airlines, Northeast Airlines, United Airlines, and Aloha Airlines, was given a 3.10-foot fuselage stretch, relabeled the Model 800, and sold to several carriers, including Continental Airlines. When production ceased in 1964, Viscount production had reached 444 transports, of which some 30 are still active.

Selected List of U.S. Operating Airlines: Atlantic Gulf Airlines; Capital Airlines; Continental Airlines; Northeast Airlines; United Airlines; (1984-1985): Go Air; Royal American Airways; Trans-Florida Airlines ■

With the acquisition of Capital and its transports (one of which is shown here in new livery) on June 1, 1961, United Airlines became the largest air carrier in the Western World, a position it still maintains. Courtesy United Airlines

Northeast Airlines operated a fleet of nine Vickers Viscounts between 1958 and 1963, in the latter year, due to financial losses, returning the lot to Vickers, despite an average load factor of 60 percent per plane. Courtesy Delta Airlines

■ CONVAIR CV-440

First Service: 1956

Type/Purpose: Twin-engined, commercial, medium-haul transport

Number of Seats: 3 crew, 52 passengers

Dimensions: Length: 81.6 feet
Height: 28.2 feet
Wingspan: 105.4 feet
Gross weight (pounds): 49,100

Engines: 2 Pratt & Whitney R-2800-CB16 or CB17 Double Wasp radials

Performance: Maximum range: 1,930 miles
Service ceiling: 24,900 feet
Maximum speed: 300 mph
Maximum cruising speed: 289 mph

Initial Test Flight: October 6, 1955

Initial U.S. Operator Service: Continental Airlines, April 1, 1956

Remarks: Essentially a slightly enlarged version of the CV-340 with weather radar, a 2.4-foot fuselage stretch, a new exhaust system, and a cabin rearrangement that offered either 44 or 52 passenger seating, a few non-reconfigured aircraft remain in service into the 1980s.

Selected List of U.S. Operating Airlines: Allegheny Airlines; American Inter-Island Airlines; Braniff International Airways; Cochise Airlines; Continental Airlines; Delta Air Lines; Eastern Airlines; Great Lakes Airlines; Hawaiian Airlines; Mohawk Airlines; National Airlines; North Central Airlines; Ozark Airlines; Southern Express; (1984-1985): Aero-Dyne Airlines; Air Resorts Airlines; Airways International; Combs Airways; Florida Air Transport; General Aviation; Liberty Airlines ■

Continental Airlines was the launch customer for the Convair CV-440 Metropolitan, placing its first into operation on April 1, 1956. Courtesy Continental Airlines

Employed as a freighter by Combs Airways, this Convair CV-440 was photographed on April 4, 1979. Courtesy James P. Woolsey

■ DEHAVILLAND DH-114 Series 2 Heron/ Turbo-Skyliner

First Service: 1957

Type/Purpose: Four-engined, light, commuter/regional transport

Number of Seats: 1-2 crew, 20 passengers

Dimensions: Length: 48.6 feet
   Height: 15.7 feet
   Wingspan: 71.6 feet
   Gross weight (pounds): 13,000

Engines: 4 DeHavilland Gipsy Queen 30 Mk.2 pistons (DH-114)/
   4 Avco Lycoming IGO-540-B1A5 turboprops (Turbo-Skyliner)

Performance: Maximum range: 805 miles
   Service ceiling: 18,500 feet
   Maximum speed: 195 mph
   Maximum cruising speed: 160 mph

Initial Test Flight: May 10, 1950 (Mk.1)/
   December 14, 1952 (Mk.2)

Initial U.S. Operator Service: Illinois Air Lines, June 1957

Remarks: The success of the twin-engined DeHavilland DH-104 Dove led to a larger successor, the DH-114 Heron. The Mark 1 possessed four engines, a fuselage 8.6 feet longer than the Dove's, and a fixed-nosewheel landing gear. Few if any Mk.1s saw U.S. service. The Mark 2, with retractable landing gear and feathering propellers, followed in 1952. Employed initially as a luxury transport by foreign governments, the aircraft soon found its way to smaller regional airlines including, after 1957, those in the United States. A total of 148 Herons were manufactured with about 80 entering U.S. commuter airline operations in the 1960s and 1970s. To extend life, performance, and profits, several operators sought to upgrade the British airliner by improving its power plant. In America, Riley Aircraft added Avco Lycoming turboprops and increased the plane's speed to 285 miles per hour. Until recently, the largest U.S. Heron operator was the Puerto Rican local-service airline, PRINAIR.

Selected List of U.S. Operating Airlines: Colorado River Airlines; Fischer Brothers Aviation; Illinois Air Lines; PRINAIR; Shawnee Airlines; Susquehanna Airlines; Wright Airlines; (1984–1985): Hawaiian Air Tour Service; PRINAIR; Seagull Air Hawaii, Semo Airways; State Airlines; Susquehanna Airlines ■

PRINAIR (Puerto Rico International Airlines) was long the nation's largest Heron operator. Unable to resolve ownership and financial problems, the one-time largest commuter closed down in mid-1985. Courtesy James P. Woolsey

■ LOCKHEED L-1649A Starliner

First Service: 1957

Type/Purpose: Four-engined, commercial, long-haul transport

Number of Seats: 4–5 crew, 74 passengers

Dimensions: Length: 116 feet
Height: 24.9 feet
Wingspan: 150 feet
Gross weight (pounds): 137,500

Engines: 4 Wright R-3350-EAZ radials

Performance: Maximum range: 6,300 miles
Service ceiling: 25,000 feet
Maximum speed: 380 mph
Maximum cruising speed: 350 mph

Initial Test Flight: October 11, 1956

Initial U.S. Operator Service: Trans-World Airlines, June 1957

Remarks: To meet the challenge of the Douglas DC-7C, Lockheed in the mid-1950s developed for Trans-World Airlines the ultimate Constellation, the L-1649A Starliner. With a fuselage stretch of 2.7 feet over the Super Constellation and entirely new, longer, thin-section wing (with straight taper instead of the earlier curved trailing edge), of greater tankage capacity, the Starliner, of which only 43 were built, could not compete with what turned out to be its real rival, the Boeing 707. The coming of the jetliner meant the end of the line for all of Lockheed's beautiful Connies. All were retired from front-line service during the 1960s, although many survivors flew on as fast freighters. Among the records set by the Starliner was a September 29, 1957, speed mark, Los Angeles to London in 18 hours and 32 minutes. The aircraft still holds the record for the longest nonstop, commercial passenger flight in terms of time aloft—23 hours and 19 minutes—on the inaugural London to San Francisco TWA service, October 1-2, 1957. ■

TWA's Lockheed L-1649A represented a high point in piston-engined airliner development. Courtesy Trans World Airlines

■ BOEING 707 Series
707-120/707-320

First Service: 1958

Type/Purpose: Four-engined, commercial, turbojet/
turbofan, medium/long-haul transport

Number of Seats: 3 crew, 181 passengers (120)/
3 crew, 202 passengers (320)

Dimensions: Length: 145 feet (120)/ 153 feet (320)
Height: 42.5 feet
Wingspan: 131 feet
Gross weight (pounds): 248,000 (120)/ 336,000 (320)

Engines: 4 Pratt & Whitney JT3C-6 turbojets (120/320)/
4 Pratt & Whitney JT3D turbofans (120B/320B)

Performance: Maximum range: 3,000 miles (120)/
4,000 miles (320)
Service ceiling: 39,000 feet
Maximum cruising speed: 600 mph

Initial Test Flight: July 15, 1954

Initial U.S. Operator Service: Pan American World Airways
(international), October 26, 1958/
National Airlines (domestic), December 10, 1958

Remarks: Realizing that its Model 377 Stratocruiser was "the end of the line" for piston-powered transports, the Boeing Commercial Airplane Company was the first United States airliner builder to appreciate the potential of the gas-turbine engine as a power source for civil aircraft and the first to take positive steps to design and construct such a plane. In August 1952, the firm took the extremely bold gamble of investing $16 million in the manufacture for such a new civil transport, shrouding the project in secrecy with the designation 367-80 or, as it was known to company employees, "Dash-80." Knowing that this move could spell fiscal disaster if a failure, Boeing developed its initial design as a military transport/tanker. Clearly derived from its Stratocruiser, but aerodynamically closer to the Boeing B-47 Stratojet bomber, the "Dash-80" was rolled out on May 14, 1954, and test flown on July 15. The USAF, pleased with the aircraft, placed the first of more than 800 orders for what it would call the C-135/C-137. With the military option secured, the "Dash-80" was re-equipped as a civil demonstrator, offering U.S. airlines the possibility of a jetliner that would make all propeller transports in their service obsolete. Juan Trippe of Pan American was first to

grasp the potential and on October 13, 1955, he ordered six production models, then designated 707-120. Later, the 367-80 pioneer was donated to the National Air and Space Museum. Pan Am's first aircraft flew on December 20, 1957, and was delivered in August 1958. Although designed primarily for domestic service, Trippe's first plane, *Clipper America*, was employed to open the carrier's New York-London transatlantic, jetliner service. In a marvelous piece of interline cooperation, National Airlines (which would later be purchased by Pan Am) leased several 120s from Trippe and opened New York-Miami service in December 1958, becoming the first carrier to operate the world's largest and fastest airliner on domestic routes. The arrival of the Boeing 707-120 set off a jet-buying spree by most of America's airlines; as the aircraft were received by major carriers, often good piston equipment was quickly sold to smaller operators thereby indirectly improving the quality of local service. With a longer fuselage and greater wingspan, the long-haul 707-320 Intercontinental with its more powerful engines was first flown on January 11, 1959. Delivered to Pan American a few months later, it allowed that carrier to inaugurate sustained, scheduled, transatlantic flights on October 10. The arrival for the 320 allowed follow-up 120s to be employed, as designed, for domestic operations. On January 31, 1962, the 320B, with a new engine and aerodynamically refined, was first flown; it was followed by the mixed-load-capable 320C, which entered Pan Am service on June 3, 1963. Several other modifications were carried out on the aircraft, resulting in minor variants. Production ended in the fall of 1980, by which time 808 airliners had been ordered and 784 delivered during a quarter-century manufacturing program. Largely gone from U.S. front-line carriers by the 1980s, the Boeing 707 had proved as revolutionary in the late 1950s–early 1960s as the Boeing 247 or Douglas DC-2/DC-3 had been in the 1930s.

Selected List of U.S. Operating Airlines: American Airlines; Braniff International Airways; Continental Airlines; National Airlines; Pan American World Airways; Trans-World Airlines; United Airlines; World Airways; (1984-1985): American Trans Air; Arrow Air; Atlanta Skylarks; Buffalo Airways; Challenger Air Transport; Global International Airways; Independent Air; Jet Charter Service; Pan Aviation; Ports of Call; Samoa Airlines; Skystar International; South Pacific Island Airways; Westar International Airlines; Worldwide Airlines ■

TOP LEFT: Ever in the forefront of new equipment, Continental Airlines quickly came to employ the Boeing 707-320, as shown in this illustration. Courtesy Continental Airlines

TOP RIGHT: Pan Am was first to place the intercontinental range Boeing 707-320 into service, assigning it to transatlantic operations on August 26, 1959. The example shown is a 707-321B — turbofan-powered, it was the final 707 development. Courtesy Pan American World Airways

BOTTOM: At New York, a TWA 707-100 enplanes passengers for California. Howard Hughes' airline possessed only one of these Boeing jetliners when it entered transcontinental competition with American Airlines in March 1959. Courtesy Trans World Airlines

■ CONVAIR CV-540

First Service: 1959

Type/Purpose: Twin-engined, commercial, medium-haul transport

Number of Seats: 3 crew, 52 passengers

Dimensions: Length: 79.2 feet
Height: 28.2 feet
Wingspan: 105.4 feet
Gross weight (pounds): 58,000

Engines: 2 Napier Eland N.El.1 turboprops

Performance: Maximum range: 500 miles
Service ceiling: 24,900 feet
Maximum cruising speed: 300 mph

Initial Test Flight: February 9, 1955

Initial U.S. Operator Service: Allegheny Airlines, July 1, 1959

Remarks: Allegheny undertook to experimentally fly these more powerful CV-340s (redesignated CV-540s) and eventually operated six in a high-density, 52-passenger layout. When development and production of the Eland came to an end in 1962, these were reconverted to piston-engined power plants. No other American airline flew this particular version. ■

An Allegheny Airlines CV-540. The Pittsburg-based carrier was the only U.S. operator to fly the Eland-powered Convair. Courtesy US Air

■ LOCKHEED L-188 Electra

First Service: 1959

Type/Purpose: Four-engined, commercial, short/medium-haul transport

Number of Seats: 3-4 crew, 66-99 passengers

Dimensions: Length: 104.6 feet
Height: 32.1 feet
Wingspan: 99 feet
Gross weight (pounds): 116,000

Engines: 4 Allison 501-D13A turboprops

Performance: Maximum range: 2,500 miles
Service ceiling: 27,000 feet
Maximum speed: 405 mph
Maximum cruising speed: 374 mph

Initial Test Flight: December 6, 1957

Initial U.S. Operator Service: Eastern Airlines, January 12, 1959

Remarks: Designed to meet a 1955 American Airlines specification, the low-wing monoplane Electra with its turboprop engines was a transitional airliner between the earlier pistons and the later turbojets. A contemporary rival of the imported Vickers Viscount, the L-188 was the only four-engined U.S. turboprop ever to enter regular commercial service. Two planes were lost within six months of entering service and the FAA required speed reduction; although the faulty, wing-affected structure was repaired, the delay in full use caused sales to fall off fatally. Most Electras had been retired from front-line scheduled or charter service by 1975; however, as late as 1984, a number of the 41 converted by Lockheed from 1967 remained in operation.

Selected List of U.S. Operating Airlines: Air California; American Flyers; Braniff International Airways; Eastern Airlines; Evergreen International Airlines; National Airlines; Northwest Orient Airlines; Overseas National Airlines; Pacific Southwest Airlines; Reeve Aleutian Airways; Western Airlines; Zantop International Airlines; (1984-1985): CAM Air International; Evergreen International Airlines; Galaxy Airlines; Gulf Air; Interstate Airlines; Reeve Aleutian Airways; Summit Airlines; Transamerican Airlines; Zantop International Airlines ■

Eastern Airlines fleet at one time included 40 Lockheed L-188 Electras, all with fuselage stripes in two shades of blue. Courtesy Eastern Airlines

This Lockheed Electra served as the Los Angeles Dodgers' team plane between 1962 and 1969. Courtesy Los Angeles Dodgers

In January 1959, American Airlines' *Flagship New York* entered service as the first of 35 Lockheed L-188 Electras to join that carrier's fleet. Note the DC-3 in the upper right-hand corner of this photograph. Courtesy American Airlines

Reeve Aleutian Lockheed Electra on its maiden flight, May 2, 1968. Courtesy Bob Reeve Collection, Reeve Aleutian Airways

■ McDONNELL-DOUGLAS DC-8 Series 10 to 50

First Service: 1959

Type/Purpose: Four-engined, commercial, long-haul transport

Number of Seats: 3-5 crew, 179 passengers

Dimensions: Length: 150.6 feet
Height: 38.6 feet
Wingspan: 142.5 feet
Gross weight (pounds): 273,000

Engines: 4 Pratt & Whitney JT3C-6 turbojets (10)/
4 Pratt & Whitney JT4A-9 turbojets (20)/
4 Pratt & Whitney JT4A-11 turbojets (30)/
4 Pratt & Whitney JT3D-3 turbofans (50)

Performance: Maximum range: 4,150-6,555 nautical miles
Service ceiling: 30,000 + feet
Maximum cruising speed: 579 mph

Initial Test Flight: May 30, 1958 (10)/
November 29, 1958 (20)/
February 20, 1959 (30)/
December 20, 1960 (50)

Initial U.S. Operator Service: Delta Air Lines/
United Airlines, September 18, 1959 (10)/ various (20)/
Pan American World Airways, April 27, 1960 (30)/
United Airlines, April 30, 1961 (50)

Remarks: Douglas announced its intention in June 1955 to build a turbojet transport to replace its DC-7 series. To save time, the manufacturer built no prototype and, following test flights in late spring 1958, it was seen that its main competitor would be the Boeing 707. Douglas designed the airframe of its first turbojet civil aircraft with almost identical dimensions, the chief differences in the Dash-10 to -50 series being in power plant and fuel capacity. Thus the 10 and 20 were introduced for domestic service, the 30 for intercontinental operations, and the 50 (with turbofans), which offered maximum passenger seating, was made available in all freight or passenger/cargo-convertible configurations. This approach simplified the builder's planning, but was not flexible enough to meet various airline requirements. Even so, these "straight" DC-8s were extremely sturdy aircraft; indeed, to demonstrate the structural integrity of the jetliner, a Douglas crew flew a produc-

tion model in a 1961 test hop over Edwards AFB in excess of the speed of sound, reaching Mach 1.012 at 41,088 feet. Production of these initial DC-8s totaled 294; although some 75 are still in service, most American operators in 1984 and 1985 were holiday-charter concerns.

Selected List of U.S. Operating Airlines: Agro Air International; Airborne Express; Air Transport International; All-Star Airlines; Arrow Air; Challenge Air Transport; Conner Air Lines; Delta Air Lines; Eastern Airlines; National Airlines; Northwest Orient Airlines; Overseas National Airways; Pan American World Airways; United Airlines; Zantop International Airlines ■

This United DC-8-10 was photographed at Chicago. The major carrier began scheduled service with this jetliner on September 18, 1959. Courtesy United Airlines

Northwest Orient Airlines was an operator of the international-range DC-8-30, a jetliner able to match the performance of the Boeing 707-320B. Courtesy Northwest Orient Airlines

■ BOEING 720/720B

First Service: 1960

Type/Purpose: Four-engined, commercial, medium-haul turbojet/turbofan transport

Number of Seats: 3 crew, 167 passengers

Dimensions: Length: 137 feet
Height: 41.6 feet
Wingspan: 146 feet
Gross weight (pounds): 230,000

Engines: 4 Pratt & Whitney JT3C-7 turbojets (720)/
4 Pratt & Whitney JT3D turbofans (720B)

Performance: Maximum range: 3,000 miles
Service ceiling: 42,000 feet
Maximum speed: ?
Maximum cruising speed: 611 mph

Initial Test Flight: November 23, 1959 (720)/
October 6, 1960 (720B)

Initial U.S. Operator Service: United Airlines, July 5, 1960 (720)/ American Airlines, October 6, 1960 (720B)

Remarks: The success of the Boeing 707 led its builder to proceed with development of a medium-range version, which, owing to its design refinements (principally in the wing), was designated Model 720. The B variant, equipped with turbofan engines, which allowed greater efficiency and also made possible takeoffs from shorter runways, followed. There was, however, only a limited demand for the 720/720B and production ceased in 1969 after 154 had been built and sold. Rarely employed by U.S. scheduled carriers by the 1980s, several have been employed by private corporations and concerns, including the Los Angeles Dodgers major-league baseball team, which employed the 720B *Kay O II* from 1971 through 1982.

Selected List of U.S. Operating Airlines: American Airlines; Eastern Airlines; Pacific Northern Airlines; United Airlines; Western Airlines; (1984-1985): American Travelair; Silver Wings International; Windwalkers Air Country Club ■

Continental, in 1961, was one of several carriers to adopt the Boeing 720B, smaller brother of the 707. Courtesy Continental Airlines

This Boeing 720B, the KAY 0II, was employed by the Los Angeles Dodgers from 1971 through 1982. Courtesy Los Angeles Dodgers

After selecting Douglas during the nation's initial jet-buying spree, United returned to the Boeing fold as the first 720 operator, placing the medium-haul airliner into service on its Chicago-Denver-Los Angeles route on July 5, 1960. Courtesy United Airlines

■ CONVAIR CV-880

First Service: 1960

Type/Purpose: Four-engined, commercial, turbojet, medium-haul transport

Number of Seats: 3-5 crew, 124 passengers

Dimensions: Length: 129.4 feet
   Height: 36.4 feet
   Wingspan: 120 feet
   Gross weight (pounds): 253,000

Engines: 4 GE CJ805-3B turbojets

Performance: Maximum range: 5,056-5,400 miles
   Service ceiling: 35,000 feet
   Maximum speed: 615 mph
   Maximum cruising speed: 556 mph

Initial Test Flight: January 27, 1959

Initial U.S. Operator Service: Delta Air Lines, May 15, 1969 (880)

Remarks: Designed for higher performance than its Boeing 707 or Douglas DC-8 rivals, the Convair had a smaller capacity but was faster than either. Few aircraft have had as many designations as the 880 in its early stages: Skylark, Golden Arrow, Convair 600. The appearance of the Boeing 720 with its advantage of commonality with the 707 doomed the sales prospect of the 880 and when production ended in July 1962, only 65 had been built. In early 1960, a CV-880 set a transcontinental Los Angeles-Miami speed record of 3 hours and 31 minutes.

Selected List of U.S. Operating Airlines: Alaska Airlines; Delta Air Lines; Northeast Airlines; Trans-World Airlines ■

Employing the Convair CV-880, Alaska Airlines commenced charter flights over the North Pole to Leningrad in the U.S.S.R. Courtesy Alaska Airlines

Initially sponsored by TWA, financial difficulties forced the carrier to hold off its first Convair CV-880 service until January 12, 1961. Courtesy Trans World Airlines

While TWA was embroiled in a control battle with Howard Hughes, it leased six Convair CV-880s to Northeast Airlines, one of which is shown here. Courtesy Delta Air Lines

■ PIPER PA-23 Aztec Series A to F

First Service: 1960

Type/Purpose: Single-engined, light, executive, regional, air-taxi transport

Number of Seats: 1 pilot, 5–6 passengers

Dimensions: Length: 31.3 feet
Height: 10.4 feet
Wingspan: 37.2 feet
Gross weight (pounds): 5,200

Engines: 2 Lycoming TIO-540-CIA pistons (PA-23)

Performance: Maximum range: 1,018-1,317 miles
Service ceiling: 18,950 feet
Maximum speed: 215 mph
Maximum cruising speed: 192 mph

Initial Test Flight: 1959

Remarks: An improved version of the Piper Apache with a slightly longer nose, the Aztec remained in production through 1981 in both its normally aspirated and turbo-supercharged version, with only slight differences distinguishing the various models.

Selected List of U.S. Operating Airlines: (1984-1985): Air Continental; Air Vermont; Airway Express; Bangor International Airlines; Banyan Air Service; Corporate Air; Fischer Brothers Aviation; Florida Airmotive; Larry's Flying Service; Long Island Airlines; Michigan Airways; New England Airlines; Provincetown-Boston Airlines (PBA); Phillips Airlines; Phoenix Airways; Semo Airways; Virgin Air; Will's Air ■

TOP: The Piper PA-23 has long been employed by small carriers and air taxis. Shown here is the Series F of 1980. Courtesy James P. Woolsey

BOTTOM: A Piper Aztec, belonging to Jay Wolfe of Bridgeport, W.V., captured at Clarksburg Benedum Airport in August 1986.

■ AEROSPATIALE (SUD) SE-210 Caravelle VI-R

First Service: 1961

Type/Purpose: Twin-engined, short/medium-range, turbofan transport

Number of Seats: 3 crew, 70 passengers

Dimensions: Length: 105 feet
Height: 29.7 feet
Wingspan: 113 feet
Gross weight (pounds): 110,231

Engines: 2 Rolls-Royce Avon RA 29-533 R turbojets

Performance: Maximum range: 1,450 miles
Service ceiling: 32,800 feet
Maximum cruising speed: 525 mph

Initial Test Flight: February 6, 1961

Initial U.S. Operator Service: United Airlines, July 14, 1961

Remarks: The Sud-Est (later Áerospatiale) SE-210 Caravelle was the first turbojet airliner of French design and construction. One of the most successful European jetliners ever constructed, this aircraft incorporated a Comet nose section purchased from DeHavilland of Great Britain. To insure improved wing performance and a quieter cabin, the Caravelle introduced a then-unique powerplant arrangement with two engines in pods, one on each side of the rear fuselage. With the wing "clean" of engines, flaps could be installed the full length of its trailing edge, thereby enhancing low-speed control and giving greater takeoff performance. This wing and engine arrangement would subsequently be copied by the American manufacturers for some of their transports, including the McDonnell-Douglas DC-9. United Airlines purchased 20 of the 56 thrust-reverser-equipped VI-Rs built and introduced them on its short-haul routes. That carrier's aircraft went on to transport over 10 million passengers and fly in excess of 117 million miles before they were retired in October 1970. The Caravelle is no longer employed by any scheduled U.S. airline.

Selected List of U.S. Operating Airlines: Airborne Express; United Airlines ■

A United Caravelle photographed at San Francisco (with fog in the background) in September 1965. Courtesy John P. Stewart, via Robert E. Garrard.

Passengers depart a United Airlines Caravelle via the rear airstair. Courtesy United Airlines

■ CONVAIR CV-990A Coronado

First Service: 1962

Type/Purpose: Four-engined, commercial, turbofan, medium-haul transport

Number of Seats: 3-5 crew, 159 passengers

Dimensions: Length: 139.2 feet
Height: 39.6 feet
Wingspan: 120 feet
Gross weight (pounds): 239,200

Engines: 4 GE CJ805-23B turbofans

Performance: Maximum range: 5,400 miles
Service ceiling: 41,000 feet
Maximum speed: 615 mph
Maximum cruising speed: 556 mph

Initial Test Flight: January 24, 1961

Initial U.S. Operator Service: American Airlines, March 18, 1962

Remarks: Created to meet an American Airlines requirement, the 990 Coronado was a more powerful, slightly modified, and stretched (10-feet longer) version of the CV-880. Testing demonstrated a need for costly modification (which proved a great embarrassment to the manufacturer) before the plane could be delivered as a 990A to American in January 1962. Production of the 990A was soon thereafter halted after only 37 had been built; the financial losses the aircraft entailed forced Convair out of the airliner-manufacturing business. Flown operationally by U.S. front-line carriers only briefly, all 12 remaining commercial 990As are owned by the Spanish line Spantax.

Selected List of U.S. Operating Airlines: Alaska Airlines; American Airlines; Modern Air Transport; Northeast Airlines ■

The Convair CV-990 was designed to meet American Airlines specifications for a high speed transport. Initially known as the CV-600, the 990 failed to meet its guaranteed performance, requiring costly modification into the 990A. Courtesy General Dynamics Corp., Convair Division

Developed to meet American Airlines' requirement for a high-speed jetliner, the CV-990 was ordered in August 1958. Reconfigured as the 990A Coronado, only 20 were eventually built for the carrier, the first entering service on March 18, 1962. Courtesy American Airlines

■ BOEING 727 Series 100 to 200

First Service: 1964

Type/Purpose: Three-engined, commercial, short/medium-haul, turbofan transport

Number of Seats: 3 crew, 94 passengers (100)/ 3 crew, 145 passengers (200)

Dimensions: Length: 133.3 feet (100)/ 153.2 feet (200)
Height: 34 feet
Wingspan: 108 feet
Gross weight (pounds): 142,500 (100)/ 154,500 (200)

Engines: 3 Pratt & Whitney JT8D-7 turbofans (100)/ 3 Pratt & Whitney JT8D-9A/15 turbofans (200)

Performance: Maximum range: 1,800 miles
Service ceiling: 35,000 feet
Maximum speed: 632 mph
Maximum cruising speed: 592 mph

Initial Test Flight: February 9, 1963

Initial U.S. Operator Service: Eastern Airlines, February 1, 1964 (100)/
Northwest Orient Airlines, April 23, 1966 (100C)/
United Airlines, May 1, 1966 (100QC)/
Northeast Airlines, December 14, 1967 (200)

Remarks: Boeing officials, even before their 707 entered service, elected to complement America's first jetliner with a new short/medium-range airliner capable of providing the kind of service unavailable from the 707/720 group. Somewhat influenced by the Aerospatiale Caravelle, the resulting project, Model 727, featured an advanced wing design, many 707/720 components and systems, including the fuselage upper lobe of the former, new landing gear, a tall "T" tail, and three rear-mounted engines (two in side pods and one buried in the rear fuselage), which are the plane's most recognizable characteristic. Boeing authorized the go-ahead for the 727 in 1960 and the first orders came that year from Eastern Airlines and United Airlines. In service, the economics of the 727-100 proved more advantageous than anticipated and the popularity of the aircraft grew rapidly. In 1964, Boeing sought to widen the 727 market by announcing a convertible cargo/passenger version (100C) and the quick-change (QC) model that allowed a change from all-passenger to all-cargo configuration in less than an hour. In an effort to meet a growing demand for a higher-capacity, short-haul transport, the 727-200, a

20-foot stretch over the 100, became available in the mid-1960s and was followed in 1971 by the more powerful and internally modified Advanced 727-200. While the 707 had proved revolutionary, the 727 would prove to be the world's best selling and most widely employed short/medium-haul turbofan. When Boeing halted 727 production in August 1984 in favor of its new 757, a total of 1,832 units had been sold, of which some 1,250 had been 727-200s or Advanced 727-200s.

Selected List of U.S. Operating Airlines: (1984-1985): *727-100* – Air Atlanta; Air Express International; Air One; Alaska Airlines; American Trans Air; Arrow Air; CAM Air International; Century Airways; Continental Airlines; DHL Airlines; Eastern Airlines; Evergreen International Airlines; Federal Express; Flight International Airlines; The Flying Tiger Line; Frontier Horizon Airlines; Gulf Air Transport; Interstate Airlines; Jet East International; Key Airlines; Northeastern International Airways; Northwest Orient Airlines; Orion Air; Pacific Interstate Airlines; Pan American World Airways; Pan Aviation; Ports of Call; Reeve Aleutian Airways; Regent Air; Ryan International Airlines; Trans-World Airlines; United Airlines; UPS; Westar International Airlines; *727-200* – Air One; Air Via; Alaska Airlines; American Airlines; Arrow Air; Braniff, Inc.; Capitol Air; Delta Air Lines; Eastern Airlines; Federal Express; Gulf Air Transport; Jet Express; Northeastern International Airways; Pan American World Airways; People Express Airlines; Republic Airlines; Southwest Airlines; Trans-World Airlines; United Airlines; UPS; USAir; Western Airlines; Wien Air Alaska ■

Eastern Airlines was the launch customer for the Boeing 727, placing its first into service on its Philadelphia-Washington-Miami route on February 1, 1964. That carrier's fleet in 1985 included 32 Dash-100s and 95 Dash-200s, one of the latter shown here. Courtesy Eastern Airlines

Some 21 months after suspending operations as Braniff International Airways and filing for bankruptcy in May 1982, a revitalized Braniff, Inc., relaunched operations on March 1, 1984. Despite reversals, the slimmed-down carrier, which operated an all Boeing 727-200 fleet (20 aircraft) in 1985 (one of which is here shown), continues to survive as a low-fare airline. Courtesy Braniff, Inc.

Better known for its long-haul operations, Pan Am in 1985 flew 38 Boeing 727-235s over its shorter routes. Courtesy Pan American World Airways.

On April 12, 1964, American Airlines became the third major carrier to send the Boeing 727 thundering off the nation's runways. Today, the Dallas-based carrier's fleet includes 39 model 100s and 125 of the 200s. Courtesy American Airlines

Alaska Airlines Boeing 727-200 high over the 49th state. The carrier currently operates twenty-two of these aircraft (2 Dash-100 and 20 Dash-200) to points in Alaska, the Pacific Northwest, and California. Courtesy Alaska Airlines.

■ CESSNA 206 Stationair/ 207 Skywagon

First Service: 1964

Type/Purpose: Single-engined, utility transport/air taxi

Number of Seats: 1 pilot, 5-7 passengers

Dimensions: Length: 28 feet (206)/ 31.9 feet (207)
Height: 9.7 feet (206)/ 9.6 feet (207)
Wingspan: 35.1 feet
Gross weight (pounds): 2,600 (206)/ 3,800 (207)

Engines: 1 Continental IO-520-F piston (206/207)/
1 Continental TSIO-520-M piston (Turbo Stationair/
Turbo Skywagon)

Performance: Maximum range: 443-702 miles
Service ceiling: 14,800 feet (206)/ 13,300 feet (207)
Maximum speed: 156 kt (206)/ 150 kt (207)
Maximum cruising speed: 147 kt (206)/ 143 kt (207)

Initial Test Flight: 1964 (206)/ May 11, 1968 (207)

Remarks: A high-wing braced monoplane, the Cessna 206 was originally known as the Super Skywagon, a name that was changed in 1970 to Stationair to avoid confusion with the builder's Model 180/185 series. A total of 4,802 206s had been delivered by late 1878 when attention turned to the generally similar, but stretched 207, first introduced in 1969. Both aircraft could be obtained with turbo-super-charged power plants and have been employed not only in business operations, but extensively by air-taxi and bush concerns and small regionals. Nearly 500 207s were in service in the early 1980s and like the Model 185, the 207 has proven extremely popular with Alaskan operators.

Selected List of U.S. Operating Airlines: (1984-1985): *206*—Air Sedona; Alaska Air Charter; Alaska Air Guides; Alaska Air Service; Alaska Bush Carrier; Arctic Circle Air; Armstrong Air Service; Bard Air; Bering Air; Capitol Airlines; Channel Flying; Coastal Aviation; Colorado Airlines; Ellis Air Taxi; Executive Charter; Flirite; Frontier Flying Service; Glacier Bay Airways; Gulkana Air Service; Ketchum Air Service; Lake Union Air; Larry's Flying Service; Seair Alaska Airlines; South Central Air; Wright Air Service of Alaska; *207*— Air Nevada; Alpha Air; Arctic Circle Air; Astor Air; Audi Air; Aurora Air Service; Bering Air; Birchwood Air Service; Bush Air; Bush Pilots Air Service; Cape Smythe Air; Capitol Airlines; Coastal Aviation; Executive Charter; 40-Mile Air; Frontier Flying Service; Galena Air Service; Grand Canyon Airlines; Grayling Air Service; Harold's Air Service; Hermen's Air; Inter Valley Airline; Island Airlines; Larry's Flying Service; Ryan Air Service; Saber Aviation; San Juan Airlines; South Central Air; Wings of Alaska; Wright Air Service of Alaska; Yukon Air North; Yute Air Alaska ■

A Cessna 206 of San Juan Airlines, photographed at Bellingham, Wash., in June 1972. Established in 1947, this small regional currently provides scheduled service in the Puget Sound area, to San Juan Island and British Columbia from its base at Port Angeles. Courtesy John P. Stewart, via Robert E. Garrard

■ CONVAIR CV-580 Super Convair CV-600/CV-640

First Service: 1964

Type/Purpose: Twin-engined, commercial, medium-haul transport

Number of Seats: 3 crew, 48-56 passengers

Dimensions: Length: 81.6 feet
Height: 29.2 feet
Wingspan: 105.4 feet
Gross weight (pounds): 58,140

Engines: 2 Allison 501-D13H turboprops (CV-580)
2 Rolls-Royce RDa.10/1 Dart 542-4 turboprops (CV-600/CV-640)

Performance: Maximum range: 1,614-2,866 miles
Service ceiling: 24,900 feet
Maximum cruising speed: 342 mph

Initial Test Flight: January 19, 1960 (CV-580)/
May 20, 1965 (CV-600/640)

Initial U.S. Operator Service: Frontier Airlines, June 1, 1964 (CV-580)/ Central Airlines, November 30, 1965 (CV-600)/ Caribair, December 22, 1965 (CV-640)

Remarks: PacAero Engineering Corporation of Santa Monica initiated a conversion program for Convairs that involved the installation of Allison turboprops and provision of larger tails; when the conversion program was completed in the mid-1960s, 175 former CV- 240s, -340s, and -440s had been altered, the former having 48-passenger layouts and the latter two 56. Initial acceptance of the Super Convair was slowed by Lockheed's introduction of the L-188 Electra, but following that aircraft's accidents and subsequent speed restrictions, local-service carriers were forced to turn to the Convair option and once in hand, the strong old aircraft received a new lease on life. In the mid-1960s, the Convair division of General Dynamics took 39 Convair CV-240s in hand, put in Rolls-Royce Dart turboprops, and sold them CV-600s; 28 Convair 340s/440s also had engine replacements and were sent to the airlines as CV-640s. Like the 580s, many of the 600s/640s are still in active carrier service.

Selected List of U.S. Operating Airlines: CV-580 – Allegheny Airlines; Evergreen International Airlines; Frontier Airlines; Lake Central Airlines; (1984-1985): Air Nevada; Air Resorts Airlines; Alaska Airlines; Aspen Airways; Atlantic Gulf Airlines; Corporate Air; ERA Aviation; Freedom Airlines; Frontier Commuter; Gulf Air; Jet Alaska; Key Airlines; Metro Airlines; PRINAIR; Republic Airlines; Saber Aviation; Seair Alaska Airlines; Sierra Pacific Airlines; Summit Airlines; *CV- 600* – Central Airlines; Trans-Texas Airlines; (1984-1985): Bar Harbor Airlines; Emery Worldwide; SMB Stage Lines; Viking International Airlines; Wright Airlines; *CV-640* – Caribair; Hawaiian Airlines; (1984-1985): Corporate Air; SMB Stage Lines; Viking International Airlines; Wright Airlines; Zantop International Airlines ■

Lake Central Airlines began Convair CV-580 service on September 6, 1966, passing along these aircraft when it merged into Allegheny Airlines on March 14, 1968. Courtesy USAir

On June 1, 1964, Frontier Airlines became the first U.S. operator to place the Allison-powered Convair 580 into service. The carrier, recently acquired by People Express Airlines, had retired its last Convairs by 1984. Courtesy General Dynamics Corp., Convair Division

■ AEROSPATIALE (Nord) 262 and Fregate/Mohawk 298 Series

First Service: 1965

Type/Purpose: Twin-engined, commercial, commuter /regional transport

Number of Seats: 2 crew, 26-29 passengers

Dimensions: Length: 63.3 feet
Height: 20.4 feet
Wingspan: 71.9 feet
Gross weight (pounds): 23,369

Engines: 2 Turboméca Bastan VII turboprops (Frégate 262)/
2 Pratt & Whitney of Canada PT6A-45 turboprops (Mohawk 298)

Performance: Maximum range: 1,325 miles
Service ceiling: 23,500 feet
Maximum speed: 239 mph
Maximum cruising speed: 233 mph

Initial Test Flight: December 24, 1962

Initial U.S. Operator Service: Lake Central Airlines, October 31, 1965 (Frégate 262)/
Allegheny Airlines, April 1978 (Mohawk 298)

Remarks: Designed as a poor-field, regional airliner, the high-wing, Nord-Aviation 262 monoplane was based on the unpressurized M.H. 250 super Broussard utility aircraft developed by Max Hoste. The Nord employed the simple tricycle landing gear of the Super Broussard with the main units retractable into fuselage blisters, but introduced a new circular-section, pressurized fuselage, the top and bottom bulkheads of which had to be cut away to allow headroom. Paradoxically, the first four production aircraft were labeled Series B; however, later early-production units, given a few improvements, were designated Series A. Production of the Series A totaled 72 planes. Following creation of the giant Áerospatiale manufacturing firm in 1970, the 262 was further developed in 33 examples of the Series C and Series D, but none of these entered service with U.S. civil operators. Despite the maufacturer's proposal for a revised version, 262 production ended in 1976 after 110 deliveries, of which less than 30 remain in U.S. airline fleets. Meanwhile, in 1974, the Allegeheny Airlines subsidiary Mohawk Air Services contracted with Frakes Aviation to modify the carrier's 9 262s.

With help from Aérospatiale, these were given new interiors (for accommodation of up to 30 passengers), air conditioning, new wing tips for the improvement of low-level performance, and most importantly, Pratt & Whitney of Canada PT6A-45 turboprop engines with five-bladed propellers. Known as Mohawk 298s, the first of these entered Allegheny service in early 1977.

Selected List of U.S. Operating Airlines: (1984–1985): Air Midwest (Skyways); Atlantic Gulf Airlines; Pennsylvania Airlines; Pocono Airlines; Pompano Airlines; Ransome Airlines ■

A Ransome Airlines Mohawk 298, a reengined and upgraded Nord 262. The former Allegheny Commuter partner still flies four of these French aircraft. Courtesy Ransome Airlines

Lake Central Airlines, with eight, was the U.S. launch-customer for the French Nord 262, inaugurating service on October 31, 1965. Following the carrier's acquisition by Allegheny Airlines in early 1968, the aircraft were repainted in purple-and-gold livery. Shown here is the *Claudette d'Allegheny*. Courtesy USAir

■ BRITISH AEROSPACE (BAC)
One-Eleven Series 200 to 500

First Service: 1965

Type/Purpose: Twin-engined, commercial, turbofan, short/medium-haul transport

Number of Seats: 2 crew, 89 – 119 passengers

Dimensions: Length: 93.6 feet (200/300/400)/ 107 feet (500)
Height: 24.6 feet
Wingspan: 93.6 feet
Gross weight (pounds): 92,000-98,500

Engines: 2 Rolls-Royce Spey 512DW turbofans

Performance: Maximum range: 1,705-1,865 miles
Service ceiling: 35,000 feet
Maximum cruising speed: 541 mph

Initial Test Flight: August 20, 1963 (200)/ June 30, 1967 (500)

Initial U.S. Operator Service: Braniff International Airways, April 25, 1965

Remarks: Originally designed as the 32-seat Hunting Aircraft H-107, the aircraft was continued as the 59-seat British Aircraft Corporation BAC-107 following Hunting's acquisition by BAC in 1960. The endeavor having failed to gain interest led to the 70-seat BAC-111, later renamed One-Eleven. Intended as a replacement for the Vickers Viscount, the One-Eleven was the first of the short-haul jetliners. The initial Dash-200 was followed by the increased-capacity 300 and the Series 400, specifically modified to meet U.S. requirements. The larger-capacity 500 with a fuselage stretch of 13.6 inches was followed by a final variant, the 475, which combined a Series-400 fuselage with Series-500 power plant and wings. When production ceased in 1982, 230 One-Elevens had been constructed; in the U.S., they were largely employed by trunk and local-service carriers in the 1960s, before moving down into the ranks of the larger regionals in the late 1970s.

Selected List of U.S. Operating Airlines: (1984-1985): Air Illinois; Air Wisconsin; Atlantic Gulf Airlines; Britt Airways; Cascade Airways; Florida Express; Jet Fleet International Airlines; Pacific Express; USAir ■

An Allegheny Airlines BAe (BAC) One-Eleven taxis at Greater Pit. Allegheny acquired a number of these British jetliners when it took over Mohawk Airlines on April 12, 1972. Courtesy USAir

A Cascade Airways BAe (BAC) One-Eleven photographed at Spokane, Washington. A prominent Pacific Northwest regional, Cascade formerly operated five of these British jetliners. Courtesy Cascade Airlines

American Airlines ordered fifteen (later thirty) BAe (BAC) One-Elevens in July 1963 and upon delivery in 1966, placed several into New York state service in competition with the prominent local One-Eleven operator, Mohawk Airlines. Courtesy American Airlines

■ McDONNELL-DOUGLAS DC-9
Series 10 to 50

First Service: 1965

Type/Purpose: Twin-engined, commercial, turbofan, medium/short-haul transport

Number of Seats: 2 crew, 90–139 passengers

Dimensions: Length: 104.4 feet (10/20)/ 133.7 feet (30/40/50)
Height: 28 feet
Wingspan: 89.5 feet (10/20)/ 93.5 feet (30/40/50)
Gross weight (pounds): 77,700 (10)/ 90,700 (20)/ 121,000 (30/40/50)

Engines: 2 Pratt & Whitney JT8D-5,-1,-7 turbofans (10)/
2 Pratt & Whitney JT8D-7 turbofans (20)/
2 Pratt & Whitney JT8D-9,-11,-15,-17 turbofans (30)/
2 Pratt & Whitney JT8D-9,-15,-17 turbofans (40)/
2 Pratt & Whitney JT8D-15,-17 turbofans (50)

Performance: Maximum range: 2,065 miles
Service ceiling: 30,000+ feet
Maximum cruising speed: 575 mph

Initial Test Flight: February 25, 1965 (10)/
December 17, 1974 (50)

Initial U.S. Operator Service: Delta Air Lines, December 8, 1965 (10)/ not U.S. employed (20)/ Eastern Airlines, February 1, 1967 (30)/ not U.S. employed (40)/ Swissair, August 24, 1975 (50)

Remarks: A complete family of short or medium-haul jet-liners of various sizes, payloads, ranges, and engines, the DC-9 was not a follow-up to the DC-8, but was, in fact, a completely new design. With a self-contained boarding stair to eliminate expensive ground facilities, the aircraft became quite popular, particularly with passengers at smaller airports. To help circumvent some of the high costs of single-manufacturer jetliner development, Douglas began a practice, now common, of sharing production, risks, and costs with another smaller builder, DeHavilland-Canada. So successful was the initial production model (10) with 137 built, that Douglas proceeded to the next variant, Model 30, skipping for the moment designation 20. The DC-9-30 saw a fuselage stretch of 14.1 feet and increased wingspan. The Model 20 next built combined the fuselage of variant 10 with the increased wingspan of Model 30; it was followed by Model 40, derived from the DC-9-30 but with greater fuel capacity. Neither the Model 20 nor 40 were employed by U.S. carriers, which, instead, elected to go with the Model 50. This last version featured a fuselage stretch of 14.3 feet and a modernized interior. Later units were available in passenger, cargo, and passenger/cargo-convertible configurations. The aircraft in appearance is outwardly distinguishable by its rear-mounted engines and tall "T" tail, reminiscent of the Aérospatiale Caravelle. With orders and options for nearly 1,200 aircraft (all but 5 percent delivered), this airliner has proven to be Douglas' most successful turbine-powered commercial transport to date.

Selected List of U.S. Operating Airlines: (1984-1985): *DC-9-10* – All Star Airlines; Best Airlines; Continental Airlines; Emerald Air; Great American Airways; Midway Airlines; Midwest Express; Northeastern International Airways; Ozark Airlines; Purolator Courier; Ross Aviation; Sunworld International Airlnes; *DC-9-30* – Delta Air Lines; Eastern Airlines; Evergreen International Airlines; Midway Airlines; New York Air; Ozark Airlines; Pacific Southwest Airlines; Republic Airlines; Trans-World Airlines; USAir; *DC-9-50* – Eastern Airlines; Hawaiian Airlines; Muse Air; Ozark Airlines; Republic Airlines ■

Resembling its BAC One-Eleven competitor, the DC-9-10 was an immediate success. One of the earliest carriers placing orders was Continental, which began Douglas service in 1966. Today, the revitalized airline flies 19 Dash-30s. Courtesy Continental Airlines

As Allegheny Airlines, USAir had first acquired the McDonnell-Douglas DC-9-10 September 1966. With only slightly higher operating costs, the stretched Dash-30 found even greater favor and by 1985 a total of 71 were in the fleet of the Pittsburgh-based carrier. Courtesy USAir

Eastern Airlines is a major DC-9 operator and its fleet includes 21 examples of the stretched Dash-51 version of the popular McDonnell-Douglas twin-jet transport. Courtesy Eastern Airlines

Launch-customer for the DC-9, Delta Air Lines placed its initial order in April 1963 and following the aircraft's rapid development, testing, and certification, was able to inaugurate service on December 8, 1965. Today, the Atlanta-based carrier's fleet includes three dozen Dash-30s, one of which is shown here taking off. Courtesy Delta Airlines

■ PIPER PA-32 Cherokee Six

First Service: 1965

Type/Purpose: Single-engined, light, executive/air-taxi/regional transport

Number of Seats: 1 pilot, 6-7 passengers

Dimensions: Length: 27.8 feet
    Height: 9.1 feet
    Wingspan: 32.9 feet
    Gross weight (pounds): 3,400

Engines: 1 Lycoming -540-E or -K piston

Performance: Maximum range: 857 miles
    Service ceiling: 25,000 feet
    Maximum speed: ?
    `Maximum cruising speed: 168 mph

Initial Test Flight: December 6, 1963

Initial U.S. Operator Service: East Coast Air Taxi, 1965

Remarks: The PA-32 is a slightly stretched and improved model of the Piper PA-28 Cherokee and can be operated as a floatplane. The aircraft has proved extremely popular with smaller carriers, scheduled and unscheduled alike.

Selected List of U.S. Operating Airlines: (1984–1985): AAA Air Enterprises; Action Airlines; American Flag Airlines; Armstrong Air Service; Bangor International Airlines; Bay Air; California Air Charter; Flamenco Airways; Green Hills Aviation; Harold's Air Service; Hub Air Service; LAB Flying Services; Las Vegas Airlines; New England Airlines; Peninsula Airways; Resort Airlines; Rover Airways; Saber Aviation; Sunbird, Inc., Wheeler Airlines; Tanana Air Service; Vieques Air Link; Yute Air Alaska ■

LEFT: This Piper Cherokee Six of the little-known Allen Aviation company was photographed in March 1973. Courtesy Robert E. Garrard

RIGHT: This Beech B80 of Hub Airlines was captured at its Fort Wayne base in June 1970. The former Hoosier commuter first began service in December 1966 over a Fort Wayne-Chicago route. Courtesy Robert E. Garrard

■ BEECHCRAFT Queen Air B80

First Service: 1965

Type/Purpose: Twin-engined, commuter/regional transport and air taxi

Number of Seats: 2 crew, 11 passengers

Dimensions: Length: 35.3 feet
    Height: 14.8 feet
    Wingspan: 50.3 feet
    Gross weight (pounds): 8,500

Engines: 2 Avco Lycoming IGSO-540-A1A pistons

Performance: Maximum range: 1,565 miles
    Service ceiling: 29,000 feet
    Maximum speed: 252 mph
    Maximum cruising speed: 230 mph

Initial Test Flight: June 22, 1961

Remarks: Featuring a low-set, cantilevered wing, the B80, sometimes called the "Queen Airliner," was developed in 1965 from the earlier A80 and was designed to provide economy of operation suitable for executive or commuter use. Some 500 unpressurized Queen Air/ Queen Airliners were delivered before production ceased in 1977, and the aircraft would serve as inspiration for the highly successful Beech 99, which largely replaced the B80 in American commuter ranks by 1984. Still widely employed as an air taxi and in scheduled service by several carriers.

Selected List of U.S. Operating Airlines: (1984–1985): Bemidji Aviation Services (Minnesota); Catskill Airways; Midwest Aviation (Minnesota); North Pacific Airlines ■

■ DEHAVILLAND-CANADA DHC-6 Twin Otter Series 100 to 300

First Service: 1966

Type/Purpose: Twin-engined, STOL, utility transport

Number of Seats: 2 crew, 13-20 passengers

Dimensions: Length: 51.9 feet
Height: 19.6 feet
Wingspan: 65 feet
Gross weight (pounds): 12,500

Engines: 2 Pratt & Whitney of Canada PT6A-20 turboprops (100/200)/
2 Pratt & Whitney of Canada PT6A-27 turboprops (300)

Performance: Maximum range: 806 miles
Service ceiling: 26,700 feet
Maximum cruising speed: 210 mph

Initial Test Flight: May 20, 1965

Initial U.S. Operator Service: Air Wisconsin/
Pilgrim Airlines, November 1966

Remarks: This unpressurized twin-engined turboprop is a braced, high-wing monoplane with fixed, tricycle landing gear (which can be replaced by optional skis or floats). Intended for use by commuters and marketed on the basis of its excellent STOL (short-takeoff-and-landing) capabilities, the DHC-6 was seen by its manufacturer as an enlarged and improved version of its successful Beaver/Otter models. The Model 100 was soon followed by the Dash-200 with its extended rear cabin and lengthened nose. Equipped with more powerful engines and a 20-seat interior, the Model 300 is the version most commonly employed by current, American, regional carriers. Over 820 of the extremely versatile $2 million Twin Otters have been delivered to customers worldwide and although fewer of the aircraft are now going to airlines, many are still being purchased by utility and bush operators.

Selected List of U.S. Operating Airlines: (1984-1985): Alaska Aeronautical Industries; Alaska Airlines; Atlantis Airlines; Cape Smythe Air; Capitol Airlines; Conner Air Lines; Coral Air; Crown Airways; Eastern Atlantis Express; Eastern Metro Express; ERA Aviation; Evergreen Airspur; Golden Eagle Air Tours; Grand Canyon Airlines; Holiday Airlines; Horizon Air; Island Airlines; Jet Alaska; Metro Airlines; Mississippi Valley Airlines; Mountain Air Cargo; NewAir; North Continent Airlines; Pennsylvania Airlines; Pilgrim Airlines; Princeville Airways; Rio Airways; Rocky Mountain Airways; Ross Aviation; Royal Hawaiian Air Service; Scenic Airlines; Seair Alaska Airlines; South Pacific Island Airways; Southern Jersey Airways; Suburban Airlines; Sunaire; Trans-North Air; Walker's Cay Airline ■

Takeoff of an Alaska Airlines DeHavilland Canada DHC-6 Twin Otter. Courtesy Alaska Airlines

DeHavilland DHC-6 Twin Otter of the former Allegheny Commuter associate Aeromech Airlines, photographed at Clarksburg, W.V. in 1978. Courtesy USAir

Scenic Airlines' new 19-passenger DeHavilland Twin Otters have been modified exclusively for the purpose of aerial sightseeing and feature the largest windows of any Grand Canyon touring aircraft. Courtesy Scenic Airlines

■ FAIRCHILD-HILLER FH-227

First Service: 1966

Type/Purpose: Twin-engined, commercial, commuter/
regional transport

Number of Seats: 2–4 crew, 44-52 passengers

Dimensions: Length: 83.8 feet
Height: 27.7 feet
Wingspan: 95.2 feet
Gross weight (pounds): 45,500

Engines: 2 Rolls-Royce Dart Mk. 532-7 turboprops (FH-227
to -227C)/
2 Rolls-Royce Dart Mk. 532-7L turboprops (FH-227
D and E)

Performance: Maximum range: 1,580 miles
Service ceiling: 28,000 feet
Maximum cruising speed: 294 mph

Initial Test Flight: January 27, 1966

Initial U.S. Operator Service: Mohawk Airlines, April 1966

Remarks: In April 1956, the Dutch builder Fokker concluded a license agreement with the U.S. manufacturer
Fairchild Engine and Airplane Corporation whereby the
latter would construct and market a variant of the Fokker
F-27 in the Western Hemisphere. The first American-made
Fokker since the 1930s was test flown April 15, 1958, but it
was not until the introduction of the F-27-500 that Fairchild (by then known as the Fairchild-Hiller Corporation)
undertook significant modification of the design. A cantilevered, high-wing monoplane of the same lines as the
F-27, the FH-227 was stretched 6 feet in the fuselage to
allow seating for up to 52 passengers. That aircraft was followed by the 227B, structurally strengthened for operation
at higher weights, and the 227C, which included many
227B improvements while retaining the original operating
weight of the 227. Later, upon the arrival of more powerful
Dart turboprops, several FH-227s became 227Es and
227Bs became 227Ds. A total of 78 FH-227s were built by
Fairchild before its agreement with Fokker expired and
production ended.

Selected List of U.S. Operating Airlines: Delta Air Lines;
Mohawk Airlines; Northeast Airlines; Ozark Airlines;
Piedmont Airlines; (1984–1985): Air Pac; Britt Airways;
Emerald Air; Ross Aviation ■

Ozark Airlines introduced its Fairchild-Hiller FH-227s on December 19, 1966, the second carrier (after Mohawk) to do so. Shown here is one of the St. Louis-based company's 227Bs.
Courtesy Ozark Airlines

When Delta Air Lines acquired Northeast Airlines in August 1972, it also received several of
the latter's Fairchild-Hiller FH-227s, one of which, repainted in Delta colors, is shown here at
Washington National Airport, ca. 1973. Courtesy Delta Air Lines

NIHON (NAMC) YS-11
Series 100 to 700

First Service: 1966

Type/Purpose: Twin-engined, commercial, short/medium-haul transport

Number of Seats: 2 crew, 52-60 passengers

Dimensions: Length: 86.3 feet
Height: 29.5 feet
Wingspan: 104.11 feet
Gross weight (pounds): 54,013

Engines: 2 Rolls-Royce Dart Mk.542-10K turboprops

Performance: Maximum range: 2,000 miles
Service ceiling: 22,900 feet
Maximum cruising speed: 291 mph

Initial Test Flight: August 30, 1962

Initial U.S. Operator Service: Hawaiian Airlines (lease)/Piedmont Airlines, 1966

Remarks: In 1957, the Japanese elected to build their first postwar transport of original design and two years later, the Nihon Aircraft Manufacturing Company (NAMC) was established to coordinate (as Airbus Industrie would later with the A-300) the work of the six member companies building components for this YS-11 airliner: Kawasaki, Fuji, Nippi, Showa, Shin Meiwa, and Mitsubishi. Following testing with two prototypes and certification in 1964, production deliveries began in 1965. With a circular-section, pressurized fuselage, retractable, tricycle landing gear, and two wing-mounted turboprops, the YS-11 is a low-wing monoplane, which became available in four versions: 100—initial, A-200—passenger, A-300—mixed passenger/cargo, and A-400—freighter. The A-500, A-600, and A-700 variants that followed were equivalent to the original series save increased maximum take-off weights. When production ended in 1974, 182 aircraft had been built, of which some 120 remain in service.

Selected List of U.S. Operating Airlines: (1984-1985): Airborne Express; Far West Airlines; Fort Worth Airlines; Mid-Pacific Airlines; Provincetown-Boston Airlines (PBA); Reeve Aleutian Airways; Simmons Airlines; Trans-Central Airlines ■

Founded in 1978 Simmons Airlines currently flies three Nikon YS-11s to 20 points in the Midwest. Courtesy Simmons Airlines

Reeve Aleutian's first YS-11 began scheduled service on November 28, 1972. Courtesy Bob Reeve Collection, Reeve Aleutian Airways

■ PIPER PA-31/PA-31-300/PA-31-310/PA-31P Navajo

First Service: 1966

Type/Purpose: Twin-engined, light, commuter/regional, executive, air-taxi transport

Number of Seats: 1 pilot, 5–8 passengers (Navajo)/ 2 crew, 8-10 passengers (Navajo Chieftain)

Dimensions: Length: 32.7 feet (PA-31 to PA-31-310)/
34.7 feet (PA-31P)/
34.7 feet (PA-31-350/PA-31-325)
Height: 13 feet
Wingspan: 40.8 feet
Gross weight (pounds): 7,800-8,500

Engines: 2 Avco Lycoming IO-540-K pistons (PA-31-310)/
2 Avco Lycoming TIO-540-A pistons (PA-31-300 Turbo Navajo)/
2 Avco Lycoming TIO-540-A2C pistons (PA-31-310)/
2 Avco Lycoming TIGO-540-E1A pistons (PA-31P)/
1 Avco Lycoming TIO-540-J2BD piston and 1 Avco Lycoming LTIO-540-J2BD piston (PA-31-350)/
1 Avco Lycoming TIO-540-F2BD piston and 1 LTIO-540-F2BD piston (PA-31-325)

Performance: Maximum range: 1,285 miles (Navajo)/
1,094 miles (Navajo Chieftain)
Service ceiling: 24,000 feet
Maximum cruising speed: 266 mph (Navajo)/
254 mph (Navajo Chieftain)

Initial Test Flight: September 30, 1964 (Navajo)/
summer 1973 (Navajo Chieftain)

Initial U.S. Operator Service: West Coast Airlines, 1966 (Navajo)

Remarks: In an effort to break into the executive/commuter market, Piper in 1963 designed a low-wing monoplane with retractable, tricycle landing gear. The resulting PA-31 Navajo featured a dutch door at the rear of the portside cabin, the top half of which swung upward, the lower half hinged down (built-in steps). The basic Navajo PA-31/PA-31-300 remained in service from 1967 to 1982 with a few changes allowing other models: the more powerful, Turbo Navajo and PA-31-310. Production of the Navajo ended in 1982. By stretching the fuselage 2 feet, changing the power plant, and allowing pressurization, the Navajo was offered between 1970 and 1977 as the PA-31P. This stretch led to the Navajo Chieftain, the current production variant, which has been in service since 1973. An all-cargo conversion kit for this aircraft is available and like the straight Navajo before it, the Navajo Chieftain has proven extremely popular with small airlines, scheduled and unscheduled alike.

Selected List of U.S. Operating Airlines: (1984-1985): *Piper Navajo*—AAA Airlines; Air Continental; Air L.A.; Air-Lift Commuter; Air Logistics; Airmarc Airlines; Air New Orleans; AirPac Airlines; Air Transport Services; Air Vermont; Airway Express; Alpha Aviation; Alpine Aviation; Arctic Circle Air; Arkansas Traveler Airlines; Audi Air; Bas Airlines; Bering Air; Bighorn Airways; Business Express; California Air Charter; California Seaboard Airlines; Catalina Vegas Airlines; Corporate Air; Cumberland Airlines; East Hampton Aire; General Aviation; Great Lakes Aviation; Green Hills Aviation; Harold's Air Service; Havasu Airlines; Kenai Air Alaska; L.A.B. Flying Service; Panorama Air Tour; Phillips Airlines; Phoenix Airways; Pocono Airlines; Precision Airlines; Resort Airlines; Sajen Air; Semo Airways; South Central Air; Susquehanna Airlines; Tanana Air Service; Trans-Midwest Airlines; Will's Air; Wright Air Service; *Piper Navajo Chieftain*—Air Vectors; Air Vermont; American Central Airlines; Arctic Circle Air; Atlantis Airlines; Aztec Air East; California Air Charter; Christman Air System; Cumberland Airlines; Desert Sun Airlines; Direct Air; Eagle Airlines; East Coast Airways; Flight Line; Harbor Airlines; Havasu Airlines; Iowa Airways; Jetstream International Airlines; Kitty Hawk Airways; L.A.B. Flying Service; Las Vegas Airlines; Long Island Airlines; Mall Airways; National Executive Airlines; Pickel Air; Precision Airlines; Sair Aviation; Sajen Air; Silver Kris Services; Skyway Commuter; South Central Air; Southern Express; Sunaire; Sun West Airlines; Tri-State Airlines; Yute Air Alaska ■

This Piper PA-31 Navajo, owned by Bob Larson of Lock Haven Aircraft, was photographed next to a DeHavilland Canada DHC-6 Twin Otter at Clarksburg (W.V.) Benedum Airport in August 1986.

■ CESSNA 402

First Service: 1967

Type/Purpose: Twin-engined, convertible, passenger/cargo transport

Number of Seats: 1 crew, 9 passengers

Dimensions: Length: 36.4 feet
Height: 11.5 feet
Wingspan: 44.1 feet
Gross weight (pounds): 6,850

Engines: 2 Continental TSIO-520-VB pistons

Performance: Maximum range: 1,420 miles
Service ceiling: 26,900 feet
Maximum cruising speed: 245 mph

Initial Test Flight: 1966

Remarks: An outgrowth of the sister airplane the 401, the $420,000, unpressurized Cessna 402 is a cantilevered, low-wing monoplane with retractable, tricycle landing gear. Following 401 phaseout in 1971, production of the 402 continued with over 1,500 constructed by the end of the seventies. Convertible for both passenger and freight carriage, the 402 has also been developed into an executive aircraft. Widely employed as a transport with small regionals and air taxis.

Selected List of U.S. Operating Airlines: (1984–1985): Aero Coach; Air L.A.; Air Logistics; Airmarc Airlines; Air Nevada; Air Sunshine; Air Vegas; Airways International; Airways of New Mexico; Alpha Aviation; Altus Airlines; AmericAir; American Flag Airlines; Aurora Air Service; Bankair; Banyan Air Service; Bar Harbor Airlines; Bard Air; Bas Airlines; Big Sky Airlines; Capitol Airlines; Caribbean Express; Central Airways; Central Pacific Airlines; Coastal Air Transport; Coastal Aviation; DHL Airlines; Express Air; Flight Line; Golden Pacific Airlines; Great Lakes Aviation; Gull Air; Hermen's Air; Indian Wells Airlines; Jimsair; Mountain Air Cargo; North American Airlines; Provincetown-Boston Airlines (PBA); Pumpkin Air; Reeves Air; Royal Hawaiian Air Service; Ryan Air Service; Saber Aviation; San Juan Airlines; Scenic Airlines; State Airlines; Sunbelt Airlines; Transair; Trans-Mo Airlines; Valley Airlines; Virgin Air; Wilbur's Flight Operation; Westair ■

The Cessna 402 shown in flight and on the ground. Courtesy Cessna Aircraft Company

■McDONNELL-DOUGLAS DC-8 Super Sixty/Super Seventy Series

First Service: 1967

Type/Purpose: Four-engined, commercial, long/medium-haul, turbofan transport

Number of Seats: 3-5 crew, 259 passengers (61/71)/
3-5 crew, 201 passengers (62/72)/
3-5 crew, 259 passengers (63/73)

Dimensions: Length: 187.5 feet
Height: 28.5 feet
Wingspan: 148.5 feet
Gross weight (pounds): 328,000 (61/71)/
350,000 (62-63/72-73)

Engines: 4 Pratt & Whitney JT3D-3 turbofans (61)/
4 Pratt & Whitney JT3D-7 turbofans (62-63)/
4 GE/SNECMA CFM-56 turbofans (71-73)

Performance: Maximum range: 4,500 miles
Service ceiling: 30,000+ feet
Maximum speed: ?
Maximum cruising speed: 583 mph

Initial Test Flight: March 14, 1966 (61)/ August 29, 1966 (62)/
April 10, 1967 (63)/ August 15, 1981 (71)

Initial U.S. Operator Service: United Airlines, February 24,
1967 (61)/ Braniff International Airways, September 4,
1967 (62)/ Seaboard World Airlines, June 30, 1968 (63)/
Delta Air Lines, 1983 (71-73)

Remarks: Douglas in 1965 announced its intention to develop improved variants of the basic DC-8 series with greater capacity. First off the mark was the Super 61, with a fuselage stretch of 36.8 feet; designed for domestic service, it retained the same power plant as the DC-8-50. The Super 62 that followed was aimed at extra-long-haul service; it featured an increased length of 6.8 feet, a greater wingspan, greater fuel capacity, and a new power plant. The last in the Super Sixty series was the 63, which combined the improvements of the 62 with the longer fuselage of the 61. As with the DC-8-50, the 63 offered convertible and all-cargo options. A total of 262 Super Sixties were built, of which some 200 remain in service worldwide. Twelve years after the first Super 63 was delivered, Douglas (by now merged into McDonnell-Douglas) announced its intention to upgrade the Super Sixty series with new, quiet, fuel-efficient power plants and redesignate those so modified as units of a Super Seventy series. Managed by Cammacorp of Los Angeles, the first DC-8-71 appeared in 1981 and in addition to the engine change, offered an optional auxiliary power system and different environmental control system. Since the initial test flight that year, Douglas has received some 130 orders and options for conversions of existing Super Sixty aircraft. The aircraft was certified in April 1982, but relatively few are yet in service.

Selected List of U.S. Operating Airlines: Super Sixty Series – Airlift International; Air Transport International; Arrow Air; Braniff International Airways; Capitol International Airways; Conner Air Lines; CP Air; Delta Airlines; Eastern Airlines; Emery Worldwide; Evergreen International Airlines; Flying Tiger Line, The; Hawaiian Airlines; ICB International Airlines; National Airlines; Pacific East Air; Rich International Airways; Seaboard World Airlines; Southern Air Transport; Transamerican Airlines; Trans-Global Airlines; Trans-International Airlines; United Airlines; UPS; World Airways; Zantop International Airlines; *Super Seventy Series* – Arrow Air; Delta Air Lines; Emery Worldwide; Evergreen International Airlines; Flying Tiger Line, The; Orion Air; Transamerica Airlines; United Airlines; UPS ■

A United Airlines DC-8-71 about to touch down. The Free World's largest air carrier, United's fleet includes 29 of these reworked Douglas transports. Courtesy United Airlines

United's DC-8-60s, one of which is shown here, have been reengined into DC-8-71s. Courtesy United Airlines via James P. Woolsey

The first Allegheny Commuter partner, Hagerstown-based Henson Airlines, launched Beech 99 service on July 1, 1968. Today a Piedmont affiliate, the carrier's fleet includes seven of the popular 99s. Courtesy Henson Airlines via Tom Valentine.

■ BEECHCRAFT B99 Airliner/ C99 Commuter-liner

First Service: 1968

Type/Purpose: Twin-engined, light, commuter/regional transport

Number of Seats: 2 crew, 9-15 passengers

Dimensions: Length: 44.7 feet
 Height: 14.4 feet
 Wingspan: 45.1 feet
 Gross weight (pounds): 10,900

Engines: 2 Pratt & Whitney of Canada PT6-A28 turboprops (B99)/
 2 Pratt & Whitney of Canada PT6-A34 turboprops (C99)

Performance: Maximum range: 1,173 miles
 Service ceiling: 26,300 feet
 Maximum speed: 308 mph
 Maximum cruising speed: 285 mph

Initial Test Flight: December 1965 (B99)/ June 20, 1980 (C99)

Initial U.S. Operator Service: Commuter Airlines, Inc., May 2, 1968 (B99)/ Pilgrim Airlines, 1982 (C99)

Remarks: One of the most popular of commuter airlines, the unpressurized Beech Model 99 was a more powerful and stretched version of the B80 Queen Airliner. Able to accommodate up to 15 passengers, the 99 entered service in 1968 and a total of 164 were built and delivered to 64 carriers before production ended in 1978. In May 1979, Beech announced its intention to reenter the commuter market with an updated model, the Commuter C99. A prototype was developed from a B99 and incorporated more powerful turboprop engines, slight system changes, and certain standard equipment formerly optional. Deliveries of the $1.869 million aircraft began on July 30, 1982, and 64 had been placed by late fall 1985.

Selected List of U.S. Operating Airlines: (1984-1985): Air Kentucky Airlines; Air New Orleans; Air Pac Airlines; Airways of New Mexico; Bar Harbor Airlines; Britt Airways; Business Express; Cascade Airways; Catskill Airways; Centennial Airlines; Chaparral Airlines; Chautauqua Airlines; Christman Air System; Colgan Airways; Desert Sun Airlines; East Hampton Aire; Great Lakes Aviation; Henson Airlines; Mall Airways; Mesa Air Shuttle; Mesaba Airlines; Mountain Air; Northern Airways; Panorama Air Tour; Pilgrim Airlines; Precision Airlines; Rio Airways; Royale Airlines; Ryan Air Service; Skyway Commuter; Sunbird Airlines; Sun West Airlines; Susquehanna Airlines; Wheeler Airlines; Wings West Airlines ■

■ BOEING 737 Series 100 to 200

First Service: 1968

Type/Purpose: Twin-engined, commercial, turbofan, short-haul transport

Number of Seats: 2 crew, 103 passengers (100)/ 2 crew, 115 passengers (200)

Dimensions: Length: 94 feet (100)/ 100.2 feet (200)
Height: 37 feet (100/200)
Wingspan: 93 feet
Gross weight (pounds): 111,000 (100)/ 116,000 (200)

Engines: 2 Pratt & Whitney JT8D-7 or 9 turbofans (100)/ 2 Pratt & Whitney JT8D-17A turbofans (200)

Performance: Maximum range: 2,913 miles
Service ceiling: 33,000 feet
Maximum speed: 586 mph
Maximum cruising speed: 532 mph

Initial Test Flight: April 9, 1967

Initial U.S. Operator Service: United Airlines, April 29, 1968 (200)

Remarks: To complete a "family" of transport, Boeing announced in 1965 its intention to build a short-haul jetliner, Model 737. This aircraft would abandon the three rear-mounted engines of the 727 in favor of two power plants in underwing pods. Of similar configuration to the 707, the 737 employed a 727 fuselage and tail unit, as well as other systems amounting to 60 percent commonality between the two planes. The ventral air stair of the 727 was not retained and air stairs and doors were provided at the forward and rear ends of the cabin, port side. Only 29 737-100s were built; only a few are now in U.S. service. The next step, taken immediately on the heels of the original announcement, was the development of a higher-capacity model, the 737-200, which was stretched 6.4 feet in the fuselage over its predecessor. In May 1971, the aircraft was made more powerful once again and offered in two new configurations, the passenger/cargo-convertible 200C and the "quick-change" 200QC, both following similar improvements first offered with the Boeing 727, and both equipped to operate from short (4,000-foot) runways. By 1980, more than 760 Model 737s had been ordered by 90 airlines and those in service to that date had transported over 600 million passengers.

Selected List of U.S. Operating Airlines: (1984-1985): *737-100* – Air Cal; People Express Airlines; United Airlines; *737-200/200C/200QC* – Air Berlin U.S.A.; Air Cal; Alaska Airlines; Aloha Airlines; America West Airlines; Challenge International Airlines; Delta Air Lines; Frontier Airlines; MarkAir; Midway Express; Pacific Express; Pan American World Airways; People Express Airlines; Piedmont Airlines; Southwest Airlines; United Airlines; Western Airlines; Wien Air Alaska ■

Although better known for its long-haul aircraft, Pan Am operates a dozen 737-200s on its shorter routes. Shown here is the *Clipper Schöneberg.* Courtesy Pan American World Airways

Piedmont Airlines chose the Boeing 737-200 as its standard jetliner during the early 1970s and today its fleet includes 63. Courtesy Piedmont Airlines

A 737-200 of Hawaii's Aloha Airlines, which inaugurated Boeing service in March 1969 and currently operates a fleet of eight, with six others leased out to other carriers. Courtesy Aloha Airlines

Colorful 737-200 of Alaska Airlines, which operates six of these Boeings on routes in the Pacific Northwest and the 49th state. Courtesy Alaska Airlines

Colorful Boeing 737-200 of Frontier Airlines. Several of these aircraft were sold before the carrier was acquired by People Express Airlines in late 1985, and sold to United in spring 1986. Courtesy Frontier Airlines

■ BRITTEN-NORMAN (Pilatus) BN-2 Islander

First Service: 1968

Type/Purpose: Twin-engined, commuter/regional transport

Number of Seats: 1 pilot, 9 passengers

Dimensions: Length: 35.7 feet
Height: 13.8 feet
Wingspan: 49 feet
Gross weight (pounds): 6,300

Engines: 2 Avco Lycoming 0-540-E4C5 pistons or 2 Avco Lycoming IO-540-K1B5 pistons or 2 Avco Lycoming TIO-540-K pistons (BN-2)/
2 Avco Lycoming LTP101 turboprops (BN-2-40 Turbo-Islander)

Performance: Maximum range: 783-870 miles
Service ceiling: 13,000 feet
Maximum speed: 170-230 mph
Maximum cruising speed: 160-220 mph

Initial Test Flight: June 13, 1965 (BN-2)/ April 6, 1977 (BN-2-40 Turbo-Islander)

Initial U.S. Operator Service: La Posada, January 1968

Remarks: Originally designed to meet the requirements of the company's partially owned Cameroon Air Transport, the BN-2 is a high-wing monoplane, which provides economical transport, good takeoff performance, and minimal maintenance demands. Following modification and installation of various power plants, Britten-Norman announced development of the Turbo-Islander in late 1975. Made more powerful and with a strengthened undercarriage and an optional nose stretch of 3.9 feet, the BN-2-40 entered service in early 1978. By 1983, well over 1,000 Islanders/Turbo-Islanders had been sold worldwide making it one of Great Britain's most successful multi-engined airliners. A number of small regionals in the United States operate the aircraft for which the Jonas Aircraft and Arms Co. (New York City) serves as American distributor.

Selected List of U.S. Operating Airlines: (1984–1985): Air Logistics; AmericAir; Arctic Circle Air; Carolina Air Parcel Service; Air South; Flamenco Airways; Florida Airmotive; L.A.B. Flying Service; Manu'a Air Transport; Munz Northern Airlines; New England Airlines; Peninsula Airways; Royal Hawaiian Air Service; Ryan Air Service; San Juan Airlines; Silver Kris Services; Slocum Air; South Central Air; South Pacific Island Airways; Talarik Creek Air Taxi; Tyee Airlines; Vieques Air Link; Wings Airways; Yute Air Alaska ■

This Harbor Airlines BN-2 Islander was photographed at Seattle on March 15, 1977. Courtesy James P. Woolsey

■ BEECHCRAFT Model 58 Baron

First Service: 1969

Type/Purpose: Twin-engined, commercial, executive/commuter/air-taxi transport

Number of Seats: 1 pilot, 4–5 passengers

Dimensions: Length: 29.1 feet
Height: 9.6 feet
Wingspan: 37.1 feet
Gross weight (pounds): 5,700

Engines: 2 Continental IO-520-C pistons (58)/
2 Continental TSIO-520-L (58P/58TC)

Performance: Maximum range: 1,300 miles
Service ceiling: 17,800 feet
Maximum speed: 242 mph
Maximum cruising speed: 231-251 mph

Initial Test Flight: February 29, 1960

Remarks: Introduced in November 1960 to succeed the lower-powered Model 95 Travel Air, the Baron, equipped with swept fin and rudder, was originally a 4-5 seater known as the 95-55. The Model 58, available after fall 1969, was made more powerful and had a lengthened fuselage the cabin of which was equipped to seat six. The Baron series was later extended to include the pressurized 58P and the unpressurized 58TC with a turbo-supercharge power plant. Over 4,400 Barons of all types have been built, with the majority as business aircraft.

Selected List of U.S. Operating Airlines: (1984-1985): Arkansas Traveler Airline; Astro Airways; Catskill Airways; Corporate Air; East Coast Airways; Flight Line; Great Lakes Aviation ■

This Beech Baron of the small Texas carrier Hood Airlines was photographed at Dallas (Love Field) in September 1970, just prior to the company's acquisition by Rio Airways. Courtesy Robert E. Garrard

■ FOKKER F-28 Fellowship

First Service: 1969

Type/Purpose: Twin-engined, commercial, turbofan, short-haul transport

Number of Seats: 2 crew, 85 passengers

Dimensions: Length: 97.2 feet
Height: 27.9 feet
Wingspan: 82.3 feet
Gross weight (pounds): 72,995

Engines: 2 Rolls-Royce RB.183-2 Spey Mk. 555-15H turbofans

Performance: Maximum range: 1,969 miles
Service ceiling: 35,000 feet
Maximum speed: 524 mph
Maximum cruising speed: 421 mph

Initial Test Flight: May 9, 1967

Initial U.S. Operator Service: Piedmont Airlines, 1969

Remarks: Designed as a short-haul, larger-capacity, turbofan complement to the F-27, the F-28 Fellowship entered production in 1964. Recognized by its T-tail and jet engines pod-mounted on the rear fuselage, the airliner is a low-wing monoplane with a circular-section, pressurized fuselage and retractable, tricycle landing gear. Plans to co-manufacture the F-28 with Fairchild in the U.S. were dropped in 1968. The Fellowship has appeared in several models, each offering a slightly different cargo or passenger configuration. The earlier Dash-100/200 were respective equivalents of the current production variants, the 3000/4000, which have been stretched and can accommodate up to 65 and 85 passengers respectively. Although a Model 5000 was not built, the 6000 features a lengthened fuselage with a wingspan increased 4 feet. Approximately 230 F-28s have been delivered; however, manufacture of the $12 million jetliner will cease once production of the F-100 begins.

Selected List of U.S. Operating Airlines: (1984-1985): Empire Airlines; Horizon Air; Mid-Pacific Airlines; Piedmont Airlines; Pilgrim Airlines ■

Top Left: Piedmont Airlines currently flies 20 Fokker F-28-1000s, and 2 F-28-4000s, has 6 Dash-4000s on order, and is in the process of assimilating the 15 Fellowships acquired as a result of the recent Empire Airlines takeover. Courtesy Fokker Aircraft U.S.A.

Top Right: Presently being absorbed by Business Express, Pilgrim Airlines took delivery of its Fokker F-28 MK 3000 Fellowship in early 1984 for service on the carrier's New York-Ottawa route. Courtesy Fokker Aircraft U.S.A.

Bottom: Beginning Hawaiian service in 1981, mid-Pacific Airlines currently operates this F-28 Fellowship as part of its mainly Nikon YS-11 fleet. Courtesy Fokker Aircraft U.S.A.

■ BOEING 747 Series 100 to 300

First Service: 1970

Type/Purpose: Four-engined, wide-bodied, commercial, turbofan, long-haul transport

Number of Seats: 14 crew, 452 passengers (100/200)/
14 crew, 496 passengers (300B)/
14 crew, 550 passengers (SR)

Dimensions: Length: 231.9 feet
Height: 63.2 feet (100)/ 63.5 feet (200/300)
Wingspan: 195.7 feet
Gross weight (pounds): 564,000 (100-300)/
525,000 (SR)

Engines: 4 Pratt & Whitney JT9D-7 or -7A turbofans

Performance: Maximum range: 5,988 miles
Service ceiling: 45,000 feet
Maximum speed: 640 mph
Maximum cruising speed: 602 mph

Initial Test Flight: February 9, 1969

Initial U.S. Operator Service: Pan American World Airways, January 22, 1970

Remarks: On April 13, 1966, Boeing announced that it would soon begin production of a new, long-range civil transport, the Model 747, and that Pan Am had concluded a $525 million contract for 25 of history's premier wide-body jetliner. Within a year, Boeing would receive $1.8 billion in 747 orders, one of the largest backlog of production requests in aviation history. Built in its own special plant, the aircraft quickly became known as the "Jumbojet" and was destined to become the giant of commercial aviation. Designed to carry more people than any other airliner ever, this monster is essentially an up-scaled Boeing 707, which can transport some 15 tons of cargo per flight, in addition to crew, baggage, and passengers. Everything about this transport is huge, including its massive 18-wheel undercarriage, which was developed to cushion landing and evenly distribute the plane's 390-ton weight on runways, a number of which had to be extended worldwide to accommodate the aircraft. Additionally, the 747 features 11 lavatories, six galleys, five movie screens, and three classes of service: first, business, and coach/economy/tourist. The most prestigious airliner in current service, the standard 747 was initially offered as a Dash-100, but since has become available in several other configurations: 100B

1970s

with strengthened structure; the SR (short-range) version of the 100B; 200B, which operates at higher weights; the 200B Combi, for all-passenger or passenger/cargo operations; the 200C convertible, for all-passenger, all-cargo, or combinations of both; the 200F freighter; the EUD (Extended Upper Deck) now called the 300, with the upper forward fuselage stretched 23.4 feet aft; and Model 400, currently under development for introduction late in this decade. Just under 400 standard 747s had been constructed by the early 1980s and these had logged over 8 million hours of flight time and had transported more than 300 million passengers. Freight, too, had been flown, including the most famous cargo of all, NASA's Space Shuttle Orbiter, carried atop a specially modified 747-100. Although widely employed by major U.S. carriers early in its history, the Jumbojet is presently flown by more foreign flag lines than by American operators.

Selected List of U.S. Operating Airlines: (1984-1985): *747-100* – The Flying Tiger Line; Northwest Orient Airlines; Pan American World Airways; Tower Air; Trans-World Airlines; United Airlines; *747-200* – The Flying Tiger Line; Northwest Orient Airlines; Pan American World Airways; People Express Airlines; Regent Air; Trans-America Airlines; Trans-World Airlines; World Airways ■

Three TWA Boeing 747s prepare to receive passengers. The carrier currently operates nearly 20 Jumbojets. Courtesy Trans World Airlines

Frontal view of Trans World Airlines Boeing 747 showing massive under-carriage. Courtesy Trans World Airlines

A Pan Am Boeing 747 demonstrates wing action, the retraction of its huge undercarriage, and a distinctive livery during a takeoff photographed in early 1985. Courtesy Pan American World Airways

A United Airlines 747-100 taxis at Honolulu International Airport. United began service with this Boeing in July 1970 and currently operates a fleet of fifteen. Courtesy United Airlines

Continental Airlines began transcontinental 747 service on July 1, 1970, but no longer operates the Boeing Jumbojet. Courtesy Continental Airlines

■ BRITTEN-NORMAN (Pilatus) BN-2A Trislander/Tri-Commutair

First Service: 1971

Type/Purpose: Trimotor, light, commuter/regional transport

Number of Seats: 1-2 crew, 16-17 passengers

Dimensions: Length: 47.6 feet
Height: 14.2 feet
Wingspan: 53 feet
Gross weight (pounds): 10,000

Engines: 3 Avco Lycoming 0-540-B4C5 pistons

Performance: Maximum range: 1,000 miles
Service ceiling: 13,150 feet
Maximum speed: 180 mph
Maximum cruising speed: 166 mph

Initial Test Flight: September 11, 1970

Remarks: The problem of stretching the BN-2 Islander so as to combine its well-demonstrated performance with increased payload was nearly solved through the addition of a third engine uniquely mounted on the tail and by lengthening the fuselage by 7.6 feet. A total of 73 Trislanders were built in the U.K.; however, the aircraft was never widely employed by U.S. operators. When production of the Trislander ended in 1982, its manufacturing license and marketing rights were obtained by the Homestead (Florida)-based International Aviation Corporation, which sold the aircraft as the Tri-Commutair.

Selected List of U.S. Operating Airlines: (1984-1985): Air South; Coral Air; Slocum Air; Vieques Air Link; Wings Airways ■

Air South's BN-2A Trislander over the ocean off Homestead, Florida. Founded in 1981 as Bahamas Caribbean Airlines and known as Aero International Airlines between 1982 and late 1984, this carrier operates scheduled and charter service in Florida and to the Bahamas. Courtesy Air South

A BN-2A Trislander lifts off. Air Pacific is the flag carrier of Fiji. Courtesy James P. Woolsey

■ McDONNELL-DOUGLAS DC-10 Series 10 to 40

First Service: 1971

Type/Purpose: Three-engined, commerical, turbofan, long/ medium-haul transport

Number of Seats: 3 crew, 250-380 passengers

Dimensions: Length: 182.3 feet (10)/ 180.6 feet (15/40)/ 181.6 feet (30)
Height: 58.1 feet
Wingspan: 155.3 feet (10/15)/ 165.3 feet (30/40)
Gross weight (pounds): 440,000 (10)/ 455,000 (15)/ 572,000 (30/40)

Engines: 3 GE CF6-6D turbofans (10)/
3 GE CF6-50C2F turbofans (15)/
3 GE CF6-50C2 turbofans (30)/
3 Pratt & Whitney JT9D-59A turbofans (40)

Performance: Maximum range: 4,123-6,357 miles
Service ceiling: 33,400 feet
Maximum speed: 600+ mph
Maximum cruising speed: 564 mph

Initial Test Flight: August 29, 1970 (10)/
January 1981 (15)/
June 21, 1972 (30)/
February 28, 1972 (40)

Initial U.S. Operator Service: American Airlines, August 5, 1971 (10)

Remarks: Douglas undertook development of the widebody DC-10 in March 1966 to meet a domestic requirement of American Airlines; the aircraft has since become the major (and dominant) participant in a rivalry with the Lockheed L-1011 TriStar. The three-engined jetliner incorporated advances in environmental compatibility, flight-control systems, structure, propulsion, aerodynamics, and avionics. Firm orders from both American and United Airlines were delivered in spring 1968 and production moved steadily ahead with the first Model 10 delivered to those carriers on the same day, July 29, 1971. The next step was development of an intercontinental range variant, the 30; this aircraft was stretched 10 feet in its wingspan, carried additional fuel tanks and an extra main-wheel unit on the fuselage centerline, and was made more powerful. The intercontinental-range Model 40 (which was to have been variant 20) and the longer-range Model 30ER differ from the Model 30 in terms of power plant. Both the Model 10 and Model 30 are also available in passenger/cargo-convertible versions and a freighter version (30F) is under development. A Model 15, with more powerful engines and a higher gross weight, was developed in the early 1980s. The DC-10's engines include a prominently mounted, high tail location for one, which forms the plane's most important visual feature and, with its somewhat blunter nose (in profile), distinguishes it from the Lockheed TriStar. Its reputation apparently unaffected by a series of crashes (the worst in Chicago in 1979), the DC-10 is widely employed by U.S. and foreign carriers; nearly 400 have been constructed in the past fifteen years.

Selected List of U.S. Operating Airlines: (1984-1985): *DC-10-10* – American Airlines; Arrow Air; Continental Airlines; Federal Express; United Airlines; Western Airlines; World Airways; *DC-10-30* – American Airlines; Continental Airlines; Eastern Airlines; Federal Express; United Airlines; World Airways; *DC-10-40* – American Trans Air; Jet Charter Service; Northwest Orient Airlines ■

The sun shines off an American Airlines DC-10-10. American was the launch customer for this McDonnell-Douglas widebody and currently operates a fleet of 45 Dash-10s and 7 Dash-30s. Courtesy American Airlines

United, the second DC-10 operator, also inaugurated transcontinental widebody service with the McDonnell-Douglas transport in 1971. It presently flies 44 Dash-10s and 6 Dash-30s. Courtesy United Airlines

A Northwest Orient Airlines DC-10-40 en route to the Orient. The carrier flies 19 of these long-range models on its transpacific routes and incidentally, the dark tail unit is actually bright red. Courtesy Northwest Orient Airlines

Continental Airlines McDonnell-Douglas DC-10-30. The Houston-based carrier flew nine Dash-10s and four Dash-30s in 1985. Courtesy Continental Airlines

Eastern's most notable new route of 1985 was Miami-London, for which the carrier purchased three DC-10-30s, one of which is shown here. Courtesy Eastern Airlines

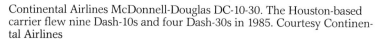

■ PIPER PA-34 Seneca Series I to III

First Service: 1971

Type/Purpose: Twin-engined, light, executive/regional/air-taxi transport

Number of Seats: 1 pilot, 5 passengers

Dimensions: Length: 28.6-27.7 feet
Height: 9.9-9.1 feet
Wingspan: 38.9-38.1 feet
Gross weight (pounds): 4,570-4,750

Engines: 2 Avco Lycoming IO-540-K pistons (Seneca I)/
2 Continental TSIO-360-E pistons (Seneca II)/
2 Continental TSIO-360-KB-440 pistons (Seneca III)

Performance: Maximum range: 700-904 miles
Service ceiling: 25,000 feet
Maximum speed: 228-240 mph
Maximum cruising speed: 187-222 mph

Initial Test Flight: 1970

Remarks: First test flown in 1970, deliveries of the Seneca I began in 1971. The aircraft was derived from the PA-32 Cherokee Six, of which it became, in effect, a twin-engined version with a slightly longer wingspan and a new nose cone. The 1975 Seneca II switched to Continental engines, retained in a more powerful format by the Seneca III of the 1980s. The Seneca has been popular not only with the business market at which it was first aimed, but with small airlines, scheduled and unscheduled alike, plus bush and air-taxi operators.

Selected List of U.S. Operating Airlines: (1984-1985): Action Airlines; Air Logistics; Air Pac Airlines; Air South; Air Vermont; Alaska Air Services; Alliance Airlines; Alpha Aviation; Alpine Aviation; Bankair; Central Airways; Crystal Shamrock Airlines; Desert Airlines; Executive Charter; 40-Mile Air; Four Star Aviation; Harold's Air Service; Hermens Air; Kitty Hawk Airways; L.A.B. Flying Service; Pocono Airlines; Sair Aviation; State Airlines; Sunaire; Wilbur's Flight Operations ■

A side view of the KCI Aviation Piper PA-34 Seneca preparing for overhaul in the FBO's hangar at Benedum Airport, Bridgeport, W. V. in August 1986.

■ LOCKHEED L-1011 TriStar Series 1 to 200

First Service: 1972

Type/Purpose: Three-engined, commercial, turbofan, short/medium-haul transport

Number of Seats: 2 crew, 256-400 passengers

Dimensions: Length: 177.8 feet
Height: 55.4 feet
Wingspan: 155.4 feet
Gross weight (pounds): 466,000

Engines: 3 Rolls-Royce RB. 211-22B turbofans (1/100)/
3 Rolls-Royce RB.211-524 turbofans (200)

Performance: Maximum range: 4,145 miles
Service ceiling: 42,000 feet
Maximum speed: 605 mph
Maximum cruising speed: 553 mph

Initial Test Flight: November 16, 1970

Initial U.S. Operator Service: Eastern Airlines, July 1, 1972

Remarks: The first Lockheed airliner since the unhappy L-188 Electra and the company's premier turbine-powered widebody, theTri Star is a dual-aisle transport, which has proven a technical success, if not the financial triumph of its rival, the McDonnell-Douglas DC-10. Originally designed to meet the same American Airlines requirement as gave birth to its competitor, the project would prove an exciting and costly challenge for a manufacturer which had not, of late, been building commercial aircraft. Lockheed announced production of the TriStar in March 1968, after a decision had been taken to allow the British firm of Rolls-Royce to supply the power plant. Work continued into late 1970, when both companies ran into severe financial problems, eventually controlled through the economic backing of their respective governments. Following the renegotiation of the contracts, production was resumed. As certified on April 14, 1972, the TriStar was a low-wing monoplane with swept-back wings of 35 degrees. Closely resembling the DC-10, the L-1011 is chiefly distinguishable from it by the merger of its third engine into the rear fuselage and a slightly sharper nose (in profile). In addition to the basic Dash-1, variants have included the extended-range Model 100 (with increased fuel tankage) and Model 200 with more powerful engines. Certified by the Federal Aviation Administration for operation in Category IIIA weather

conditions, the L-1011 can fly on automatic pilot from takeoff to landing. Indeed, in May 1972, a TriStar flown by a Lockheed crew made the first fully automatic coast-to-coast flight (without human hands on the controls) from departure to arrival. By early 1983 when production ceased, Lockheed had received orders and options for 247 L-1011s.

Selected List of U.S. Operating Airlines: (1984-1985): Delta Air Lines; Eastern Airlines; Federal Express; Five Star Air; Pan American World Airways; Total Air; Trans-World Airlines; United Airlines; World Airways ■

As launch-customer, Eastern started initial L-1011 service on April 26, 1972. Today, the carrier flies 25 Tristars. Here N305EA lifts off – note the retracting landing gear. Courtesy Eastern Airlines via James P. Woolsey

Another early Tristar customer was Trans World Airlines, which now flies 33 on its various long-haul routes. Courtesy Trans World Airlines

■ FAIRCHILD-SWEARINGEN
Metro/Metro II

First Service: 1973

Type/Purpose: Twin-engined, commuter/regional transport

Number of Seats: 2 crew, 20 passengers

Dimensions: Length: 59.4 feet
Height: 16.8 feet
Wingspan: 46.3 feet
Gross weight (pounds): 12,500

Engines: 2 Garrett-AiResearch TPE-331-3UW-303G
turboprops

Performance: Maximum range: 1,000 miles
Service ceiling: 27,500 feet
Maximum cruising speed: 279-294 mph

Initial Test Flight: August 26, 1969

Initial U.S. Operator Service: Commuter Airlines, Inc.,
1973 (Metro)

Remarks: Developed by the late Ed Swearingen as a commuter version of his successful Merlin executive transport, the SA226-TC did not enter regional service until 1973. A conventional, low-wing, pressurized monoplane, the Metro featured retractable, tricycle landing gear and wing-mounted, turboprop engines. Forced to close in 1971 due to financial difficulties, the Swearingen Aviation Corporation was taken over by Fairchild Industries and production of the Metro was resumed, being known for awhile as a Fairchild-Swearingen product, a label now gone. Only 20 aircraft were delivered between 1973 and 1975, but the market increased following introduction of the Metro II in the latter year. With detail refinements and larger cabin windows, Metro IIs were placed with over a dozen U.S. regionals before the manufacturer again refined the aircraft in 1981 and 1982.

Selected List of U.S. Operating Airlines: (1984-1985): Air Midwest; Atlantis Airlines; AVAir; Big Sky Airlines; Britt Airways; Chautauqua Airlines; DHL Airlines; Empire Airlines; Freedom Airlines; Horizon Air; Midstate Airlines; Pocono Airlines; Resort Airlines/TWA Express; Saber Aviation; Sun Aire Lines; Trans-Colorado Airlines; Wings West Airlines ■

A Fairchild-Swearingen Metro II of Wisconsin's Midstate Airlines. Founded in 1964, the carrier's 1985 fleet included an even dozen metroliners. Courtesy Midstate Airlines

Palm Springs, California-based Sun Aire Lines numbered several Fairchild Metros in its fleet. The carrier was sold to Sky West Airlines in September 1984. Courtesy James P. Woolsey

Tucson-based Cochise Airlines flew over 100,000 passengers in 1979, many in its Fairchild Metro IIs, one of which is pictured here. The carrier, in deep financial trouble, shut its doors in 1982. Courtesy James P. Woolsey;

■ SHORTS S-25 Sandringham

First Service: 1974

Type/Purpose: Four-engined, commercial, long-range flying boat

Number of Seats: 5 crew, 22 passengers

Dimensions: Length: 86.3 feet
Height: 22.1 feet
Wingspan: 112.9 feet
Gross weight (pounds): 60,000

Engines: 4 Pratt & Whitney R-1830-92D Twin Wasp radials

Performance: Maximum range: 2,450 miles
Service ceiling: 20,000 feet
Maximum speed: 238 mph
Maximum cruising speed: 221 mph

Initial Test Flight: Spring 1946

Initial U.S. Operator Service: Antilles Air Boats, 1974

Remarks: A high-wing monoplane, the Sandringham was a civil development of the World War II British flying boat, the Sunderland III. Stretched and with interior refinements, the aircraft was available in several versions, Marks 1 to 7. A total of 25 were built. Initial front-line service by the Sandringham was flown by BOAC, the Norwegian Airlines DNL. Aviacion del Litoral Fluvial Argentino, Tasman Empire Airways (now Air New Zealand), Quantas, RAI (now Air Polynesia), Barrier Reef Airways, and Trans-Oceanic Airways/Ansett Flying Boat Services. The latter operated two S-25s on the Lord Howe Island route from 1953 until 1974, when the pair were sold to Charles Blair's Antilles Air Boats. AAB became the only U.S.-registered airline to fly the Sandringham, operating them on scheduled service between the Virgin Islands and Puerto Rico until the late 1970s. ■

With its name proudly printed on the bow, one of the two Antilles Air Boats, S-25 Sandringham was photographed at St. Thomas in April 1973. Courtesy Robert E. Garrard

■ GOVERNMENT AIRCRAFT FACTORIES N2 Nomad

First Service: 1975

Type/Purpose: Twin-engined, commercial, regional/utility transport

Number of Seats: 1-2 crew, 16-17 passengers

Dimensions: Length: 43.2 feet (N22)/ 47.1 (N24)
　　Height: 18.2 feet
　　Wingspan: 54.2 feet
　　Gross weight (pounds): 9,400
Engines: 2 Allison 250-B17C turboprops

Performance: Maximum range: 840 miles
　　Service ceiling: 23,300 feet
　　Maximum cruising speed: 193 mph

Initial Test Flight: July 23, 1971

Remarks: A strut-braced, high-wing monoplane (with a low-set stub wing to which the upper, wing-bracing struts are attached as well as fairings for the main units of the retractable, tricycle landing gear), the Australian GAF Nomad STOL (short-takeoff-and-landing) transport has a rectangular-section fuselage. Following basic, simple lines, the aircraft has included the initial production N-22 and the stretched N24, the latter currently retailing for $900,822. Debate raged "Down Under" during the early 1980s as to continuation of production, but no decision had been reached as of late 1985. Some 147 of the unpressurized transports have been delivered; however, they have not found much of a market in the United States.

Selected List of U.S. Operating Airlines: Princeton Airways; Southeast Airlines ■

Founded in 1960, the former Princeton, New Jersey carrier Princeton Airways employed a variety of aircraft on its routes, including this GAF Nomad photographed at Boston in May 1981. Courtesy Robert E. Garrard

This GAF Nomad of Southeastern Airlines was photographed at Atlanta in June 1982, approximately one year before the small regional was acquired by Atlantic Southeast Airlines. Courtesy Robert E. Garrard

■ BOEING 747SP

First Service: 1976

Type/Purpose: Four-engined, widebody, commercial, turbofan, long-haul transport

Number of Seats: 14 crew, 331 passengers

Dimensions: Length: 184.7 feet
Height: 65.6 feet
Wingspan: 195.7 feet
Gross weight (pounds): 465,000

Engines: 4 Pratt & Whitney JT9D-7FW turbofans

Performance: Maximum range: 6,736 miles
Service ceiling: 45,100 feet
Maximum speed: 640 mph
Maximum cruising speed: 625 mph

Initial Test Flight: 1975

Initial U.S. Operator Service: Pan American World Airways, 1976

Remarks: Boeing developed the 747SP (SP = Special Purpose) as a lighter, but longer-legged Jumbojet for use on low-density routes. First orders were received from Pan Am in September 1973. Similar to the 100B, the SP was reduced 47.1 feet in length, passengers were seated more compactly, and fuel tankage was increased. Total production by the early 1980s had reached 40, including 2 for Trans-World Airlines and 10 for Pan Am. The long-range aircraft has established several speed and distance records. On May 1-3, 1976, a Pan Am 747SP flew a new round-the-world speed record of 502.8 miles per hour. This followed on the heels of a March 23-24 nonstop distance achievement in which an SP flew 10,290 nonstop miles between the Boeing plant at Seattle and Cape Town, South Africa. In late 1985, Pan Am sold its Pacific Division to United Airlines together with its 11 747SPs, which, repainted in the colors of the Chicago-based colossus, reentered the trans-Pacific arena on February 11, 1986.

Selected List of U.S. Operating Airlines: Pan American World Airways; Trans-World Airlines; United Airlines ■

The Pan Am Boeing 747SP *Clipper Constellation.* On May 1-3, 1976, a sister clipper established a new round-the-world speed record of 502.8 mph. Courtesy Pan American World Airways

One of two Boeing 747SPs in the 1985 fleet of Trans World Airlines. Courtesy Trans World Airlines

■ CESSNA 404 Titan

First Service: 1976

Type/Purpose: Twin-engined, commercial, commuter/ regional transport and executive aircraft

Number of Seats: 1-2 crew, 8-9 passengers

Dimensions: Length: 39.6 feet
 Height: 13.3 feet
 Wingspan: 46.4 feet
 Gross weight (pounds): 8,400

Engines: 2 Continental GTSIO-520-M pistons

Performance: Maximum range: 2,119 miles
 Service ceiling: 26,000 feet
 Maximum cruising speed: 250 mph

Initial Test Flight: February 26, 1975

Remarks: With its model number dropped early on, the Cessna Titan was a stretched version of the model 402, which it closely resembles, with a slightly longer fuselage and wingspan. When deliveries began in 1976, the aircraft was originally marketed in three variants: Ambassador (passenger); Courier (passenger/cargo convertible); and Freighter. Nearly 380 aircraft were in service by 1982, when production ceased. In 1985, Titan Aviation, Ltd./Omni-Titan Corporation began marketing Titans converted to operate with Pratt & Whitney of Canada PT6A-34 turboprops and stretched to accommodate two crew up front and 12 passengers.

Selected List of U.S. Operating Airlines: (1984-1985): AAA Airlines; Air Logistics; Air Pac Airlines; Bas Airlines; Emery Worldwide; General Aviation; Imperial Airlines; Jimsair; Mississippi Valley Airlines; Mountain Air Cargo; Pompano Airways; Pro Air Services; Scenic Airlines; Silver Kris Services; Sunbird Airlines; Trans-North Airlines; Viking Express ■

Shown in flight over Kansas, the Cessna 404 Titan joined that builder's range of aircraft in 1976. With a large cabin and excellent short field capability, the plane was aimed at the commuter/air cargo market. Courtesy Cessna Aircraft Company

Although now retired from its fleet, Las Vegas-based Scenic Airlines long flew Cessna 404 Titans on sightseeing tours over the Grand Canyon. Founded in 1967, the carrier also provides scheduled service to points in both Nevada and Arizona. Courtesy Scenic Airlines

■ SHORTS 330

First Service: 1976

Type/Purpose: Twin-engined, commuter/regional transport

Number of Seats: 2 crew, 30 passengers

Dimensions: Length: 58 feet
    Height: 16.3 feet
    Wingspan: 74.8 feet
    Gross weight (pounds): 22,900

Engines: 2 Pratt & Whitney of Canada PT6A-45R
    turboprops

Performance: Maximum range: 872 miles
    Service ceiling: 18,000 feet
    Maximum cruising speed: 219 mph

Initial Test Flight: August 22, 1974

Initial U.S. Operator Service: Golden West Airlines,
    June 1976

Remarks: At first known as the SD3-30, the Shorts 330 was based on the SC-7 Skyvan/Skyliner, 19 passenger and cargo utility liner. The $3.6 million, unpressurized aircraft retains many of the features of its predecessor, including a high-wing-monoplane configuration and a practical, if graceless, wide and unobstructed cabin, lengthened by 12.5 feet. Additionally, the 330 was given improved lines and a retractable, tricycle landing gear. Manufactured in Belfast, Northern Ireland, the 330 is available in an improved passenger model (200), freighter, and passenger/cargo-convertible variants. Something over 120 are in airline service worldwide.

Selected List of U.S. Operating Airlines: (1984-1985): Brockway Air; Chautauqua Airlines; Comair; Command Airways; Crown Airways; Fischer Brothers Aviation; Hawaiian Airlines; Henson Aviation; Mississippi Valley Airlines (now part of Air Wisconsin); Pennsylvania Commuter Airlines; Suburban Airlines; Sunbird Airlines; Westair ■

Based at Wappingers Falls, New York, Command Airways operates nine Shorts 330s on its routes in New Hampshire, Massachusetts, and New York. Courtesy Short Brothers Limited

ComAir currently operates three of the Irish-built Shorts 330s from its base at Cincinnati. Courtesy ComAir

Recently taken over by USAir, Pennsylvania Airlines still flies 5 Shorts 330s. Courtesy USAir

■ AIRBUS INDUSTRIE A-300 Airbus

First Service: 1978

Type/Purpose: Twin-engined, short/medium-haul turbofan transport

Number of Seats: 8-10 crew, 220-375 passengers

Dimensions: Length: 175.9 feet (A300-B2/B4/C4)/
    177.4 feet (A300-B4-600/600C)
    Height: 54.2 feet
    Wingspan: 147.1 feet
    Gross weight (pounds): 302,030 (A300-B2)/
    363,760 (A300-B4/B4-600/600C)/ 347,200 (A300-C4)

Engines: 2 GE CF6-50C or 2 Pratt & Whitney JT9D-59A
    turbofans (A300-B2/B4/C4)/
    2 GE CF6-80C2 or 2 Pratt & Whitney JT9D-7R4H1 or
    2 Rolls-Royce RB.211-524-D4 turbofans
    (A300-B4-600/600C)

Performance: Maximum range: 2,649 miles
    Service ceiling: 35,020 feet
    Maximum cruising speed: 566 mph

Initial Test Flight: October 28, 1972 (A300-B1)/
    June 28, 1973 (A300-B2)

Initial U.S. Operator Service: Trial service by Eastern Airlines (6 months, 1977-1978); four A300-B4-200s were purchased by Eastern on April 6, 1978, and placed in service.

Remarks: At about the same time as the Boeing 747 widebody was being finished in America, studies were undertaken in Great Britain for the design of an airliner for short-haul operations on European routes. In late 1965, major European airlines met to consider their needs and determined that not only was a new short-range transport required, but one with high-capacity, low-operating cost, and fuel efficiency was demanded. Continuing discussions led the major Western European airframe and component manufacturers with government backing to join forces in December 1970 under the banner of Airbus Industrie. With U.S.-made engines, the Europeans would create their own wide-bodied, short-haul airliners, which were given the then-generic name of Airbus. The successful gamble to build an aircraft easy to fly, operate, and maintain and which could carry hundreds of passengers was confirmed after Eastern Airlines in 1978 purchased its 4 test aircraft. The American major, which gave the Euro-

peans entry into the previously impenetrable American market, then ordered 34 more aircraft. Eastern remained the only American owner-operator of the A300 until 1985 when Pan American World Airways leased 4 A300-B4-200s (pending delivery in 1986 of an order for 12 A310-300s) and Continental Airlines announced it would acquire 6 A300-B4s.

Selected List of U.S. Operating Airlines: Eastern Airlines; Pan American World Airways. ■

Pan Am's A300B4 *Clipper America*. Courtesy Pan American World Airways

Eastern Airlines A300 Airbus departs Washington National Airport. Courtesy Eastern Airlines

■ DEHAVILLAND-CANADA DHC-7 (Dash 7)

First Service: 1978

Type/Purpose: Four-engined, commercial, STOL, medium/short-haul transport

Number of Seats: 2 crew, 50 passengers

Dimensions: Length: 80.5 feet
Height: 26.2 feet
Wingspan: 93 feet
Gross weight (pounds): 44,000

Engines: 4 Pratt & Whitney of Canada PT6A-50 turboprops

Performance: Maximum range: 795 miles
Service ceiling: 21,000 feet
Maximum cruising speed: 266 mph

Initial Test Flight: March 27, 1975

Initial U.S. Operator Service: Rocky Mountain Airways, February 3, 1978

Remarks: Backed by the Canadian government, DHC in 1972 began development of a small airliner that could offer the amenities of larger aircraft while still exhibiting STOL (short-takeoff-and-landing) capabilities that would allow takeoff from runways of only 3,000 feet. Designated DHC-7/Dash-7, the plane is a cantilevered, high-wing monoplane with a circular-section, pressurized fuselage and retractable, tricycle landing gear, and is easily recognizable by its tall "T" tail. The aircraft is available in all-passenger, all-cargo, or mixed cargo/passenger configuration. Travellers board the DASH-7 via a single air-stair door at the rear of the cabin, port side; for cargo operations, a large freight door can be fitted at the forward end of the cabin, port side. The DHC-7, which sells for $7.5 million, has proved extremely popular with 105 deliveries by late fall 1985. Company officials have recently elected to turn some of their research toward changing the engine of the aircraft.

Selected List of U.S. Operating Airlines: (1984-1985): AirPac; Airwest Airlines; Air Wisconsin; Alaska Airlines; Atlantic Southeast Airlines; ERA Helicopters; Golden West Airlines; Hawaiian Airlines; Henson Aviation; Jet Alaska; Ransome Airlines; Rio Airways; Rocky Mountain Airways; Southern Jersey Airways ■

Scheduled to be acquired by Pan Am in 1986 and previously a Delta Connection carrier, Ransome Airlines was a longtime Allegheny Commuter associate. Today it flies eight Dash-7s, one of which is shown here in an earlier livery. Courtesy DeHavilland Canada

Four parked Dash-7s of Rio Airways. Founded in 1967, the Killeen-based carrier currently operates these STOL airliners to eight points in Texas and Arkansas. Courtesy DeHavilland Canada.

■ BRITISH AEROSPACE (HS) 748
Series 2B Intercity

First Service: 1979

Type/Purpose: Twin-engined, commuter/regional transport

Number of Seats: 2 crew, 48 passengers

Dimensions: Length: 67 feet
   Height: 24.1 feet
   Wingspan: 98.6 feet
   Gross weight (pounds): 46,500

Engines: 2 Rolls-Royce Dart RDa.7 Mk.536-2 turboprops

Performance: Maximum range: 1,635 miles
   Service ceiling: 25,000 feet
   Maximum cruising speed: 281 mph

Initial Test Flight: August 31, 1961

Initial U.S. Operator Service: Air Illinois, 1979

Remarks: Originally designed as a 20-seat DC-3 replacement in 1958, the Type 748 was gradually scaled upward in capacity through Series 1 and into Series 2. A low-wing monoplane with its two engines mounted high on the wing leading edge, this British airliner was certified on January 9, 1962. Made more powerful, the Series 2B, introduced by BAe in 1979 and marketed in America as the Intercity, featured a slight increase in wingspan, better "hot-and-high" performance, and other refinements aimed at better economics for U.S. commuter operators. Some 380 of the pressurized, $6 million aircraft have been sold worldwide; however, many of those purchased by American regional airlines are now being phased out of service in favor of more recent equipment.

Selected List of U.S. Operating Airlines: (1984-1985): Air Illinois; AVAir; Cascade Airways; Midwest Airlines ■

Air Virginia's Intercity 748 sits on the ramp at Aero Spacelines' Santa Barbara, California, facility prior to its delivery on September 18, 1981. Courtesy James P. Woolsey

Cascade Airways BAe(HS)748. The Spokane-based regional currently operates two of these British turboprops. Courtesy Cascade Airways

■ CASA C-212 Series 200 to 300 Aviocar

First Service: 1979

Type/Purpose: Twin-engined, STOL, commuter/regional transport

Number of Seats: 2-3 crew, 28 passengers

Dimensions: Length: 49.9 feet (200)/ 53.2 feet (300)
Height: 20.8 feet
Wingspan: 62.3 feet (200)/ 66.11 feet (300)
Gross weight (pounds): 16,975

Engines: 2 Garrett AiResearch TPE 311-10-501C turboprops (200)/
2 Garrett AiResearch TPE 331-1OR turboprops (300)

Performance: Maximum range: 1,094 miles
Service ceiling: 28,400 feet
Maximum cruising speed: 227 mph

Initial Test Flight: March 26, 1971

Remarks: Originally designed by the Spanish firm Construcciones Aeronauticas S/A (CASA) to a Spanish military requirement, an unpressurized, passenger version of this STOL (short-takeoff-and-landing) transport was simultaneously developed. Civil models have included the 10-passenger configuration (211-5), the 28-passenger variant (200), and the latest, a "dash" 300, differentiated mainly by some airframe stretch and more powerful engines. The $2.45 million aircraft has sold well for CASA with 349 delivered worldwide, with 37 more on order as of late fall 1985.

Selected List of U.S. Operating Airlines: Air Guam; Bader Express; Chaparral Airlines; Fischer Brothers Aviation; Gull Air; National Air; PRINAIR; Transair ■

A CASA C-212 of the Allegheny Commuter associate Fischer Bros. Aviation of Galion, Ohio. One of the nation's oldest commuters, this carrier began operations in 1948 and affiliated with Allegheny in 1969. Currently, it provides scheduled service to cities in Ohio, Michigan, and Pennsylvania with a fleet that includes three CASAs. Courtesy USAir

A Chaparral Airlines CASA C-212 photographed at the carrier's Abilene (Texas) base. Formed in 1975, the company currently operates three Aviocars to points in Texas and Louisiana. Courtesy James P. Woolsey

◼ EMBRAER EMB-110 Bandeirante P/P2

First Service: 1979

Type/Purpose: Twin-engined, commuter/regional transport

Number of Seats: 2 crew, 19-21 passengers

Dimensions: Length: 49.6 feet
   Height: 16.1 feet
   Wingspan: 50.3 feet
   Gross weight (pounds): 12,500

Engines: 2 Pratt & Whitney of Canada PT6A-34 turboprops

Performance: Maximum range: 1,244 miles
   Service ceiling: 22,500 feet
   Maximum speed: 286 mph
   Maximum cruising speed: 257 mph

Initial Test Flight: October 26, 1968

Initial U.S. Operator Service: Aeromech Airlines, 1979

Remarks: Resembling and rivaling the Beech 99, the unpressurized, Brazilian, multipurpose transport (named for the seventeenth century pioneers of western Brazil) is a cantilevered, low-wing monoplane possessed of swept-tail surfaces, a conventional fuselage, and retractable, tricycle landing gear. The airliner is available in several configurations, including the 110P 19-passenger model, the 110P2 21-passenger commuter, the passenger/cargo-convertible 110P1 version of the 110P2, and the higher-weight 110P1/41 and 110P2/41. A pressurized 110P3 21-passenger variant is under development. The $1.9 million Bandeirante was the first indigenous South American transport sold to U.S.-regional carriers, beginning with the former Clarksburg, West Virginia, commuter Aeromech Airlines. By 1985, the plane had gained wide acceptance with American airlines for its reliability and economy of operation. Production has exceeded 450 units.

Selected List of U.S. Operating Airlines: (1984-1985): AAA Airlines; Aero Coach; Air Spirit; Alaska Aeronautical Industries; American Central Airlines; Arctic Circle Air; Atlantic Southeast Airlines; Cascade Airways; ComAir; Dolphin Airlines; Harold's Air Service; Imperial Airlines; Iowa Airways; Jetstream International Airlines; NewAir; North American Airlines; Provincetown-Boston Airlines (PBA); Royale Airlines; San Juan Airlines; Simmons Airlines; Southern Express; Sunbelt Airlines; Tennessee Airways; Trans-North Air; Valdez Airlines; Wright Airlines ◼

Several other U.S. regional carriers also employ the EMB-110 Bandeirante, including Cincinnati-based ComAir, which owns a fleet of ten. Courtesy ComAir

An Aeromech Airlines Bandeirante flies high above West Virginia in 1982. Launch-customer for the EMB-110, the Clarksburg-based commuter's fleet was expanded to 10 prior to the airline's merger with Wright in late 1983. Courtesy Angelo C. Koukoulis

■ LOCKHEED L-1011 TriStar 500

First Service: 1979

Type/Purpose: Three-engined, commercial, turbofan, long-haul transport

Number of Seats: 2 crew, 222 – 330 passengers

Dimensions: Length: 164.2 feet
Height: 55.4 feet
Wingspan: 164.4 feet with winglets
Gross weight (pounds): 510,000

Engines: 3 Rolls-Royce RB. 211-524B or -B4 turbofans

Performance: Maximum range: 6,154 miles
Service ceiling: 43,000 feet
Maximum speed: 605 mph
Maximum cruising speed: 553 mph

Initial Test Flight: October 1978

Initial U.S. Operator Service: Pan American World Airways, 1979

Remarks: The first TriStar L-1011 was retained by Lockheed for developmental work and became known as the Advanced TriStar. That L-1011 was modified with such features as an all-moving tailplane, active aileron control, automatic takeoff thrust and brakes, extended wing tips, and advanced systems and avionics. Carrier interest in a long-range version of the Model 200 led to the Model 500, which began testing in fall 1978. It differs from earlier variants by having a 13.6-foot shorter fuselage, the smaller capacity of which allows for increased center-section tankage, similar to that employed by Boeing for the 747SP as well as active aileron, extended wing tips and various internal layouts. As with the earlier models, L-1011-500 production has ceased.

Selected List of U.S. Operating Airlines: (1984-1985): Delta Air Lines; Pan American World Airways; Trans-World Airlines; United Airlines ■

Pan Am was the U.S. launch customer for the L-1011-500. In late 1985, that carrier's Pacific Division was sold to United Airlines together with six of the company's nine Lockheeds. Courtesy James P. Woolsey

A Delta Air Lines Lockheed L-1011-500 Tristar in flight. The Atlanta-based carrier currently numbers six in its fleet. Courtesy Delta Airlines

■ GRUMMAN-GULFSTREAM AEROSPACE G-159 Gulfstream Series I/G-1C

First Service: 1980

Type/Purpose: Twin-engined, commuter/regional transport

Number of Seats: 2 flight crew, 10-14 passengers (I/G)/ 2 flight crew, 37 passengers (1C)

Dimensions: Length: 63.9 feet (I/G)/ 75.4 feet (1C)
Height: 23 feet
Wingspan: 78.4 feet
Gross weight (pounds): 36,000

Engines: 2 Rolls-Royce Dart Mk. 529 turboprops

Performance: Maximum range: 500 miles
Service ceiling: 30,000 feet
Maximum speed: ?
Maximum cruising speed: 345 mph

Initial Test Flight: August 14, 1958 (I/G)/ October 25, 1979 (1C)

Initial U.S. Operator Service: Air North, December 1, 1980 (1C)

Remarks: Originally designed in the late 1950s as an executive transport, the G-159 Gulfstream I is a cantilevered, low-wing monoplane with a pressurized fuselage, tricycle landing gear, and wing-mounted turboprop engines. The aircraft was certified on May 21, 1959, and when production ended in 1969, 200 had been built. When Grumman was reorganized in 1978, responsibility for the G-159 was turned over to Gulfstream American Corporation (now Gulfstream Aerospace) which, in early 1979, began to investigate stretching this "baby airliner" for the commuter market. As a result, the plane was given a lengthened fuselage (10.8 feet), lavatory, baggage compartments, two additional passenger windows per side, and seating for 37 passengers. The updated aircraft, relabeled the G-159C, was marketed beginning in 1980, but relatively few regional airlines have elected to purchase it.

Selected List of U.S. Operating Airlines: (1984-1985): Brockway Air (formerly Air North); Chaparral Airlines; Emerald Air; Excellair; Executive Air Fleet; Flight International Airlines; Jet Fleet International Airlines; Mall Airways; Orion Air; Royale Airlines; Susquehanna Airlines ■

A Gulfstream I-C of Air U.S. photographed in late summer 1983. Formed in 1974, the Denver-based carrier changed its name to Excellair in January 1984, but ceased operations that spring. Courtesy Gulfstream Aerospace Corporation.

Now part of Brockway Air, Air North was the first U.S. commuter carrier to inaugurate Gulfstream I-C service in December 1980. The initial route was Rochester, N.Y. to Washington, D.C. Courtesy Gulfstream Aerospace Corporation.

■ McDONNELL-DOUGLAS DC-9 Series 81 to 87 Super Eighty (Dash 80/MD-80)

First Service: 1980

Type/Purpose: Twin-engined, commercial, medium/short-haul, turbofan transport

Number of Seats: 2 crew, 137-172 passengers (81/82)/
2 crew, 155 passengers (83)/
2 crew, 110-130 passengers (87)

Dimensions: Length: 147.1 feet
Height: 29.8 feet
Wingspan: 107.1 feet
Gross weight (pounds): 128,000 (81/87)/ 130,000 (82)/
139,500 (83)

Engines: 2 Pratt & Whitney JT8D-209 turbofans (81)/
2 Pratt & Whitney JT8D-217A turbofans (82)/
2 Pratt & Whitney JT8D-219 turbofans (83)/
2 Pratt & Whitney JT8D-217B turbofans (87)

Performance: Maximum range: 3,990-4,350 miles
Service ceiling: 25,000-35,000 feet
Maximum speed: 576 mph
Maximum cruising speed: 550mph

Initial Test Flight: October 18, 1979 (81)/
December 17, 1984 (83)/
December 1986 (87)

Initial U.S. Operator Service: Swissair, September 12,
1980 (81)

Remarks: In the first new Douglas design since the company's merger with McDonnell in 1967, officials announced in 1978 the production of an improved DC-9-50 with greater capacity and quieter, more fuel-efficient engines. Also known as the Dash-80 and marketed as the MD-80, -81, -82, and -83 (with the -87 to come), the Super 80s are available in several configurations. The Super 81 features a 14.3-foot-fuselage stretch and increased wingspan of 14.5 feet and a 16 percent increase in gross weight owing to the addition of advanced new Pratt & Whitney engines. The Dash-82 is similar, but still more powerful, and the longer-range MD-83 is just becoming available. The short-haul Dash-87 is expected to begin deliveries in 1987. To date, orders and options for available units in the series exceed 300.

Selected List of U.S. Operating Airlines: (1984-1985): AirCal; Alaska Airlines; American Airlines; Continental Airlines; Frontier Airlines; Hawaiian Airlines; Jet America; Midway Airlines; Muse Airlines; New York Air; Ozark Airlines; Pacific Southwest Airlines (PSA); Republic Airlines; Trans-World Airlines ■

Continental Airlines currently operates nineteen MD-80s, one of which is shown in level flights over the Rocky Mountains. Courtesy Continental Airlines

American Airlines is a major MD-80 operator with 56 in its current fleet, 64 on order, and options on 80 more. Courtesy American Airlines

Established in January 1980 and recently acquired by Southwest Airlines, Muse Air changed its name to Transtar in February 1986. The carrier's current fleet includes six MD-80s. Courtesy Muse Air

■ GRUMMAN G-111 Albatross

First Service: 1981

Type/Purpose: Twin-engined, commuter/regional amphibian

Number of Seats: 2-3 crew, 28 passengers

Dimensions: Length: 61.3 feet
Height: 25.1 feet
Wingspan: 96.8 feet
Gross weight (pounds): 31,150

Engines: 2 Wright R-982-C9HE3 radials

Performance: Maximum range: 2,850 miles
Service ceiling: 21,500 feet
Maximum speed: 236 mph
Maximum cruising speed: 150 mph

Initial Test Flight: October 24, 1947

Initial U.S. Operator Service: Chalk's International Airlines, 1983

Remarks: Experience with the Grumman Goose led the U.S. military, during World War II, to seek a larger amphibian of greater range. Of similar configuration to the G-21, the aircraft, which would long be known as the HU-16, incorporated a number of refinements not known by the Goose. Among these were: a redesigned, drag-reducing structure; cantilevered tailplane; pylons beneath the wing, outboard of the engines; retractable, tricycle landing gear; increased wingspan and, later, a cambered-wing leading-edge and increased fin/rudder area. With provision for a crew of 4, 10 passengers and cargo, it was expected that, when a few HU-16s became surplus, their more powerful (if fuel hungry) engines and long range would make them attractive to civil operators. The Albatross did not, however, offer that many advantages over the smaller and more economical Goose and thus airlines did not find the G-64 a desirable purchase. As a subcontractor to the U.S. Department of the Interior, Pan American World Airways operated two G-64s (nicknamed "Clipper Ducks") for the Trust Territory Air Services (serving the U.S.-administered islands of Micronesia) between 1960 and 1968. No other large-scale civil use was seen until Resorts International redesigned a HU-16B in 1979 to fill a long-existing need for a medium-sized amphibian in the Caribbean island-hopping scene. Having begun to reacquire 57 of some 200 yet in civil/military use or available for modification (out of 464 constructed), Grumman Aerospace Corporation began remanufacture of Resorts' 28-passenger design at its St. Augustine modification center in 1980. Christened the G-111, Grumman delivered the first of 13 G-111s to the Resorts subsidiary, Chalk's International Airlines, which promptly placed the Albatross into service between southern Florida and Nassau's Paradise Island (in the Bahamas) in 1981.

Selected List of U.S. Operating Airlines: (1984-1985): Chalk's International Airline ■

One of Chalk's Grumman G-111 Albatross amphibians takes off on a Caribbean flight in 1985. Courtesy Grumman Corporation

■ BOEING 767 Series 200 to 300

First Service: 1982

Type/Purpose: Twin-engined, commercial, turbofan, medium/long-haul transport

Number of Seats: 2 crew, 211-290 passengers (200/200ER)/ 2 crew, 261-330 passengers (300)

Dimensions: Length: 159.1 feet (200/200ER)/ 180.3 feet (300)
Height: 52 feet
Wingspan: 156.2 feet
Gross weight (pounds): 300,000 (200)/ 345,000 (200ER/300)

Engines: 2 Pratt & Whitney JT9D-7R4 turbofans or 2 GE CF6-80A turbofans

Performance: Maximum range: 3,200+ miles
Service ceiling: 30,000 feet
Maximum speed: 593 mph
Maximum cruising speed: 506 mph

Initial Test Flight: September 26, 1981 (200)/ January 30, 1986 (300)

Initial U.S. Operator Service: United Airlines, September 8, 1982

Remarks: The major U.S. competitor to the European Airbus A300, the 767 was Boeing's first all-new aircraft since the 747 was unveiled in September 1968. Although smaller than the 747, the McDonnell-Douglas DC-10, or the Lockheed L-1011, the twin-aisled, wide-bodied, flying mate of the B-757 narrowbody still offers three classes of passenger service. The 767 is fuel efficient, burning its spirit up to 35 percent more efficiently than, say, a Boeing 727; its advanced wing (actually longer than that of the larger Lockheed TriStar) reduces drag, thereby reducing engine-power requirements. The new Boeing is also the first commercial jetliner built with a significant number of structural components fabricated of advanced composites, which are lighter and stronger than the traditional aluminum or fiberglass and reduce fuel consumption through weight savings. The aircraft is currently available in three variants, depending upon mission, with the 200/300 differentiated primarily by length and capacity. On February 1, 1985, a TWA 200ER (Extended Range) became the first twin-jet airliner to fly the transatlantic route in scheduled passenger service. The 767 has not yet been widely adopted by America's airlines.

Selected List of U.S. Operating Airlines: (1984-1985): American Airlines; Delta Air Lines; Trans-World Airlines; United Airlines ■

On September 8, 1982, United Airlines became the first U.S. carrier to place the Boeing 767 into service. As of early 1986, the Free World's largest air transport company owned 19. Courtesy United Airlines

A Delta Air Lines Boeing 767 shows its two large engine pods. The second largest 767 operator in 1985, Delta currently owns fifteen with orders for nine more and options on eighteen others. Courtesy Delta Air Lines

American Airlines operates 15 Boeing 767s as part of its fleet with orders for 15 more to be delivered through 1987. Courtesy American Airlines

■ FAIRCHILD-SWEARINGEN Metro III/III-A

First Service: 1982

Type/Purpose: Twin-engined, commuter/regional transport

Number of Seats: 2 flight crew, 20 passengers

Dimensions: Length: 59.4 feet
    Height: 16.8 feet
    Wingspan: 57 feet
    Gross weight (pounds): 14,500

Engines: 2 Garrett AiResearch TPE 331-11U-601G
    turboprops (Metro III)/
    2 Pratt & Whitney of Canada PT6A-45R turboprops
    (Metro III-A)

Performance: Maximum range: 1,000 miles
    Service ceiling: 27,500 feet
    Maximum speed: ?
    Maximum cruising speed: 320 mph

Initial Test Flight: 1981

Initial U.S. Operator Service: Horizon Air, 1982

Remarks: Fuel efficient and the fastest aircraft in its class, the Metro III was introduced with many improvements over its predecessor. These included: a 10-foot wingspan increase, system refinements, new main-landing-gear doors, stowing/folding seats, movable bulkheads, a large, and upward-swinging, hinged rear door, a baggage compartment in the nose, split cowlings, and an option for increasing gross take-off weight to 16,000 pounds. This increased flexibility has brought increased sales; over 70 Metro IIIs were sold in the first three quarters of 1985 leading to a favorable backlog of 57 orders by November. Although no orders were received by the end of 1985 for the III-A, Fairchild had succeeded in placing some 250 of the three variants of its clean-lined, pressurized passenger transport in service with some 44 airlines worldwide.

Selected List of U.S. Operating Airlines: (1984-1985): Air Midwest; Britt Airways; Cascade Airways; ComAir; Fairchild Air; Horizon Air; Mesaba Airlines; Midstate Airlines; Pioneer Airlines; Resort Air/TWA Express; Skyway Airlines; Trans-Colorado Airlines; Wing West Airlines ■

A rapidly expanding California commuter, founded in 1979, Wings West numbers five Metro IIIs as part of its fleet. Courtesy Fairchild Aircraft Corporation

A member of the American Eagle commuter network, AV Air, formerly Air Virginia, currently operates ten Metro IIIs from its Lynchburg base. Courtesy American Airlines

The Cincinnati-based regional ComAir flies ten Metro IIIs in 1986, including this example shown over the Queen City. Sports fans—Riverfront Stadium appears in the center of this photograph on the northern bank of the Ohio River. Courtesy ComAir

■ SHORTS 360

First Service: 1982

Type/Purpose: Twin-engined, commuter/regional transport

Number of Seats: 3 crew, 36 passengers

Dimensions: Length: 70.1 feet
    Height: 23.8 feet
    Wingspan: 74.1 feet
    Gross weight (pounds): 25,700

Engines: 2 Pratt & Whitney of Canada PT6A-65R
    turboprops

Performance: Maximum range: 655 miles
    Service ceiling: 18,000 feet
    Maximum cruising speed: 243 mph

Initial Test Flight: June 1, 1981

Initial U.S. Operator Service: Suburban Airlines,
    November 1982

Remarks: Announced by Shorts on July 10, 1980, as the SD3-60, the new aircraft retains the basic configuration of the 330 with a fuselage stretch of 3 feet and a cabin height and width of 6.6 feet. The 360, a high-wing, braced, and unpressurized monoplane with outer wing panels, retails for $4.6 million. The aircraft's most conspicuous change over the 330 is its adoption of a revised rear fuselage, which incorporates a conventional single fin/rudder that reduces drag and allows greater baggage capacity. By fall 1985, 80 360s had been delivered worldwide with orders outstanding for 120 more.

Selected List of U.S. Operating Airlines: (1984-1985): Atlantic Southeast Airlines; Fischer Brothers Aviation; Imperial Airlines; Mississippi Valley Airlines; NewAir; Pennsylvania Airlines; Simmons Airlines; Suburban Airlines; Sunbelt Airlines ■

In British pre-delivery registration, these Shorts 360s are shown in the liveries of Simmons Airlines (top) and the Allegheny Commuter associate Pennsylvania Airlines (bottom). Courtesy Short Brothers Limited

Suburban Airlines' Shorts 360 is shown (still in British registry) prior to delivery. Courtesy Short Brothers Ltd.

■ BEECHCRAFT B1900 Airliner

First Service: 1983

Type/Purpose: Twin-engined, light, commuter/regional transport

Number of Seats: 2 crew, 19 passengers

Dimensions: Length: 57.9 feet
Height: 14.9 feet
Wingspan: 54.5 feet
Gross weight (pounds): 16,600

Engines: 2 Pratt & Whitney of Canada PT6A-65B turboprops

Performance: Maximum range: 979 miles
Service ceiling: 30,000 feet
Maximum cruising speed: 295 mph

Initial Test Flight: September 3, 1982

Initial U.S. Operator Service: Bar Harbor Airlines, 1983

Remarks: A cantilevered, low-wing monoplane with a pressurized fuselage, the Model 1900 is not a stretch of the C99, but an entirely new design for a commuter airliner that can operate at higher altitudes. Production continues at a modest pace with 47 airplanes delivered by late fall 1985. An interesting feature of the 1900 is its auxiliary, horizontal tail surfaces (Beech calls them "stabilons"), which are complemented by new vertical tail surfaces that have been added beneath the tips of the "T" tail.

Selected List of U.S. Operating Airlines: (1984-1985): Bar Harbor Airlines; Brockway Air; Business Express; Cascade Airways; Colgen Airways; North Continent Airlines; Pennsylvania Airlines; Rio Airways; Ryan Air Services ■

This Ryan Air Service Beech 1900 was photographed over Kansas prior to its delivery to the carrier's base at Unalakleet, Alaska. Currently serving 40 points in southern and western Alaska, Ryan absorbed the well-known Nome-based Munz Northern Airlines in 1983. Courtesy Beech Aircraft

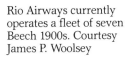

Rio Airways currently operates a fleet of seven Beech 1900s. Courtesy James P. Woolsey

Forced into bankruptcy in August 1985, Cascade suspended operations in early 1986, at which time the manufacturer was forced to repossess the carrier's six Beech 1900s, one of which is shown here in happier times. Courtesy Cascade Airways

■ BOEING 757-200

First Service: 1983

Type/Purpose: Twin-engined, commercial, turbofan, short/medium-haul transport

Number of Seats: 2 crew, 186-200 passengers

Dimensions: Length: 155.3 feet
Height: 44.6 feet
Wingspan: 124.5 feet
Gross weight (pounds): 220,000

Engines: 2 Rolls-Royce RB.211-535 C or E turbofans or 2 Pratt & Whitney PW 2037 turbofans

Performance: Maximum range: 2,380 miles
Service ceiling: 30,000 feet
Maximum speed: 593 mph
Maximum cruising speed: 528 mph

Initial Test Flight: February 19, 1982

Initial U.S. Operator Service: Eastern Airlines, January 1, 1983

Remarks: Boeing officials in early 1978 announced their plans for a new "family" of fuel-efficient, high-technology jetliners. Key to this group would be a 727 replacement, the Model 757, for which firm orders were received in 1979. Lagging somewhat behind the production program of its twin, the 767, the 757 narrowbody benefitted from lessons learned in manufacture of the widebody. Employing the 727 fuselage, the aircraft's wing is swept back less than its predecessor's and the use of Rolls-Royce engines marked the first time Boeing had introduced a new airliner with a foreign power plant. Passengers are accommodated in a single-aisle body of identical width to the 707. Not yet widely adopted by American airlines, the plane, with its advance flight deck/avionics and predatory appearance, is also advertised as "the world's most fuel-efficient airplane."

Selected List of U.S. Operating Airlines: (1984-1985): Delta Air Lines; Eastern Airlines; Northwest Orient Airlines; Republic Airlines; on order by UPS, 757PF (Package-Freight) ■

On January 1, 1983, Eastern Airlines became the first airline to commence 757 operations. The launch-customer's fleet currently includes 22 of these Boeings with 5 more on order. Courtesy Eastern Airlines

View of a Delta Air Lines Boeing 757. The Atlanta-based airline's fleet currently includes 12 examples, with 48 on order, and options on an additional 10. Courtesy Delta Air Lines

A Delta Air Lines Boeing 757 captured on the taxiway (moving to 27R on the south side) of Atlanta Airport in July 1986. Courtesy Walter C. White

■ BRITISH AEROSPACE (HS) 146
Series 100 to 300

First Service: 1983

Type/Purpose: Twin-engined, commercial, turbofan, short-haul transport

Number of Seats: 2 crew, 93 passengers (100)/
 2 crew, 111 passengers (200)/
 2 crew, 120 passengers (300)

Dimensions: Length: 85.8 feet (100)/ 93.1 feet (200)/
 103.1 feet (300)
 Height: 28.3 feet
 Wingspan: 86.5 feet
 Gross weight (pounds): 76,000 (100)/ 89,500 (200)/
 94,000 (300)

Engines: 4 Avco Lycoming ALF-520F-3 or -5 turbofans

Performance: Maximum range: 1,700 nautical miles
 Service ceiling: 30,000 feet
 Maximum cruising speed: 500 mph

Initial Test Flight: September 1, 1981 (100)/
 August 1, 1982 (200)

Initial U.S. Operator Service: Air Wisconsin, June 27, 1983

Remarks: A high-wing, cantilevered monoplane with a pressurized, circular-section fuselage, the fuel-efficient BAe 146 features retractable, tricycle landing gear, under-wing engine pods, and a T-tail with swept surfaces. Originally designed by Hawker-Siddeley before its 1977 absorption into British Aerospace, the aircraft seeks to offer low operating costs and capability from short, semi-prepared airfields. The Model 200 introduced by Air Wisconsin is a basic 100 stretched 7.1 feet in the fuselage. The Model 300 now under study would stretch the fuselage an additional ten feet. Not yet widely adopted by U.S. carriers, a total of 30 146s had been delivered by fall 1985 with 61 others on order (worldwide).

Selected List of U.S. Operating Airlines: Air Wisconsin; Air-Pac, Inc.; Alaska Airlines; Aspen Airways; Pacific South-west Airlines (PSA) ■

One of Aspen Airways' two BAe 146s. First offering scheduled service to Colorado ski resorts in 1962, the carrier currently flies in that state, as well as several other Western and Midwestern locales, and holds an option for one more British jetliner. Courtesy British Aerospace

A BAe 146 of Air Wisconsin, which, on June 27, 1983, became the first U.S. carrier to operate this British jetliner, and which currently includes eight in its fleet. Courtesy British Aerospace

■ BRITISH AEROSPACE (HP) Jetstream 31

First Service: 1983

Type/Purpose: Twin-engined, commercial, commuter/ regional transport

Number of Seats: 1-2 crew, 18-19 passengers

Dimensions: Length: 47.2 feet
Height: 17.5 feet
Wingspan: 52 feet
Gross weight (pounds): 15,212

Engines: 2 Garrett AiResearch TPE331-1OUG turboprops

Performance: Maximum range: 1,210 nautical miles
Service ceiling: 25,000 feet
Maximum cruising speed: 282 mph

Initial Test Flight: March 18, 1982

Initial U.S. Operator Service: Appolo Airways, 1983

Remarks: This conventional, low-wing monoplane began as the last design of Great Britain's Handley-Page Company and was originally called the HP-137. With a new engine and improved, British Aerospace relaunched the aircraft as the Jetstream 31 on December 5, 1978, and by fall 1985 had delivered 60 aircraft, with 34 more on order. The United States has been the top market for the $2.85 million, pressurized aircraft with five carriers ordering a total of 56 planes between them.

Selected List of U.S. Operating Airlines: (1984-1985): Air Illinois; Atlantis Airlines; Eastern Metro Express; Excellair; Flight Line, Inc.; JetAire Airlines; Jetstream International Airlines; Metro Airlines; Pacific Coast Airlines; Skywest; Republic Express ■

The holding company Phoenix Airline Services entered an association with Republic Airlines in spring 1985 to provide feeder service through the latter's Memphis hub, employing a fleet of 19 Jetstream 31s under the name Republic Express. Courtesy British Aerospace

Based in Florence, South Carolina, Atlantis Airlines entered into an association with Eastern Airlines in 1985 and began operating as Eastern Atlantis Express. The company operates 6 Jetstream 31s. Courtesy British Aerospace

■ DORNIER GmbH. Do-228
Series 100 to 200

First Service: 1983

Type/Purpose: Twin-engined, commuter/regional transport

Number of Seats: 2 crew, 15-16 passengers (100)/
2 crew, 19-20 passengers (200)

Dimensions: Length: 49.4 feet (100)/ 54.4 feet (200)
Height: 15.9 feet
Wingspan: 55.8 feet (100)/ 55.7 feet (200)
Gross weight (pounds): 13,260

Engines: 2 Garrett AiResearch TPE331-5 turboprops

Performance: Maximum range: 620 miles (100)/
1,065 miles (200)
Service ceiling: 16,000 feet
Maximum speed: 245 mph
Maximum cruising speed: 166 mph

Initial Test Flight: April-May 1981

Initial U.S. Operator Service: Precision Airlines, 1983

Remarks: Equipped with an advanced-design, "TNT" high wing, the $2 million plus, unpressurized Do-228 retains the basic, if lengthened, fuselage of the Do-28D-2 Skyservant introduced in 1980 and is capable of STOL (short-takeoff-and-landing) from runways of about 3,000 feet. The high wing and graceless nose are the recognition points of this flexible and economic transport. Some 58 aircraft were delivered worldwide by fall 1985, with orders outstanding for 119 more. As yet, the plane is little known in America.

Selected List of U.S. Operating Airlines: (1984-1985): Precision Airlines ■

Showing her fuselage, stretched slightly over the Dash-100, a Dornier Do-228-200 (in manufacturer's livery) flies near Munich. Courtesy Dornier via *Air Transport World*

Based at Springfield, Vermont, Precision Airlines provides scheduled service throughout the Northeast with its fleet of six Dornier Do-228s. Courtesy James P. Woolsey

■ PIPER T-1020/T-1040

First Service: 1983

Type/Purpose: Twin-engined, commercial, commuter/air-taxi transport

Number of Seats: 1 pilot, 9 passengers

Dimensions: Length: 34.6 feet (T-1020)/ 36.7 feet (T-1040)
Height: 13 feet (T-1020)/ 12.8 feet (T-1040)
Wingspan: 40.7 feet (T-1020)/ 41.1 feet (T-1040)
Gross weight (pounds): 7,000 (T-1020)/ 9,000 (T-1040)

Engines: 2 Avco Lycoming T10-540 J2B pistons (T-1020)/
2 Pratt & Whitney of Canada PT6A-11 turboprops (T-1040)

Performance: Maximum range: 895 nautical miles (T-1020)/ 990 nautical miles (T-1040)
Service ceiling: 24,000 feet
Maximum cruising speed: 211 knots (T-1020)/ 238 knots (T-1040)

Initial Test Flight: 1981

Remarks: Employing components from other successful Piper aircraft and a mix of engines, these low-wing, unpressurized monoplanes have seen only limited success and sales have slowed since Piper began to move its production facilities in Florida. Only six units were delivered in 1984.

Selected List of U.S. Operating Airlines: (1984-1985): *T-1020*—Air New Orleans; Bering Air; Sky West; Southern Express; Tennessee Airways; *T-1040*—Atlantis Airlines; Corporate Air; Flight Line; South Central Air; Texas Airlines; Trans-Southern Airways ■

The Piper T-1020 employs a mix of components from other of the builder's successful aircraft and Avco-Lycoming piston engines. Courtesy Piper Aircraft Corporation

With wing-tip tanks and turboprop engines, the T-1040 is faster and longer-legged than its T-1020 stablemate. Courtesy Piper Aircraft Corporation

■ BOEING 737 Series 300

First Service: 1984

Type/Purpose: Twin-engined, commercial, turbofan, short-haul transport

Number of Seats: 2 crew, 132-148 passengers

Dimensions: Length: 109.6 feet
    Height: 36.5 feet
    Wingspan: 94.9 feet
    Gross weight (pounds): 125,000

Engines: 2 CFM International CFM 56-3 turbofans

Performance: Maximum range: 2,913 miles
    Service ceiling: 33,000 feet
    Maximum speed: 550 mph
    Maximum cruising speed: 532 mph

Initial Test Flight: February 24, 1984

Initial U.S. Operator Service: USAir, 1984

Remarks: Work began on a larger-capacity 737 in 1980. Modifications include wing refinements, new-generation, fuel-efficient, turbofan engines, and a fuselage stretch of 8.8 feet. Advertised as "the perfect step up from smaller jetliner service," the Dash-300 offers a variety of marketing options and makes it Boeing's best-selling production airliner in late 1985 to early 1986.

Selected List of U.S. Operating Airlines: America West Airlines; Continental Airlines; New York Air; Piedmont Airlines; Southwest Airlines; USAir; Western Airlines ■

Formed in December 1980, New York Air provides scheduled service to points in the Northeast, Midwest and Florida with a fleet which includes four Boeing 737-300s. Courtesy James P. Woolsey

A USAir Boeing 737-300 enroute to Pittsburgh from the manufacturer's Seattle plant. By early 1986, the carrier was operating 15 of the advanced airliners and had orders placed for 25 more. Courtesy USAir

■ DEHAVILLAND-CANADA DHC-8 (Dash 8)

First Service: 1984

Type/Purpose: Twin-engined, commercial, STOL, short-haul transport

Number of Seats: 2 crew, 36-39 passengers

Dimensions: Length: 73 feet
Height: 25 feet
Wingspan: 85 feet
Gross weight (pounds): 21,590

Engines: 2 Pratt & Whitney of Canada PT7A-2R turboprops

Performance: Maximum range: 1,266 miles
Service ceiling: 25,000
Maximum cruising speed: 310 mph

Initial Test Flight: June 20, 1983

Initial U.S. Operator Service: Henson Airlines/Metro Airlines, 1984

Remarks: To complete its family of STOL (short-takeoff-and-landing) transports, DHC has developed a downgrade of its popular DASH-7 for the 30–40-seat market. With a circular-center-section fuselage, retractable, tricycle landing gear, and T-tail, the cantilevered, high-wing monoplane is outwardly similar to its stablemate, except that its power plant consists of not four, but two advanced-technology turboprops. The $5.5 million airliner is available in both commuter and corporate versions, the latter distributed exclusively by Innotech Aviation of Montreal. Over 100 orders/options had been received for the plane by late 1985, with 60 percent of those from U.S. regionals.

Selected List of U.S. Operating Airlines: (1984-1985): Henson Airlines; Horizon Air; Metro Airlines ■

An Eastern Metro Express DHC-8 at the company's Atlanta ramp in July 1986. Note the BAe Jetstream 31 behind the fuel truck. Courtesy Walter C. White

Still in Canadian registration, a new Dash-8 is prepared for delivery to Henson Airlines. The Hagerstown (Maryland) based regional currently operates five of these DHCs, with orders for three more. Courtesy DeHavilland Canada

■ SAAB SF-340

First Service: 1984

Type/Purpose: Twin-engined, commuter/regional transport

Number of Seats: 2–3 crew, 35 passengers

Dimensions: Length: 64.6 feet
   Height: 22.6 feet
   Wingspan: 70.4 feet
   Gross weight (pounds): 27,000

Engines: 2 G.E. CT7-5A turboprops

Performance: Maximum range: 1,048 miles
   Service ceiling: 18,000+ feet
   Maximum speed: 322 mph
   Maximum cruising speed: 315 mph

Initial Test Flight: January 25, 1983

Initial U.S. Operator Service: Comair, 1984

Remarks: A cantilevered, low-wing monoplane, the 340 is the result of a joint venture between Saab-Scania S/A of Sweden and Fairchild Industries of the United States. As a result of recent financial reversals, Fairchild withdrew from full partnership on November 1, 1985, to become a sub-contractor; Saab-Scania, which assumed full program control, renamed the commuter-liner from Saab-Fairchild to Saab SF-340. Quiet, fuel efficient, economical to operate, the $5.75 million, pressurized airliner can be employed without any need for airport ground-handling equipment. By fall 1985, 28 planes had been delivered worldwide with orders outstanding for 70 more.

Selected List of U.S. Operating Airlines: Air Midwest; Comair; Ransome Airlines; Republic Express; on order: Bar Harbor Airlines; Ransome Airlines ■

A Saab-Fairchild SF-340 of Air Midwest. The first of four now flown was delivered to the carrier's Wichita base in July 1985. Courtesy Air Midwest

Cockpit of the SF-340. Courtesy Saab-Fairchild International

■ CESSNA 208 Caravan I

First Service: 1985

Type/Purpose: Single-engined, commercial, passenger/cargo transport and air taxi

Number of Seats: 1 crew, 9 passengers

Dimensions: Length: 37.6 feet
    Height: 14.2 feet
    Wingspan: 52.1 feet
    Gross weight (pounds): 9,650

Engines: One Pratt & Whitney of Canada PT6A-114 turboprop

Performance: Maximum range: 1,500 miles
    Service ceiling: 27,600 feet
    Maximum cruising speed: 174 knots

Initial Test Flight: December 1982

Initial U.S. Operator Service: Federal Express, February 28, 1985

Remarks: The first single-engine turboprop to be designed and certified for civil use by a major U.S.-general-aviation manufacturer, the Caravan I is a high-wing, single-engine, unpressurized turbine-powered, passenger/cargo-convertible airliner with STOL capabilities. A long life is forecast for this aircraft both as regional transport and a utility/ air-taxi aircraft.

Selected List of U.S. Operating Airlines: (1985): Baron Aviation (Missouri); Federal Express; Herman's Air Service (Alaska); Union Flight (California) ■

Loading the high-wing Cessna Caravan I turboprops in a manufacturer's demonstration. Courtesy Cessna Aircraft Company

A Cessna 208 Caravan I banking. The aircraft is the first single-engined turboprop designed and certified for civil use by a major U.S. general aviation manufacturer. Courtesy Cessna Aircraft Company

■ EMBRAER EMB-120 Brasilia

First Service: 1985

Type/Purpose: Twin-engined, commuter/regional transport

Number of Seats: 2 crew, 30 passengers

Dimensions: Length: 65.6 feet
   Height: 20.1 feet
   Wingspan: 64.1 feet
   Gross weight (pounds): 21,165

Engines: 2 Pratt & Whitney of Canada PW 115 turboprops

Performance: Maximum range: 628 miles
   Service ceiling: 32,000 feet
   Maximum speed: 338 mph
   Maximum cruising speed: 288 mph

Initial Test Flight: mid-1983

Initial U.S. Operator Service: Atlantic Southeast Airlines,
   fall 1985

Remarks: Encouraged by the success of its EMB-110, Embraer began studies in late 1979 for a stretched, more powerful, and pressurized variant capable of transporting up to 30 passengers. A cantilevered, low-wing monoplane with a circular-section fuselage, the new Brasilia commuter-liner sports a T-tail with all swept surfaces and retails for $4.985 million fully equipped. By November 1985, the manufacturer had received orders for 52 EMB-120s and various carriers had taken options on 95 more.

Selected List of U.S. Operating Airlines: In addition to Atlantic Southeast, other airlines placing orders or requesting options on the Brasilia have included: Air Midwest; Cascade Airways; Metro Airlines; Provincetown-Boston Airlines; Sky West; West Air ■

Embraer EMB-120 of Atlantic Southeast Airlines. Founded in June 1979 and presently an associate in the Delta Connection commuter network, Atlanta-based ASA placed two Brasilias into service and held options for five more. Courtesy Embraer Aircraft Corporation

One of ten Atlantic Southeast Airlines EMB-120s on an Atlanta taxiway in July 1986. Courtesy Walter C. White

■ AERITALIA/AEROSPATIALE ATR-42

First Service: 1986

Type/Purpose: Twin-engined, commercial, commuter/ regional transport

Number of Seats: 5 crew, 42–50 passengers

Dimensions: Length: 74.5 feet
Height: 24.9 feet
Wingspan: 80.6 feet
Gross weight (pounds): 34,720

Engines: 2 Pratt & Whitney of Canada PW120 turboprops

Performance: Maximum range: 808 miles
Service ceiling: 25,000 feet
Maximum cruising speed: 319 mph

Initial Test Flight: 1984

Initial U.S. Operator Service: Command Airways, January 1986

Remarks: Just entering service, the ATR-42 is a pressurized, $7 million commuter-liner jointly developed by the Italian builder Aeritalia and the French concern Áerospatiale under the joint title Avions Transport Regional (ATR). A fuel-efficient widebody, fast and quiet, the ATR-42 employs the advanced technologies developed by the two manufacturers during their work on the Concorde, Boeing 767, and McDonnell-Douglas DC-9-80. Current plans call for introduction of a stretched 70-passenger version, ATR-72, now scheduled for flight testing in April 1988. Certified by the FAA in late fall 1985, 53 ATR-42s have been ordered worldwide with options outstanding for 37 others.

Selected List of U.S. Operating Airlines: Orders or options have been made by Air Midwest; Command Airways; Pennsylvania Airlines; Pioneer Airlines; Ransome Airlines; Simmons Airlines ■

Command Airways ATR-42. Courtesy Áerospatiale Aircraft Corporation

Three ATR-42s fly formation during tests. Courtesy Áerospatiale Aircraft Corporation

■ AIRBUS INDUSTRIE
A310-300 Airbus

First Service: 1986

Type/Purpose: Twin-engined, short/medium-range, turbofan transport

Number of Seats: 9-11 crew, 210-265 passengers

Dimensions: Length: 153.1 feet
Height: 51.9 feet
Wingspan: 144 feet
Gross weight (pounds): 330,690-337,300

Engines: 2 Pratt & Whitney JT9D-7R4D/E turbofans

Performance: Maximum range: 2,810 miles
Service ceiling: 37,000 feet
Maximum cruising speed: 414 mph

Initial Test Flight: April 3, 1982

Initial U.S. Operator Service: Scheduled for Pan American World Airways in 1986

Remarks: Motivated by the interest of European carriers for a 200-seat variant, Airbus Industrie in July 1978 elected to proceed with development and sale of a shortened version of the A300. Taking advantage of much component commonality, the A310 features new engine pylons, tail-unit and landing-gear modifications, and new British-designed and aerodynamically more efficient wings. Accommodation can be varied from a 210 mixed-class layout to a high-density, one-class configuration with seating for 265 passengers. In 1985, Pan American World Airways elected to become the airliner's first American operator when it placed an order for 12 A310-300s, with options for 13 more. ■

Pan American World Airways Airbus Industrie A-310 Airbus lifts off. Courtesy Airbus Industrie

The A310: Airbus Industrie's most advanced 210-280 seat twin-aisle twin. Combines experience of the A300 with a maximum in fuel efficiency, advanced flight deck, cabin comfort and cargo capacity. Courtesy Airbus Industrie

Shown taking off at Miami in March 1983, this colorfully marked Nord 262 belonged to the former Florida regional National Commuter Airlines.

This Mohawk 298 of the Allegheny Commuter associate Ransome Airlines was photographed at Philadelphia in March 1981.

A fine side-view of a United Caravelle photographed in October 1970, the last month in which the aircraft was operated by the large U.S. carrier.

Formerly owned by Air Texas, this Beech B99 became the first airliner of Colgan Airways and was photographed at Manassas, Virginia, in April 1971.

Following purchase of the prototype Beech 1900, photographed at Manassas, Virginia, Colgan Airways, like other commuter airlines, became affiliated with a major carrier, in this case New York Air, and in what has become common practice, began painting its aircraft to reflect the association.

One of Aspen Airways two BAe 146s photographed at Denver, Colorado, in September 1985. First offering scheduled service to Colorado ski resorts in 1962, the carrier currently flies in that state, as well as several other Western and Midwestern locales, and has options for the purchase of six more 146s.

A Jetstream International BAe Jetstream 31 lifts off from Washington National Airport in May 1985. Beginning operations as Vee Neal Airlines in May 1980, the Erie, Pennsylvania-based regional changed its name in 1983 in celebration of its re-equipment with the British turbo-prop, of which it currently operates six.

A Cessna 207 Stationair owned by Island Airlines and photographed at Put-in-Bay, Ohio, in 1980. Established in 1929, the carrier was long known for its scenic Ford Tri-Motor flights to the Lake Erie Islands.

Blue Bell, Pennsylvania-based Wings Airways was founded in 1976 and currently operates a fleet which includes three BN-2A Trislanders; this one was photographed while landing at Philadelphia in March 1985.

This CASA C-212 in the markings of Air Florida Commuter was photographed at Miami in March 1984.

A BN-2 Islander of the former Tennessee commuter Volunteer (Vol Air) photographed at Knoxville in April 1973.

Based at El Paso, Texas, the former small regional Aztec Airways began service in 1966 with a fleet of light planes which included this Cessna 206.

This Cessna 402 of the former Denver-based small regional Trans Central Airlines was photographed at College Station, Texas, in September 1970. Founded in 1966, the carrier flew to several points in Colorado, Texas, and New Mexico.

One of five Convair 580s of the former Cleveland-based regional Freedom Airlines shown taking off from Washington National Airport in May 1983. The photographer snapped this shot from a canoe in the Potomac River.

One of the original sponsors of the STOL (short take off and landing) DHC-6 was Pilgrim Airlines, which currently operates six models, including this colorfully marked Twin Otter photographed at Boston in May 1981.

A DHC-6 Twin Otter of Shawnee Airlines, captured at Herndon Field, Orlando, Florida, in April 1972.

A Dash-7 of Rocky Mountain Airways photographed at Denver in September 1985. Rocky Mountain was the U.S. launch customer for the Canadian STOL aircraft and currently has six in its fleet.

Henson's first Dash-8 lifts off from Washington National Airport in June 1985. Note the extremely clean lines revealed.

Precision Airlines, which began passenger service in 1977, remains the major Do-228 operator in the United States. This example was photographed while landing in Philadelphia in March 1985.

Aeromech Airlines merged with Cleveland-based Wright Airlines on October 1, 1983. One of the carrier's EMB-110 Bandeirantes, painted in the Aeromech color scheme with Wright titles, is shown landing at Washington National Airport in December 1983.

American Eagle commuter network associate AVAir, formerly Air Virginia, operated a fleet of 17 Fairchilds in early 1985, including this Metro II shown in the carrier's earlier livery while landing at Washington National Airport in June 1985.

An Empire Airlines Fokker F-28 Fellowship photographed while on its final approach to Washington National Airport in January 1985. Founded in 1974, the carrier, recently acquired by Piedmont Airlines as a separate division, owned a fleet of eleven Dutch jets.

The Grumman Gulfstream executive transport from whence the Gulfstream I-C evolved saw only limited airline service. This example, owned by Susquehanna Airlines, was photographed at Sidney, New York, in May 1985.

A Delta Air Lines Lockheed L-1011-500 departs Miami in December 1983. The Atlanta-based major numbered three of the advanced TriStars in its 1985 fleet.

An Arrow Air DC-8-63, identical to that involved in the tragic December 1985 Newfoundland crash, photographed at Miami in March 1984. A major charter operator, Arrow operated a number of DC-8s including -54s, -62s, -63s, and -73s prior to its bankruptcy on February 11, 1986.

Showing off its new CFM engines, a Delta Air Lines DC-8-71 comes into Baltimore-Washington International Airport in January 1985. Delta was one of the first carriers to operate the Super Seventies.

This Piper Apache of the former small airline Central American Airways was photographed at Louisville, Kentucky, in September 1970.

A Cumberland Airlines Piper Aztec photographed at the company's Cumberland, Maryland, base in March 1980.

A Piper Navajo Chieftain of Mall Airways photographed at Albany, New York, in 1985. The New York regional currently provides scheduled service to cities in the Northeast, Ontario and Quebec, with a fleet which includes three Chieftains.

In its original livery, a new Colgan Airways Shorts 330 lands at Baltimore-Washington International Airport in May 1983.

BAe Jetstream 31 of Jetstream International. Courtesy British Aerospace

A brand new USAir Boeing 737-300 near Pittsburgh in early 1985. Formerly known as Allegheny Airlines, this company operated only eight Dash-300s in early 1985, but had orders for 22 more (for delivery through late 1987) and options for 10 others. Courtesy USAir

A Convair CV-580 of the American Eagle commuter associate Metro Airlines photographed at Dallas-Fort Worth International Airport in 1985. Courtesy American Airlines.

Cutaway view of the Martin 130 *China Clipper*. Courtesy Pan American World Airways

THE AUTHOR

Myron J. Smith, Jr., Director of Libraries and Aviation, Professor of Library Science and History, at Salem College, Salem, West Virginia, is an internationally known bibliographer and historian. The author of over 50 guides and histories, his works include: *Airlines: The Salem College Guide to Sources in English*; *Air War Bibliography/Chronology, 1939-1945*; *World War I in the Air: A Bibliography and Chronology*; *Air War Southeast Asia, 1961-1973: A Bibliography and 16mm Film Guide*; Mountaineer Battlewagon: *U.S.S. West Virginia* (BB-48); *Keystone Battlewagon: U.S.S. Pennsylvania (BB-38)*; *Golden State Battlewagon: U.S.S. California (BB-44)*; and *The Baseball Bibliography*. First American to receive West Germany's Richard Franck Medal (1981) for historical bibliography, Smith is past president of the Association for the Bibliography of History. He resides with his wife, Dennie, in Salem, West Virginia.